MODERN MISOGYNY

MODERN MISOGYNY: ANTI-FEMINISM IN A POST-FEMINIST ERA

Kristin J. Anderson

OXFORD
UNIVERSITY PRESS

OXFORD

UNIVERSITY PRESS

Oxford University Press is a department of the University of
Oxford. It furthers the University's objective of excellence in research,
scholarship, and education by publishing worldwide.

Oxford   New York
Auckland   Cape Town   Dar es Salaam   Hong Kong   Karachi
Kuala Lumpur   Madrid   Melbourne   Mexico City   Nairobi
New Delhi   Shanghai   Taipei   Toronto

With offices in
Argentina   Austria   Brazil   Chile   Czech Republic   France   Greece
Guatemala   Hungary   Italy   Japan   Poland   Portugal   Singapore
South Korea   Switzerland   Thailand   Turkey   Ukraine   Vietnam

Oxford is a registered trademark of Oxford University Press
in the UK and certain other countries.

Published in the United States of America by
Oxford University Press
198 Madison Avenue, New York, NY 10016

Library of Congress Cataloging-in-Publication Data
Anderson, Kristin J., 1967–
Modern misogyny : anti-feminism in a post-feminist era / Kristin J. Anderson.
    pages cm
Includes index.
ISBN 978–0–19–932817–8
1. Misogyny.   2. Feminism.   I. Title.
HQ1233.A686 2015
305.42—dc23   2014012169

9 8 7 6 5 4 3 2 1
Printed in the United States of America
on acid-free paper

For Alana and Alyssa

CONTENTS

ACKNOWLEDGMENTS

I am grateful to many individuals whose generosity made this work possible. First, I am inestimably indebted to Christina Accomando for her friendship and her political and intellectual guidance over the past two and a half decades. I am a better teacher, writer, and activist because of her patience and persistence (and numerous alliterative suggestions). Over the past two years, it was a consistent pleasure to work with Sean K. O'Hare, who read the entire manuscript in its many versions and provided assistance with organization, editing, substantive suggestions, and superbly snarky comments in the margins. Over the course of this research and writing, many colleagues provided invaluable feedback on drafts of chapters: Christina Accomando, Bonnie Field, Melinda Kanner, Campbell Leaper, Rachael Robnett, Larissa Smith, and Tammis Thomas, all helped make this a better book. I thank my students at the University of Houston-Downtown whose meticulous work on this project was vital: Sagrario Baca, Kevin Farren, Eynar Hernandez, Lisa Ludtke, Christina Matthews, and Alicia Young. Finally, I am grateful to the following people for their friendship and support: Travis Crone, Shauna Curtis, Bonnie Field, Alex Rossman, Larissa Smith, Cindy Stewart, Fran and Kim Watson, and, most especially, Tammis Thomas.

INTRODUCTION

THE (LACK OF) SIGNIFICANCE OF FEMINISM

A strange phenomenon has accompanied the unprecedented growth of feminist
activism around the globe: the recurrent pronouncement of feminism's death.
From the 1970s through the new millennium, journalists, academics, and even
some feminist scholars have declared the demise of feminism and hailed the
advent of the post-feminist age...Given the vibrancy and the variety of proliferating
forms of feminist theory and practice, why the premature burial of feminism?

—MARY HAWKESWORTH, 2004[1]

Pundits, politicians, and the press have been declaring the demise of feminism
since the birth of the women's movement. The feminist postmortem has become
so predictable that it even has been dubbed by one feminist critic as False Feminist
Death Syndrome. "This pernicious media-borne virus...has popped up in print
and over the airwaves on and off for decades, poisoning public opinion against
the 'F-word' (feminism)[2] and contaminating our collective understanding of the
history, ideology and goals of the women's movement."[3] Some commentators
describe the state of feminism as "post-feminist," that women have come a long
way in recent decades and there really is no need for a continued feminist movement. We see "post-feminist" alongside equally questionable claims of Barack
Obama's election as U.S. president as signaling a "postracial" America. The notion
here seems to be that because the country has made so much progress on racial
equality, the election of an African American president signals our arrival into a
society that no longer needs antiracist activism or structural change. As Rinku
Sen argues, "Postracialism grows out of the trope of colorblindness, but is even
more aggressive in resisting racial justice standards. Like post-feminist, it implies
not just a destination—a society that doesn't use race to judge people—but
asserts that we have arrived at that place."[4] American women have made so much

progress, the post-feminist argument continues, as evidenced by their numbers in the workforce and in college graduation, surely we have achieved gender equality.

Modern Misogyny examines contemporary sexism and anti-feminism during what has been described as a post-feminist era in the United States and other Western countries. This book critically analyzes the notion that the feminist movement is unnecessary because the work of feminism is complete. From this point of view, women, regardless of their race, social class, sexual orientation, or geography, have achieved equality in most meaningful respects. Feminism is now merely a history lesson. In fact, the argument goes, women have been so successful in achieving equality, it is now *men* who are victims of gender discrimination. These sentiments make up modern misogyny. Contrary to the claims of the post-feminist punditry, equality has not been achieved. Instead, sexism is now packaged in a more palatable but stealthy form. This book addresses the nature, function, and implications of modern misogyny but also asserts the benefits of a continued feminist movement.

My academic training is in social psychology, and that lens informs the approach to critiquing the myths of modern misogyny. My area of specialization examines subtle, contemporary forms of prejudice and discrimination, and social psychology is particularly well equipped to examine this sort of bias. On the one hand, overt, explicit, and extreme forms of prejudice and discrimination still exist. In fact, the number of hate groups in the United States has increased steadily since the election of President Barack Obama.[5] At the same time, much contemporary prejudice and discrimination is subtle, covert, implicit, and often nonconscious. Subtle prejudice, or what I have called "benign" bigotry,[6] entails everyday, *seemingly* innocent slights, comments, overgeneralizations, othering, and denigration of marginalized groups. Subtle prejudice is insidious because (1) it can be nonconscious and unintentional, so the perpetrator may not be aware of engaging in it, (2) due to its subtlety, the target or victim may not notice it as prejudice, and (3) it can have the veneer of a "positive" stereotype. Stereotypes about subordinate groups can appear complimentary (e.g., women are nurturing, Latinos are family-oriented), but even positive stereotypes are harmful because they rob the person of individuality, they box people into certain behaviors (and, sometimes, lower-paid jobs), and the person being judged is not seen in individual terms but in categorical, less accurate, and more exaggerated terms. At the cultural level, subtle prejudice permeates all corners of society; like the air we breathe, it is everywhere and we are often unaware that we inhale it.[7] In studying subtle prejudice directed toward ethnic, religious, and sexual minorities, I have examined its devastating consequences in employment, education, and the criminal justice system. In this book, I examine misogyny from the perspective of the theories and research on subtle prejudice. Many people believe that women as a group are doing just fine, that feminism has run its course, and that the new victims of sexism are men. This book will demonstrate otherwise by illuminating manifestations of modern misogyny that are harder to see than overt sexism.

Personal anecdotes of discrimination are important in terms of honoring people's lived experiences, and they can provide vivid and memorable accounts of discrimination. However, personal reports of discrimination can be dismissed by skeptics: *Maybe you weren't qualified for the job, maybe your interview didn't go well—why would you assume sexism played a role? Maybe your boss treats everyone badly?* The experimental method is a powerful way to study and detect subtle yet pervasive forms of stereotyping, prejudice, and discrimination. Controlled experiments recreate real-life situations in which discrimination is evidenced often without the perpetrator's awareness. For instance, if we create fictitious résumés with standardized qualifications such as education and experience, attach a woman's name to some and a man's name to others, and ask people to evaluate the qualifications of otherwise comparable job candidates, we can demonstrate gender discrimination if the participants evaluate the résumés of one gender less favorably than the other gender. If the only difference in the résumé is the name at the top, we must conclude that gender discrimination has occurred, even if the evaluator has not overtly and consciously articulated sexism. In this book, I rely on the vast experimental data in social and cognitive psychology to uncover prejudice and discrimination. At the same time, I use qualitative data in the form of surveys, focus groups, and interviews from psychology, education, and the humanities, which allow individuals to share their experiences, feelings, and attitudes in their own voices.

As a field, psychology focuses on individual thinking and behavior—the micro elements of human phenomena. Psychologists study how people make sense of their surroundings, how they think, feel, process information, and behave. But individuals live in a society in which institutions and larger cultural trends and tropes shape their thinking and behavior. There are several important books that address contemporary anti-feminism and sexism that focus on these larger macro issues such as politics, prisons, schools, and popular culture. I utilize some of these works here. One aspect of contemporary misogyny that has been missing from some of the recent work in this area is the link between the cultural and social with the individual. For instance, neoliberal political trends became popular in the United States and the United Kingdom in the 1980s and emphasize individualism, consumerism, and personal responsibility. We see this same rhetoric in individuals' descriptions of themselves as they describe having myriad choices and as being ultimately responsible for their successes and failures, even those faced with grinding poverty. This book aims to bridge both the "micro" and "macro" for a more complete picture of contemporary sexism and anti-feminism.

In its six chapters, *Modern Misogyny* addresses the nature of sexism and modern anti-feminism. The first two chapters explore the political, cultural, and psychological landscape of post-feminist anti-feminism. Post-feminism is marked by the depoliticization of feminist goals and an opposition to collective feminist action. In Chapter 1, Consumerism, Individualism, and Anti-Activism, we examine the notion of post-feminism and its attendant characteristics. To this particular incarnation of anti-feminism-fronting-as-feminism, empowerment in the marketplace and in lifestyle choice has replaced the earlier political and intellectual work of feminism. Appropriating words such as "empowerment" and "choice," these elements are then converted into an individualistic discourse and deployed in a new guise as a substitute for feminism. Chapter 1 examines these trends in popular culture and politics. Chapter 1 also examines recent psychological research on the ways in which individuals' attitudes about feminism mirror this anticollectivist, individualist trend. For example, young adults are less likely than previous generations to believe that collective action is necessary to improve women's status in society.

The terror attacks of September 11, 2001, affected nearly every aspect of American culture. Chapter 2, Post-feminism Post-9/11, explores the retreat to gender traditionalism that has occurred over the past decade. Susan Faludi[8] describes the many ways in which feminism was rolled back after 9/11. For example, in the weeks and months after 9/11 many commentators observed a return to "traditional" values, with articles about single women who had previously placed careers ahead of matrimony but now were said to be hurriedly looking for husbands. The widows of 9/11 were shown in the media, while widowed men were invisible. Those women directly affected by 9/11 were celebrated as grieving wives and mothers but only so long as they adhered to that prescribed passive role of victim. When a group of 9/11 widows known as the "Jersey Girls" began to question the script by asking questions critical of the Bush Administration and its handling of the aftermath of the attacks, they were marginalized in the press in favor of more easily digestible traditional women.

Chapter 2 explores the ways these post-9/11 trends reflect the swiftness with which progress toward civil rights and equality reverts to traditional patriarchal patterns of men as breadwinners/protectors and women as homemakers/mothers. When the country is under siege and at war, progressive politics and civil rights are rendered capricious luxuries that distract from the constructed core values of male protector and female victim. In this chapter, social psychological theories such as terror management theory join political and media analysis in an effort to explain these events and trends.

A key feature of modern anti-feminism is the cornerstone belief that the work of the feminist movement is done and that feminism itself has become obsolete—an antique piece of 20th-century ideology. Women have, more or less, achieved equality through legislative changes in sexual harassment and antidiscrimination laws, and through changes in norms that now accept women in the military, in the university, and in the workplace. Thus, women do not have any reasons to complain about being oppressed. Those women who do insist on being feminists and favor a continued feminist movement must want to get *ahead* of men or believe that they are superior to men. Modern anti-feminism tells us that those who still complain about inequality just don't like men. Thus, there is a belief that feminism has gone too far and has become too extreme; there is a sort of *feminism gone wild* perception of feminists and feminist activism. Chapter 3, Manufacturing Man-Hating Feminism, addresses the myth of the antimale feminist. Anti-feminist columnists argue that discrimination against women is largely in the past and feminism in the present day is unnecessary and dangerous. Only isolated cases of overt gender discrimination against women are recognized. Today's feminists who talk about gender inequality as a *system* face allegations of man-hating. In fact, according to this view, the real victims of gender discrimination today are boys and men.

Chapter 3 also explores the empirical research on feminists' and nonfeminists' attitudes toward men. Contrary to popular opinion, systematic research finds that feminists actually hold more positive attitudes toward men than do nonfeminists. Nonfeminists tend to subscribe to traditional gender roles of male power and privilege, yet at the same time they resent men for their power and privilege relative to women. Chapter 3 explores the function and implications of the feminist-man-hater myth.

Another expression of the perception of *feminism gone wild* is seen in the contemporary construction of the "war against boys" and "the end of men." Chapter 4, The Boy Crisis and the End of Men, responds to arguments made in recent books including, *Are Men Necessary?, Save the Males, Is There Anything Good About Men?,* and *The War Against Boys.* These books fuel what has almost become a contemporary moral panic. The war-against-boys rhetoric claims that feminism brought attention to girls' needs in education but in doing so feminists subordinated boys' needs to the point that girls got ahead of boys. Chapter 4 examines mass media and education and responds to the allegation that society and schools have become "feminized," antimale, and "toxic" to boys. The analysis in this chapter demonstrates that rather than schools being anti-male, boys are socialized to view education as incompatible with masculinity. Instead of blaming too-much-feminism, this chapter examines the psychology of male privilege and entitlement as contributions to boys' and young men's disengagement from school.

The final two chapters of the book consider the role that feminism plays in today's post-feminist era and in real women's lives. Chapter 5, Women Are

Wonderful, But Most Are Disliked, explores the research on attitudes (both women's and men's) toward women. The category "women" elicits more warm feelings than the category "men." This phenomenon has been described by social psychologists as the *women-are-wonderful* effect. Many individual women embrace and find protection in the warm feelings people tend to have for women. On further examination, however, we find that most women do not benefit from this dynamic because the women-are-wonderful effect is relevant only to the most traditional women who adhere to strict gender roles (e.g., *housewives*). Most women today are nontraditional—they are working women, elected officials, athletes, feminists, prostitutes, soldiers, lesbians—and people's views of nontraditional women are quite negative. Chapter 5 explores the experimental research on nontraditional women, exposing and explaining the modern misogyny of paradoxical attitudes toward women.

Is a feminist identity good for women's well-being? This question is addressed in the final chapter, Chapter 6, Is Feminism Good for Women? This chapter considers psychological theory and research on the role that feminism plays in women's lives in terms of self-efficacy, mental health, body image, and romantic relationships. Do women differ in these areas depending on whether they hold traditional gender role attitudes or identify as feminists? Does a feminist identity operate as a *protective* identity? In addition, Chapter 6 explores the role of gender studies courses on women's and men's attitudes. There is a growing body of research on the benefits of women's and gender studies courses ranging from increases in critical thinking skills to open mindedness to self-efficacy. Gaining an understanding of the role these courses play in students' intellectual and political development will inform larger curricular questions, as well as aid the instructors who teach these courses.

If we look at gender inequality only in terms university graduation statistics or the presence of women in full-time employment, we conclude that women are doing better than forty years ago. However, sexism no longer manifests in shutting women out of the ivory tower or categorically excluding them from certain professions. Modern misogyny in this post-feminist era is subtle but sneaky. It turns the tools and principles from earlier feminist movements against women. It offers women equality in name but then provides only narrow choices that keep male dominance in place under a veneer of equality. *Modern Misogyny* calls for a revitalization of feminism and a mobilization of a feminist movement.

Notes

1. Hawkesworth, M. (2004). The semiotics of premature burial: Feminism in a post-feminist age. *Signs: Journal of Women in Culture and Society, 29*, 961–985.

2. There are a variety of definitions of a feminist, but common to most definitions is the idea that a feminist recognizes that discrimination against women exists, she experiences a sense of shared fate with women as a group, and wants to work with others to improve women's status.

3. Page 31: Pozner, J. L. (2003). The "big lie": False Feminist Death Syndrome, profit, and the media. In R. Dicker, & A. Piepmeier (Eds.), *Catching a wave: Reclaiming feminism for the 21st century* (pp. 31–56). Boston, MA: Northeastern University Press.

4. Sen, R. (2009, Fall). Taking on postracialism. *On the Issues*. Retrieved from http://www.ontheissuesmagazine.com/2009fall/2009fall_sen.php

5. Potok, M. (2012, Spring). The 'Patriot' movement explodes. *Southern Poverty Law Center*. Retrieved from http://www.splcenter.org/get-informed/intelligence-report/browse-all-issues/2012/spring/the-year-in-hate-and-extremism

6. Anderson, K. J. (2010). *Benign bigotry: The psychology of subtle prejudice*. Cambridge, UK: Cambridge University Press.

7. See page 6 in Tatum, B. D. (1997). *"Why are all the Black kids sitting together in the cafeteria?" And other conversations about race*. New York, NY: Basic Books.

8. Faludi, S. (2007). *The terror dream: Myth and misogyny in an insecure America*. New York, NY: Picador.

MODERN MISOGYNY

1

CONSUMERISM, INDIVIDUALISM, AND ANTI-ACTIVISM

The war between the sexes is over. We won okay? We won the second women started doing pole dancing for exercise.

—JACOB *(played by Ryan Gosling) in Crazy, Stupid, Love*[1]

Introducing Post-feminist Anti-feminism

The era of "post-feminism" emerged in the 1990s and continues today. Post-feminism is distinguished by the depoliticization of feminist goals and an opposition to collective feminist action. A post-feminist perspective is grounded in the assumption that women's material needs have mostly been met and that a feminist movement is no longer necessary. Post-feminist rhetoric often acknowledges the positive effects of feminism and incorporates some of the language of the feminist movement such as "empowerment" and "choice." Ostensible empowerment in the marketplace through consumerism and in lifestyle choice has replaced the earlier political and intellectual work of feminism. Whereas feminism used to focus on women wanting to have control over their bodies, for instance in the area of reproductive choice, post-feminism utilizes "choice" to pick products for purchase. Whereas feminism used to focus on pay equality and discrimination in the workplace, post-feminism encourages women to focus on their private lives and consumer capacities as a means of self-expression and agency.[2] The media help undermine feminist objectives by placing the focus of women's empowerment on *self*-transformation rather than *social* transformation. Post-feminism is assimilationist in that white, heterosexual, and middle-class women's issues are generalized to all women.[3] The assumption that women's material needs have been met and they can now demonstrate empowerment through consumer choices illustrates the Western, middle-, and upper-middle class assumptions of post-feminism. Post-feminism is especially suited to the neoliberal politics popularized in the United States and United Kingdom in the 1980s. Neoliberalism is a system that attempts to dismantle the social welfare programs (e.g., government work programs, aid to farmers) that have been in place since the New Deal in the

United States, and it is characterized by a pro-business capitalism that supports the redistribution of resources upward without regard for the widening inequalities such a system produces.

The era of post-feminism corresponds to what has been referred to as the third wave of feminism (the first wave being roughly from the 1840s to the 1920s and the second wave roughly from the 1960s to the 1980s, peaking in the 1970s). Some feminist writers see a clear distinction between third-wave feminism and post-feminism, whereas others see them as the same—both as versions of anti-feminism. Those who distinguish the two describe third-wave feminism as an extension of the historical trajectory of first- and second-wave feminism to better accommodate contemporary political culture and the logic of women as consumer citizens. Two of the most well-known of the third-wave feminists, Jennifer Baumgardner and Amy Richards, articulated third-wave feminism in their popular 2000 book, *Manifesta: Young Women, Feminism, and the Future*.[4] Their stated goal was to widen the borders of feminism to include more contemporary manifestations.[5] They argue that third-wave feminism is structured as a more diverse, inclusive, and integrated movement with the goal of diversifying its approach to activism and social change through social media and *zines* and different feminist subcultures such as *riot grrrl* culture popular in the 1990s. One important stated goal of third-wave feminism is to be explicitly inclusive in terms of race, class, gender, sexual orientation, and disability, relative to the feminism of the 1960s and 1970s (i.e., second wave).[6] Third-wave feminists, conscious of the white- and heterosexual-centered limitations of the second-wave movement, seek to include women who had been previously marginalized. Still other feminist scholars do not find utility in classifying the feminist movement into three waves, especially for Latina and African American feminism. For example, the 1980s was a vibrant period for feminists of color with the publication of now classic works such as Angela Davis's 1981 *Women, Race & Class*,[7] bell hooks's *Feminist Theory: From Margin to Center* in 1984,[8] Audre Lorde's *Sister Outsider* in 1984,[9] and Cherríe Moraga and Gloria Anzaldúa's *This Bridge Called My Back* in 1981.[10]

This chapter explores the landscape of popular culture, politics, and psychology, emphasizing relatively recent moves away from feminist activism to individualism and consumerism where "self-empowerment" represents women's progress. First, post-feminism borrows the rhetoric of feminism with references to "choice" and "empowerment." But the post-feminist version of these terms is very different from what actual feminists mean. Second, post-feminism moves away from collective action, protest, and resistance—the cornerstone of all civil rights movements—to an individualism and consumerism ethic. Third, a hyper-sexualization of girls and women is key to post-feminism—now women can "choose" to be sexual objects. Finally, in addition to examining popular culture and political illustrations of post-feminism, we examine recent psychological research on the ways in which women's attitudes about feminism mirror this anti-collectivist, individualist trend. Psychology studies find that young adults are less likely than previous generations to believe that activism is necessary to improve women's status in society.

Empowerment, Choice, and Personal Responsibility

In her book *The Aftermath of Feminism: Gender, Culture, and Social Change,* Angela McRobbie[11] describes a process in which feminism is acknowledged and then dismissed in the post-feminist era of the early 21st century. Post-feminist rhetoric recognizes the principles and accomplishments of feminism and incorporates them into a post-feminist discourse. Employing terms such as "empowerment" and "choice," these elements are refigured into an individualistic discourse, then deployed in a new guise, by media, popular culture, and politics, as a substitute for feminism. Feminism is utilized to explain and promote individual choice, and the success of feminism is cited as an argument for why further social change is unnecessary, and any negative outcome for women is their own fault.

Popular films such as *Bridget Jones's Diary* (2001) and the popular television series and films in the *Sex and the City* franchise reflect this deployment of certain palatable elements of women's liberation, such as sexual freedom and economic independence. But the elements of feminism that would question the obsession with beauty and cosmetics, rampant consumerism, and hyperfemininity are ignored. McRobbie describes *Sex and the City's* Carrie Bradshaw as displaying a "cloying girlie infantilism"[12] that undercuts any authority she might have as a writer for a reputable newspaper. U.S. films such as *The Ugly Truth* (2009) and *The Proposal* (2009) reflect additional elements of post-feminism. In *The Ugly Truth* Katherine Heigl plays a controlling, high-powered morning news TV producer who is forced to work with Gerard Butler, who plays a lewd and rude sexist tell-it-like-it-is relationship expert. In *The Proposal*, Sandra Bullock plays the controlling high-powered über-bitch executive who forces her earnest underling played by Ryan Reynolds to marry her so she can avoid deportation. In both films, we find that the main characters are independent career women—acknowledging the economic progress of women, thanks in part to the second wave of feminism. However, these professionally successful characters are portrayed as self-loathing, bossy, uptight, and utterly without personal lives. *What they need is a man.* Before they can get a man, they must experience a "mortifying comeuppance"[13]—a debasing punishment for their independent relationship-less lives. Under post-feminism, these modern shrews must be tamed. In *The*

Ugly Truth, the vulgar chauvinist Gerard Butler tames Katherine Heigl. In *The Proposal,* the decent Ryan Reynolds sweetens his boss, Sandra Bullock. Both women inevitably fall for their previously mismatched male leads. This form of backlash motivates not through fear but the promise of love. By making the right man the solution to the dilemmas of gender discrimination, these films make feminism old, tired, and laughable in the present, implying that even in the past feminism must have exaggerated problems or been a mistake altogether.[14] These films convey that love between a woman and a man is real, natural, and unchanging—despite the acceptance of women in the workplace. The backlash against 1960s and 1970s feminism attempted to frighten women back into the home, accepting traditional gender roles, and identifying such roles as the only source of personal happiness. These films reflect a post-feminist backlash. Post-feminism recognizes that it is unlikely that women all together will be pushed out of the workplace and back into the home, yet these films function to distance women from feminism and convince them that their lives should revolve around the heterosexual family, even if greater independence and work outside the home are expected.[15] While the women of *Sex and the City* experiment with transgressive sexuality, including same-sex relations, drag, and dominance/submission, they too eventually return to familiar and safe heterosexuality.[16]

What is absent in *post*-feminism is the feminist requirement that men be prepared to relinquish some of their privileges and advantages in work and in the home in order to achieve equality in the domestic sphere.[17] So post-feminism is represented by a popular culture marked by an undoing or dismantling of feminism but that is not in favor of a total re-traditionalization. Instead, aspects of feminism are now common sense and, as such, a cohesive feminist movement is something women no longer need.[18] Also absent in post-feminism is an understanding of dominant-group privilege and structural inequality. Post-feminism reduces *women* to white, middle- and upper-class, heterosexual women. That is, in post-feminism the typical woman has a job with a salary that allows her to purchase consumer goods, she has a husband and family, and she does not experience discrimination. Post-feminism erases structural inequality in that any discrimination against women that does still exist is viewed as a singular case of mistreatment against individual women, and it is probably the women's own fault.

Post-feminist choice and empowerment rhetoric is found not only in pop culture and politics but also in individual women's thinking about their own lives. The internalization of the post-feminist rhetoric of personal choice is displayed in two interview studies with women. Joanne Baker[19] interviewed Australian women from diverse ethnic and class backgrounds, and Emma Rich[20] interviewed white women from the United Kingdom about their perceived opportunities and their relationship to feminism. Participants in these studies assert that anything is possible, that there are endless options for women today, and that striving for self-improvement will be rewarded in a meritocratic system. The young women Baker interviewed were optimistic that they could do anything, even those facing terrible odds due to early motherhood and lack of formal education.[21] Although this optimism allows the imagination of a different future in which things can be better, it puts the onus solely on the shoulders of the individual—the state, politics, and any kind of collective action is irrelevant to improving people's lives. These narratives are indicative of post-feminism that draws on a notion of rational actors who can free themselves from restrictions if they simply have the motivation. This rationalization depoliticizes the inequitable social structures that have an impact on their lives.

These young women are in perfect sync with the rhetoric of neoliberalism in which opportunity is something of one's own making and failure one's own fault. In drawing on the language of individualism, these women are reluctant to associate with a group that would be seen as victims, since victimhood would undermine their carefully constructed sense of agency that is vital to their identity narratives. According to Rich's analysis, to view their circumstances through a feminist lens was to be associated with *disadvantage*, or to draw upon a position of *victim*, a pathetic female. Victimhood is strenuously avoided as it is associated with insufficient personal drive, a lack of personal responsibility for one's own life, and self-pity. [22]

During the interviews, conversations about gender inequality are either absent[23] or dismissed by the women interviewed as a thing of the past, and those who complain about inequality are stigmatized by the interviewees as unfeminine.[24] A feminist analysis would rupture an imagined sense of self-determination so intimately tied to the discourse of individualism. Baker observes that neoliberal and post-feminist discourses have foreclosed any articulation of inequality or oppression in social relations, so instead the participants emphasize their sense of agency and self-determination. Both groups of women articulate success in terms of individual responsibility. Opportunity and failure are something of one's own making.

However, the emphasis on personal responsibility means that challenges tend to be understood as psychological (as opposed to structural) and as manifestations of personal failings or inadequacies. Most notably, Baker found that among the young women, it was the *least* advantaged who distanced themselves from the specter of disadvantage. Even domestic violence is looked at in the context of a personal experience rather than as a phenomenon that is, to some degree, explained by structural circumstances and unequal power relations between women and men. The tendency to use individualizing discourse not only facilitates a misunderstanding of people's own actual circumstances, but it also forgoes empathy for others; sexism, racism, and other forms of discrimination are simply individual problems or are not problems at all. Thus, harm from men's violence against women and the difficulties of single parenthood have been individualized, thus effectively privatizing personal experience that is, in part, structurally produced and profoundly gendered.[25]

Despite the supposed access to unprecedented choice, the findings emerging from these interviews suggest that the new possibilities for young women are still grounded in traditionally gendered and classed boundaries. The women interviewed seek stereotypical careers in altruistic and people-oriented occupations rather than male-dominated jobs.[26] They position themselves as autonomous individuals free to choose whatever occupation they desire, yet ultimately they prioritized the role of women as wives and mothers.[27] The young women's aspirations reflect cultural and historical limits, but like the women in popular culture, these young women account for their restricted vision in a post-feminist framework of presumed equality and personal choice. Rather than being confined by gender inequality and pressure to play out traditional roles, these women simply "choose" to be traditional.

The personal choice and empowerment discourse goes beyond women's career choices and takes a disturbing form in Katy Day and Tammy Keys'[28] analysis of "pro-eating-disorder" websites. These websites offer tips for girls and women for maintaining and hiding an eating disorder. Their analysis of the material from websites revealed that the practice of self-starvation or binging was often reframed as an empowering lifestyle choice as opposed to a pathology or the result of a beauty industry that creates, and then profits from, women's insecurities. Starving and binging is framed as an attempt to reclaim control over the female body and as nonconformity in what is described as a fat, gluttonous world. The women who post on these websites describe themselves as enlightened, even part of an elite group. For instance, one woman posts, "This is a place for the elite who, through personal determination in their ongoing quest for perfection, demonstrate daily that Ana [anorexia] is the ONLY way to live."[29] Day and Keys' research demonstrates that destructive health behaviors such as anorexia are recoded by the girls and women as signaling empowerment and control. In this case, empowerment takes the form of unhealthy behavior rather than a feminist resistance to impossible beauty norms.

Consumerism, Individualism, but Not Activism

From the preceding discussion, we see that individualism and consumerism make collective action appear unnecessary, irrelevant, and obsolete. In this regard, post-feminism is consistent with the neoliberal corporatist[30] doctrine of Milton

Friedman and the Chicago School theory of economics. This corporatist agenda was embraced by Ronald Reagan and, to varying degrees, by every subsequent U.S. president. The corporatist doctrine seeks to privatize anything and everything. The goal is for a tiny government with huge transfers of wealth from public into private, for-profit, hands. In her book *The Shock Doctrine*, Naomi Klein[31] describes how U.S. presidential administrations beginning with Reagan in the 1980s began to sell off or outsource large, publicly owned entities such as water, electricity, highway management, and garbage collection to private companies. Likewise, in Britain under Prime Minister Margaret Thatcher, the government privatized British Telecom, British Gas, British Airways, British Airport Authority, and British Steel. By the time George W. Bush was named president in 2000, many public schools began to be replaced by vouchered private charter schools. Many U.S. prisons became privatized and for-profit, now financially dependent on a constant stream of new inmates to keep beds filled. And by the time the U.S. invaded Iraq and Afghanistan in 2001 and 2003, even war was outsourced with a record number of for-hire mercenaries employed by companies such as *Blackwater*.[32]

How does the move from public holdings to private relate to anti-feminism? Post-feminism is part of a corporatist and neoliberal political economy that encourages women to focus on their private lives and consumer capacities for self-expression and agency.[33] A central feature of neoliberalism is the implanting of market cultures across everyday life, the relentless pursuit of welfare "reform" (reducing help for the poor), and the encouragement of forms of consumer citizenship that are beneficial only to those who are already privileged. Undoing the anti-hierarchical struggles of social movements is also a priority within the discourse of neoliberalism. In a neoliberal context, there is no room for collective action. An attack on disadvantaged social groups is masked by the ostensibly nonracist and nonsexist language of self-esteem, empowerment, and personal responsibility. The post-feminist emphasis on consumerism divides women by class and by region. If empowerment for women is measured by purchasing power, those who can afford to consume and those who cannot will find little common ground and solidarity. Globally, there is little opportunity for building coalitions between the Western women who consume products made in developing countries and the girls and women who make the products that Western women purchase.

The emphasis on individualism and consumerism says a woman can be whatever she wants to be: who she becomes is up to her and is disconnected from history and uninfluenced by social movements or the struggles of past generations. With women's progress in the workplace and marketplace there is a narrative of the *successful woman*. Women have as much or more education as men[34] and, as we will see in Chapter 4, employers can pay them less.[35] At the same time there is an emphasis on girls and women as consumers. Companies draw on the language of "girl power" as if to bestow on their products a sense of dynamism, modernity, and innovation. As a consequence, girls are gender-differentiated and marketed to as consumers at younger and younger ages.[36]

Magazines targeting girls such as *CosmoGIRL!* and *Teen Vogue* emphasize this individual-empowerment-through-consumption "feminism." In her analysis of teen girl magazines, Jessalynn Keller[37] finds a defanged feminism where feminism is fun, and is a celebration of individual agency. This kind of feminism comes with the promise that hard work and dedication will lead to success and an empowered life. The individualized version of feminism offered by these mainstream teen magazines may be more easily accepted by corporate, mainstream publications because the message coincides with the larger cultural narratives about hard work, success, and the "American Dream." This version of feminism avoids any criticism of capitalism and, as a result, fails to incorporate important analysis that was the cornerstone of feminist critique, such as criticism of the beauty industry, in favor of presenting topics in a fun, playful tone. This "fun-feminism" is problematic because male dominance, power, and privilege are not addressed, and the feminism presented is merely stylistic and not directed toward social change. Keller argues that while the individualistic expression of feminism is not inherently problematic, by itself, it offers girls a grossly limited understanding of contemporary power relations. It overlooks structural barriers such as sexism, racism, classism, and heterosexism—factors that continue to impact girls' lives. Social change is rendered irrelevant, and personal change through consumerism is coded as empowerment.

A popular U.S. reality television show, *Undercover Boss*, captures this individualist worldview. The show depicts corporate CEOs who go undercover in disguise and work within their own organization. Each episode follows a specific format. The CEO, introduced as a new employee, gets to know a handful of workers in the organization, and learns of their struggles to balance work and family obligations, pay their way through part-time college, and be loyal to the company. This witnessing of the workers' tribulations in many cases brings tears to the eyes of the CEO and each episode culminates in the revelation that the new employee is actually the boss. The CEO provides gifts mostly in the form of money to the needy workers. For instance, one employee reports earlier in the episode that she hasn't been able to take a vacation with her family in years, and so the CEO pays for a family vacation. Another employee has kids but cannot afford college for them, so the CEO contributes $20,000 for a college fund for this employee's children. There are a few instances of more structural changes to accommodate workers, such as giving back a 10% wage cut the workers accepted when two companies merged, or adding smoking cessation to the employee medical plan so anyone in the company who wants to quit smoking will get help. By and large, however, the changes in the form of generous offerings made by the newly raised consciousness of the CEO are specific to three or four individual workers, keeping the struggles of all the other workers in the company (and in corporatized America) unchanged.

Even the most obvious structural racial inequality gets an individualized spin in this individualist era. Keffrelyn Brown and Anthony Brown[38] analyzed the depictions of slavery in ten popular fifth and eighth grade social studies textbooks. They found that even something undeniably systemic and structural—U.S. slavery—was framed in individualized terms. The texts failed to show how racial violence operated systematically to oppress African Americans' opportunities and social mobility in the United States. The textbooks do not present the slave trade and slavery as based in our fundamental institutions such as law and religion. Rather, the perpetrators of violence against enslaved African Americans are falsely portrayed as individual actors, or "bad men" who were deviant and not necessarily a reflection of the larger social, economic, and political structures. When discussing resistance to racial violence, stories focused again on individual, isolated efforts that concealed the organized and systematic ways that enslaved Americans and free blacks acted against their social condition. These individualized (and inaccurate) depictions of slavery and resistance prevent students from understanding the structural and institutional nature of racism.[39] Instead, students may come to view racial violence as isolated events in the past that were done by a few bad people and that only affected the individuals directly involved. Students are led to believe that present day treatment of blacks couldn't have anything to do with the legacy of structural racism rooted in slavery centuries ago.

We see a trend toward individualism in the psychological literature on *narcissism*—characterized by self-absorption, inflated ego, entitlement, and disregard for others. In her work on cultural and historic trends in narcissism, Jean Twenge finds generational differences, arguing that narcissism has increased over the last 30 years.[40] Younger people are more narcissistic than older people and young people score higher on individual traits and lower on communal and expressive traits. Interestingly, women have become more instrumental (individualistic and agentic), making them adaptive to the workplace and education, although men have not become more communal and expressive.[41] Even lyrics to popular songs demonstrate a change toward individualism. An analysis of popular songs in the United States from 1980 to 2007 found an increase in words related to a focus on *the self*. Specifically, songs showed changes toward more first-person singular pronouns (*I, me, mine*) and fewer firstperson plural pronouns (*we, us, our*) over time.[42]

Shelly Budgeon[43] finds this highly individualist focus in her interviews with young women. She interviewed 33 young women in the United Kingdom about the women's movement and gender inequality. The suggestion that their choices and opportunities might be limited by external factors was met with a strong expression of individualism. Joanne Baker's[44] interviews with young Australian women described earlier also find young women articulating their lives through an individualist lens. The ideology of neoliberalism intensifies this entrenchment of a selfhood that is individuated and that the economic and social world can be best understood as constituted of self-directed, self-sufficient individual behavior that is informed by rational choice in the pursuit of self-interest. These young women's emphasis on individual improvement is unlikely to facilitate an openness to feminism or an orientation toward collective action for social change. Even more troubling, in addition to the tendency to deny one's own difficulties, this "can-do" neoliberal discourse also appears to foreclose voicing compassion for others experiencing oppression or challenging circumstances and the recognition of how social structures act on individuals. Complementing these interviews, a recent meta-analysis of 72 studies on empathy found a decrease in empathy and perspective-taking among American college students from 1979 to 2009.[45] Therefore, the obligation to demonstrate plucky individualism has consequences that extend beyond individual psychological processes, impacting broader social consequences with the lack of regard for others' plights.

A main feature of post-feminism is the acknowledgment that choices young women have today are due in large part to the women's liberation movement before them. However, the legacy of feminism is not recognized by some of the very women who benefit from it today and who believe they have choices. That they do not recognize the role of feminism in their freedoms is an indication of the extent to which feminism in the early 21st century is not a marginalized discourse but has become an integral part of young women's lives. In order to demonstrate the empowerment and success expected of them, women in this post-feminist individualist culture seemingly need to dissociate themselves from feminism: precisely *because* young women feel empowered, they believe they no longer need feminism.[46]

Unlike the feminist movement of the 1960s and 1970s, there is little *movement* in post-feminism. A key theme of this chapter is the post-feminist focus on *self*-transformation rather than *structural* transformation, the core assumption being that any kind of collective action is unnecessary, repellent, and, as demonstrated in the previous section, shows weakness.[47] Post-feminism offers a defanged feminism, offering lifestyle and an assertive can-do attitude in place of the hard political and intellectual work that feminists have done. Angela McRobbie[48] describes a process she calls *disarticulation*, the force that devalues, negates, and makes unthinkable the possibility of coming together, on the widely promoted assumption that there is no longer any need for such actions. Disarticulation operates through the widespread dissemination of values that typecast feminism as having been fueled by anger and hostility toward men (a topic we address in Chapter 3). Feminist activists are constructed as embittered, unfeminine, and repugnant. Young women are discouraged from getting involved in controversial or confrontational political areas (particularly issues such as sex work or pornography) for fear of offending men and being branded a feminist. This reluctance results in the stifling of dissent, debate, and solidarity among women.[49]

A study by Nigel Edley and Margaret Wetherell[50] dissects the stereotype of the unattractive feminist activist. Edley and Wetherell examined men's constructions of feminists and feminism in their interviews with U.K. men ranging from age 17 to 64 from a variety of class and ethnic backgrounds. They found two competing versions of feminists and feminism. The first, the liberal feminist, was frequently presented as a woman simply wanting equality. The second version of feminist was a hyperbolic theatrical representation, with the men providing information about her physical appearance, sexual orientation, and attitudes toward men. The two versions of feminists worked in a "Jekyll and Hyde" fashion. Like Jekyll, feminists and feminism in the first version have a nonthreatening, sane, and rational character. Feminist aspirations for gender equality were reported as simple, ordinary, reasonable matters of fact. Dr. Jekyll is the ordinary woman who simply wants equality. In stark contrast, there is Ms. Hyde, the unfeminine feminist and extreme political activist. A person should be in favor of equality (Jekyll) but not be fanatical about it (Hyde). We should all want equality, but not too ardently. The men believed that change is slow and requires patience. Extremists therefore are trying to change the course of history. They are too pushy. The men interviewed by Edley and Wetherell seemed to believe that the improvement of women's position in Western society has occurred regardless of the efforts of feminists. Their belief is that we are getting there, slowly but surely, and women should be patient and tolerant of current inequalities. The most readily available ways of talking (and thinking) about feminists encourages men (and perhaps women) to identify with a definition of feminism that is patient, moderate, and stripped of any radical potential.[51]

Male dominance is also partly achieved through attempts to obscure women's resistance by characterizing collective female resistance as negative and unfeminine, implying that feminists are unattractive to men. Once such a negative category is in place, feminism can be used as an accusation, and a means of silencing assertive women.[52] No reasonable woman would want to identify as a feminist as long as the extremist caricature exists.

Indeed, recent empirical work on attitudes about feminism finds further evidence for this anticollectivist trend. Young adults in the 21st century are less likely than previous generations to believe that collective action is necessary to improve women's status in society. Also, young women are reluctant to identify as feminists if they believe feminists are activists.[53] In Chapter 6, we address the question of whether or not a feminist identity is good for women in terms of psychological and social health. We will see that there are distinct differences between women who call themselves feminists and those who agree with the principles of feminism but do not label themselves as feminists. Women who self-label as feminists, as opposed to women who merely believe in the principles of feminism, are more likely to believe that gender inequality exists and that women (and men) must work together to end sexism. Self-labeled feminists are more likely to see beyond the individualist rhetoric of post-feminism and recognize the need for societal change.[54] Consequently, feminists need to remain focused on raising women's awareness of continued gender inequity in order to motivate young women to understand that work still needs to be done.

Post-feminist Sexualization

In her book, *Enlightened Sexism: The Seductive Message That Feminism's Work Is Done*, media critic Susan Douglas[55] defines and distinguishes embedded feminism and enlightened sexism. *Embedded feminism* is the assumption that women's achievements are now simply part of the media landscape. Feminism is no longer marginal, outside of the media, as it was in, say, the 1960s. For instance, we see women on television as police captains, doctors, and lawyers. *Enlightened sexism* takes the gains of the women's movement as a given, and then uses those gains to resurrect retrograde images of girls and women as sexual objects still defined by their appearance. Now that women have it all, they should focus their energy on their true power—their bodies, attire, and sexuality—power that is fun, power that will not alienate men. Embedded feminism and enlightened sexism serve to reinforce each other: they both exaggerate women's gains and accomplishments and render feminism obsolete.[56]

Post-feminist empowerment and choice rhetoric discussed earlier tells women they can now *choose* to be sexualized and objectified, and they can disregard their second-wave feminist grandmothers who would cringe in disapproval. This trend is seen in the increased promotion and popularity of pole-dancing among suburban middle class women as exercise and at-home entertainment for their male partners. The popularity in the United States of the *Pussy Cat Dolls* in the early 2000s, the franchise dance troupe with a rotating cast made up of young women with sexually explicit dance routines, also reflects this diversion from the politics of feminism. Feminism is evoked and claimed regarding sexual freedom, but then is quickly dismissed with relief—no more feminist nagging about the sexual objectification of women. In post-feminism it is permissible once again to enjoy the scantily clad bodies of women.[57] Angela McRobbie also notes the expansion of wedding culture. The prominence of wedding culture, apart from contributing to the expansion of consumer culture, rides on this tidal wave of celebratory post-feminism, as though to say, thank goodness, girls can be girls again, the feminist Debbie Downers of the 1960s and 1970s are long gone.[58]

An implicit assumption of post-feminism is that women's status has improved. Progress has been slow perhaps, but portrayals of women in popular culture and real-world opportunities for women have progressed over the last several decades. To be sure, in some domains things have gotten better for girls and women. However, there is one area that has gotten startlingly worse in the last two decades: the sexualization and objectification of girls and women in mass media. John Mager and James Helgeson[59] examined 50 years of advertising images of women and men in major magazines. Common sense might predict that portrayals of women in print ads have gotten better. In some ways they have. For instance, early ads depicted women in the home happy to be passively domestic. More recent ads do not show such traditional images. Ads today, however, still show women as dependent on men and still in need of men's protection, such as those in previous decades. Men today are still more likely to be shown in authoritative, superior, and more powerful positions and women are in more deferential positions to men.[60] Compared to men, women are also more likely to be positioned in weakened psychological states, looking away, disoriented, and even looking dead or passed out—and these depictions have actually *increased* over the 50-year period analyzed by Mager and Helgeson.[61] Open a fashion magazine and you can find print ads depicting dead women from Marc Jacobs, Gucci, Lanvin, Jimmy Choo, and Louis Vuitton, and ads depicting gang rape by Calvin Klein, Dolce & Gabbana, and Tom Ford. These depictions are *more* prevalent today. Shock value in ads is used to break through the commercial clutter of competing ads and comes in many forms. One major strategy is to feature women's sexual objectification. Sadly, when contemporary women's own attitudes about sexual objectification in advertisements have been analyzed we find women are more accepting of and less offended by sexually objectified images of women than they were 10 or 20 years ago. We have become habituated to these images. They have become normalized. Furthermore, women report that an ad that demeans women would not influence whether or not they purchased the particular product.[62] Thus, advertising has fully embraced this post-feminist permission to objectify women and to some extent women in the early 21st century have embraced this too.

Feminists in the 1960s and 1970s fought for, among other things, control over their bodies—the right to control their reproduction, the right to love who they want, the right to extricate themselves from abusive relationships. The women's liberation movement fought for the release of women from conventional morality around sex, which had confined them to either idealized chastity on the one hand or contemptible promiscuity on the other. Feminism allowed for the possibility of women engaging in sex for their own pleasure rather than for the two previously allowed reasons for sex: to reproduce or to please a husband. In the context of post-feminism, an era in which feminism is taken into account but then swiftly dismissed and debased, women's sexual freedom manifests in porn culture and the hypersexualization of women and girls. The sexually affirming woman of the 1960s and 1970s has turned into a sexually objectified woman of post-feminism. Embedded feminism, enlightened sexism, and the lack of a collective and cohesive women's liberation movement all contribute to this climate.

Post-feminism and the Domestication of Pornography

A major hallmark of post-feminism is the post-feminist "permission" to sexualize and objectify women—often by women themselves. In her book, *Living Dolls: The Return of Sexism*, Natasha Walters[63] studies the rise of hypersexual culture. Far from giving a full range of women's freedom and potential, the new hypersexual culture redefines women's success through a narrow framework of sexual allure: *Hotness*. Once on the margins of society, pole dancing is articulated as liberating for women. Free yourself and feel empowered. And who wouldn't want to wear high heels as they exercise? The narrowing of what it means to be sexy arises from the way that the sex industry has become more pervasive and more generally acceptable. In her book, *Female Chauvinist Pigs: Women and the Rise of Raunch Culture*, Ariel Levy[64] describes women's embrace of porn culture, where the emphasis is on hotness and being *sexy* but not necessarily on being *sexual*. The distinction between sexy and sexual is important because it's the difference between women being the *subject* of their sexuality versus women being *objects* of someone else's desire. Levy writes that the intertwining of women embracing their own sexual objectification and the post-feminist culture of consumption puts sexual desire and arousal in the background, and *looking* hot and *looking* sexy in the foreground. Therefore, post-feminist hypersexuality has little to do with women feeling empowered to be in charge of their sexual desire, to explore passion, to expect sexual fulfillment, and more to do with looking like porn stars. Consistent with the principles of post-feminism, all this happens in the context of supposed free choice.

Let's consider just a few recent and current trends that mark the mainstreaming of pornography and the hypersexualization of women in popular culture. Once a widespread but sequestered industry, pornography is now abundant and permeates the cultural space.[65] This change is due in large part to the increased access to online pornography. That one can access a limitless range of pornography with just a few mouse taps means that it's accessible to anyone with a computer or phone. A person used to slink into a seedy theater, bookstore, or club—now anyone can access hardcore pornography at home or work or even while commuting. Easy accessibility goes a long way to mainstreaming pornography, but the mainstreaming of pornography isn't the only effect of Internet access to porn. A recent study found that newer pornographic media feature more violence against women than do older ones. Internet-based pornography is more likely to show sexual violence as nonconsensual with men victimizing women compared to magazine and video pornography.[66] That Internet porn contains more violence against women is significant because it is violent pornography, not pornography in general, that has been linked to men's aggression against women. In a classic experiment, Edward Donnerstein[67] showed men a neutral, erotic, or aggressive-erotic film. Compared to the other films, exposure to the aggressive-erotic film led men to be aggressive toward both women and men, and especially more aggressive toward women.

Working in the sex industry used to signal the death of a mainstream career, but work in pornography is now seen as a stepping-stone to a more legitimate career in Hollywood. The mainstreaming of porn can be seen in the intertwining of pornography and music videos. Pornographic film directors now can be found directing mainstream music videos and former porn stars can be found starring in them.[68] *Girls Next Door*—a reality TV show that debuted in 2005 on the *E!* network about *Playboy* founder Hugh Hefner's three Playboy bunny girlfriends— was a mainstream hit that spawned spinoff shows for two of the bunnies, *Holly's World* and *Kendra*. Sixteen-year-old teen actor-singer Miley Cyrus performed a pole dance at the 2009 Teen Choice Awards.[69] On a 2012 episode of MTV's *Pauly D Project* Britney Spears performs a lap dance for *Jersey Shore* reality star Paul "Pauly D" DelVecchio.[70] These examples illustrate the conventionalization of the previously marginal and seamy porn industry.

Another noted consequence of the mainstreaming of pornography is the increase in women who wax or shave their pubic hair. The complete removal of *all* pubic hair—not just waxing the "bikini line"—has become normalized in recent years. Feminist writer Caitlin Moran argues that the increase in pubic hair removal coincides with the same trend in pornography. She writes, "Hollywood waxing is now total industry standard. Watch any porn made after say, 1988, and it's all hairless down there: close-ups are like watching Daddy Warbucks, with no eyes, eating a very large, fidgety sausage."[71] Moran believes pubic hair is removed in hardcore pornography to enable viewers to see more in penetrative shots of intercourse. How does pubic hair removal become an internalized value for young women today? Moran argues that "hard-core pornography is now the primary form of sex education in the Western world. This is where teenage boys and girls are 'learning' what to do to each other, and what to expect when they take each other's clothes off."[72] This phenomenon is problematic for several reasons. First, the pubic region has become yet another part of a woman's natural body— in addition to her legs and underarms—that needs to be altered in order to be viewed as attractive and sexually desirable. Second, women seem to time their waxing, shaving, and plucking according to when they may have sex and vice versa, rather than timing sex according to when they are least likely to become pregnant, or according to when they actually desire to have intercourse. Third, pubic waxing is another consumer product/service they must purchase, adding to the bloated consumer beauty industry. Fourth, shaving pubic areas increases the likelihood of infections, including sexually-transmitted diseases.[73] Finally, that grown women's pubic area is modified to look like a prepubescent girls' area juvenilizes women, sexualizes young girls, and blurs the difference between the two.

Confusing Sexual Objectification with Empowerment

The feminist movement of the 1960s and 1970s emphasized women's control over their own bodies and their own sexuality, while simultaneously critiquing the culture's sexual objectification of women in the form of Miss America pageants or *Penthouse Pets*. Drawing on the emphasis on sexual empowerment of the 1960s and 1970s, the third-wave feminism of the mid-1990s supposedly ushered in a nonjudgmental approach to sexuality. Given the forces of neoliberal consumerism and individualism, however, *women's liberation* seems to have been reduced to *sexual liberation* and in this context *sexual liberation* has come to mean *sexual self-objectification*. In other words, the post-feminist message is that being a sexual object is now a source of power.[74] The result is that young women in the United States are encouraged by marketers, filmmakers, pornographers, and magazine publishers to participate in their own objectification. Instead of demanding the right to be seen as human beings, many of today's girls and women are cooperating with the old-fashioned notion of being seen as sex objects. It's the one kind of power that is sanctioned for women: the power to look hot and to draw attention to your hotness; the kind of power that doesn't threaten *real* power—political, economic, and cultural power. The use of the word *empowerment* is a strange distortion of what the term once meant to feminists. When feminists talked about empowerment in the past it was not in reference to a young woman in a thong twirling around a pole,[75] wearing T-shirts that say "unbelievable knockers,"[76] or wearing sweat pants with the word "juicy" on the butt. The clothing brand *Juicy Couture* prints bags and laptop sleeves that say "Fun is back."[77] Culturally, and assisted by such accouterments, girls and women can present themselves as fun and hip and distance themselves from their outdated, uptight, feminist grandmothers.

The hypersexualized marketplace is reinforcing certain behavior (i.e., the hot young woman) and punishing other behavior (i.e., a woman perceived as an uptight feminist), making it hard for many young women to find the space for alternative views of female sexuality and other ways for women to feel empowered. The smoke-and-mirrors language of choice and empowerment prevents people from seeing just how limiting such so-called choices can be.[78] *It's their choice and we shouldn't judge.* So, it's stodgy old second-wave feminists who are judging these women. Feminists are uptight and old fashioned, or worse, feminists are the *oppressors* in a post-feminist hypersexual context.

One of the most ironic domains displaying the hypersexualization, or at least hyper-*feminization*, of women may be one of the more paradoxical ones—women's sports. To acquire sponsors and appear in sports magazines, while not scaring off fans (particularly men), women athletes are pressured to present themselves as objects of femininity and obedience to traditional gender roles. Although the fact of women in sports challenges the historical and traditional association between masculinity and sport, media representations of women athletes sadly emphasize gender difference through a focus on the femininity of the athlete rather than her athletic strengths. This process of feminization constructs differences between women and men athletes and undermines challenges to the gender order.[79] Women's athleticism is rendered unthreatening and feminine whereas men's athleticism is the real deal—masculine and strong. Some women professional athletes wear full make up during competition, bows in their hair, long fingernails, and other markers of femininity when they engage in the masculine activity of sports. Indeed many well-known professional and Olympic athletes have posed for *Playboy* magazine, including Amanda Beard (swimming), Gabrielle Reece (volleyball), Mia St. John (taekwondo/boxing), and Chyna (World Wrestling Entertainment).

The process of feminizing the professional woman athlete tends to occur for white women athletes more readily than black women. Because African American women have been historically denied access to full-time homemaking and deprived of sexual protection, black womanhood has not been tied in the same way as white womanhood to activities and attributes defined as distinctive and different from masculine attributes. Therefore, African American women historically have been located outside dominant culture's definition of conventional (white) femininity. Victoria Carty argues that African American women athletes are seen as more conventionally athletic (i.e., masculine) than white women because black women's strength does not threaten traditional notions of beauty and femininity (coded as white) in the same way that white women's strength does. Therefore, media coverage of black women athletes is more about their athletic accomplishments compared to coverage of white women. For instance, Serena and Venus Williams have been described as "huge," "heavyweight fighter," "pummeling," and "masculine." African American women athletes are portrayed as lacking those features attributed to the norm of white heterosexual femininity. Carty argues that African American women athletes "may enjoy a greater expansion of gender roles and trespass more freely across the boundaries of traditional standards of femininity, because they have never been fully included in the stringent ideals of femininity and heterosexuality to begin with."[80]

The hypersexualization of women in post-feminism is indeed *raced* and *classed*. The mainstreaming of the sex industry made popular "Pimp and Ho" parties in the past two decades, as well as the domestication of the term "pimp" as a noun and verb. The actual pimp and prostitute relationship, a fundamentally exploitative relationship involving a man profiting from the use and abuse of women's bodies, is lost when we pretend these terms and roles are simply playful (and supposedly sexy). "Pimp" and "ho" are also racialized images, in contemporary media representations and with historical roots in the construction of African American men as hypersexual predators and African American women as temptresses with poor sexual morals.[81] When white men and women perform these roles, whether or not they literally don blackface or afro wigs, they are play-acting race along with gender and sexuality. In addition, playing with the "pimp and ho" dynamic has historical reverberations for African Americans about which white people can be oblivious. It's one thing for an economically privileged white woman to dress scantily and perform the role of "ho" for a party, it's another for women of color or working class women to be culturally cast as whores.[82] African American women's bodies have been sexualized and sexually abused since slavery. The image of African American women as inherently sexual and immoral functioned to justify their sexual assault by slaveholders, making the rape of a black woman no crime, literally. A 19th-century legal treatise, for example, explicitly blames interracial sex on "the *want of chastity* in the female slaves, and a *corresponding* immorality in the white males."[83] An 1859 Mississippi ruling declared that "[t]he crime of rape does not exist in this State between African slaves," because "their intercourse is promiscuous."[84] The legacies of such policies and practices continue to circulate in contemporary law and culture. In this context, for African American women, wearing revealing clothing, engaging in public displays of affection, and even wearing makeup can be seen as a confirmation of black women's promiscuity and lewdness.[85]

The mainstreaming of the sex industry has coincided with a point in history where there is less social and economic mobility than in previous generations.[86] No wonder then if the ideal that the sex industry pushes—that status can be won by any woman if she is prepared to flaunt her body—is now finding fertile ground among many young women who would never imagine a career in, say, politics.

Finally, the use of sexual attractiveness to gain status translates feminism into an act of using one's body as an object to obtain a specific type of attention, as opposed to a political movement that seeks gender equality and social justice at the structural and institutional level. Some individual women might think these "choices" work for them, but they are not necessarily good for women in general (and they might not, in fact, "work" for them, even as individuals). Post-feminists have overlooked the fact that men do not have to rely on such strategies because institutions such as education, mass media, and politics—historically and currently—privilege men and marginalize women, as we will see throughout this book. Thus, in post-feminism the structural arrangements that create and maintain sexism tend to go unacknowledged.

Conclusion

This chapter has explored post-feminism marked by the shift from feminism as a collective movement for women's liberation to superficial empowerment of the individual and her choices. In post-feminism, feminist goals are depoliticized and collective action is rendered irrelevant and unnecessary. In post-feminism, feminism is taken into account and is incorporated into political and institutional life but only as much as it allows a narrow self-empowerment. As Angela McRobbie[87] argues, there is a kind of exchange, and a process of displacement and substitution: Young women are offered equality in name, concretized in education and employment, and through membership in consumer culture and the public sphere—in place of what a reinvented feminist politics might have to offer.[88] In this neoliberal corporatist context, sexual power and purchasing power are presented as more gratifying and empowering than institutional, political or economic power.[89] Post-feminism is about the individual woman—personal choice, individual expression, and individual career success—and no recognition of the need for a united and collective social movement to liberate all women and enact structural change.[90] The language of individualism, choice, and empowerment in this consumerist context functions to tell women that a feminist movement is unnecessary, passé, and unattractive. Certainly women have choices but these choices occur in a limited context. Women are being disempowered through the rhetoric of empowerment they are offered as substitutes for feminism.[91]

Post-feminism is integral to a neoliberal framework because it undercuts feminism and doesn't threaten what neoliberals hold dear—profitability, privatization, and individualism. These strategies masquerade as common sense.[92] Post-feminism is a politics not of resistance or transformation, but of capitulation: to patriarchy, to neoliberalism, and to corporate control over public issues that affect us all.[93] Neoliberalism privileges private, corporate solutions to social problems and tends to marginalize critiques of oppression (racism and classism, as well as sexism) as subordinating practices—those who critique the system of inequality, we are told, focus too much on victimhood rather than on individual effort.[94]

The depoliticized notion that feminism is anything a woman says it is refigures the Women's Liberation Movement into a milder "women's movement" minus "liberation" (and even minus "movement"). Abandoning the analysis of structural inequality, post-feminism masks the systemic forces that continue to oppress women and undercuts the possible strategic weight of politicized feminist collectivities.[95]

This post-feminist environment makes unlikely the forging of alliances between Western and non-Western women. The sexual and consumer freedoms of some in the West now actively pitches them against the gender arrangements of other cultures.[96] Women in the West are encouraged to demonstrate their empowerment through rampant consumerism. Who is likely to make the products that these women purchase? Women in the developing world work in sweatshops for ever lower pay with each passing decade. In November 2012 a fire at a garment factory in Bangladesh killed more than 100 workers, mostly young women. The sweatshop made clothing for Wal-Mart, Disney, Sears, and other retailers.[97] Only five months later on April 24, 2013 another factory in Bangladesh that made clothing for U.S. and European companies collapsed, killing more than 1,000 sweatshop workers. Apparel companies are attracted to countries such as China and Bangladesh because the young women workers can be paid as low as 14 cents an hour and can be forced to work 14 hour days often 7 days a week.[98] If, as post-feminism dictates, empowerment is individual, not collective, the links between women globally is obscured and the potential for solidarity among women is foreclosed.

The trends of post-feminism emerging in the last two decades, in conjunction with more recent events such as the terror attacks of September 11, 2001, work in concert to limit and confine the range of possible identities and roles for women. The next chapter addresses the effect of 9/11 on gender roles, and a later chapter addresses women who resist the restricted roles of women provided by post-feminism and 9/11.

Notes

1. Carell, S. (Producer), Di Novi, D. (Producer), Ficarra, G. (Director), & Requa, J. (Director). (2011). *Crazy, stupid, love* [Motion picture]. United States: Warner Bros. Studios.

2. Genz, S. (2006). Third way/ve: The politics of post-feminism. *Feminist Theory, 7,* 333–353. doi:10.1177/1464700106069040

3. Vavrus, M. D. (2012). Post-feminist redux? *The Review of Communication, 12,* 224–236.

4. Baumgardner, J., & Richards, A. (2000). *Manifesta: Young women, feminism, and the future.* New York, NY: Farrar, Straus, and Giroux.

5. Banet-Weiser, S. (2007). What's your flava? Race and post-feminism in media culture. In Y. Tasker & D. Negra (Eds.) *Interrogating post-feminism: Gender and the politics of popular culture* (pp. 201–226). Durham, NC: Duke University Press.

6. Seely, M. (2007). *Fight like a girl: How to be a fearless feminist.* New York, NY: New York University Press.

7. Davis, A. Y. (1981). *Women, race, & class.* New York, NY: Random House.

8. hooks, b. (1984). *Feminist theory: From margin to center.* Cambridge, MA: South End Press.

9. Lorde, A. (1984) *Sister outsider.* New York, NY: Crossing Press.

10. Moraga, C., & Anzaldúa, G. (1981). *This bridge called my back: Writings by radical women of color.* Watertown, MA: Persephone Press.

11. McRobbie, A. (2009). *The aftermath of feminism: Gender, culture and social change.* London, UK: Sage.

12. Page 541: McRobbie, A. (2008). Young women and consumer culture: An intervention. *Cultural Studies, 22,* 531–550. doi:10.1080/09502380802245803

13. Powers, J. (2009, July 31). *On Hollywood's strong, self-hating* women/Interviewer: David Bianculli. Retrieved from http://www.npr.org/templates/transcript/transcript.php?storyId=111419481

14. Vint, S. (2007). The new backlash: Popular culture's "marriage" with feminism, or love is all you need. *Journal of Popular Film and Television, 34,* 160–169.

15. Vint, S. (2007). The new backlash: Popular culture's "marriage" with feminism, or love is all you need. *Journal of Popular Film and Television, 34,* 160–169.

16. McRobbie, A. (2008). Young women and consumer culture: An intervention. *Cultural Studies, 22,* 531–550. doi:10.1080/09502380802245803

17. McRobbie, A. (2009). *The aftermath of feminism: Gender, culture and social change.* London, UK: Sage.

18. McRobbie, A. (2009). *The aftermath of feminism: Gender, culture and social change.* London, UK: Sage.

19. Baker, J. (2010). Great expectations and post-feminist accountability: Young women living up to the 'successful girls' discourse. *Gender and Education, 22*(1), 1–15.

20. Rich, E. (2005). Young women, feminist identities and neo-liberalism. *Women's Studies International Forum, 28*, 495–508. doi:10.1016/j.wsif.2005.09.006

21. Baker, J. (2010). Great expectations and post-feminist accountability: Young women living up to the 'successful girls' discourse. *Gender and Education, 22*(1), 1–15.

22. Baker, J. (2010). Claiming volition and evading victimhood: Post-feminist obligations for young women. *Feminism & Psychology, 20*(2), 186–204. doi:10.1177/0959353509359142

23. Jacques, H. A. K., & Radtke, H. L. (2012). Constrained by choice: Young women negotiate the discourses of marriage and motherhood. *Feminism & Psychology, 22*, 443–461. doi:10.1177/0959353512442929

24. Rich, E. (2005). Young women, feminist identities and neo-liberalism. *Women's Studies International Forum, 28*, 495–508. doi:10.1016/j.wsif.2005.09.006

25. Baker, J. (2010). Claiming volition and evading victimhood: Post-feminist obligations for young women. *Feminism & Psychology, 20*(2), 186–204. doi:10.1177/0959353509359142

26. Baker, J. (2010). Great expectations and post-feminist accountability: Young women living up to the 'successful girls' discourse. *Gender and Education, 22*(1), 1–15.

27. Jacques, H. A. K., & Radtke, H. L. (2012). Constrained by choice: Young women negotiate the discourses of marriage and motherhood. *Feminism & Psychology, 22*, 443–461. doi:10.1177/0959353512442929

28. Day, K., & Keys, T. (2008). Starving in cyberspace: A discourse analysis of pro-eating-disorder websites. *Journal of Gender Studies, 17*(1), 1–15. doi:10.1080/09589230701838321

29. Page 11: Day, K., & Keys, T. (2008). Starving in cyberspace: A discourse analysis of pro-eating-disorder websites. *Journal of Gender Studies, 17*(1), 1–15. doi:10.1080/09589230701838321

30. Here I use Naomi Klein's definition and description of *corporatist*: "Its main characteristics are huge transfers of public wealth to private hands, often accompanied by exploding debt, an ever-widening chasm between the dazzling rich and the disposable poor and an aggressive nationalism that justifies bottomless spending on security" (p. 18). Klein, N. (2007). *The shock doctrine: The rise of disaster capitalism.* New York, NY: Picador.

31. Klein, N. (2007). *The shock doctrine: The rise of disaster capitalism.* New York, NY: Picador.

32. Klein, N. (2007). *The shock doctrine: The rise of disaster capitalism.* New York, NY: Picador.
Because of its tarnished reputation, *Blackwater* changed its name to *Xe Services*, and then changed its name again to *Academi*.

33. Genz, S. (2006). Third way/ve: The politics of post-feminism. *Feminist Theory, 7*, 333–353. doi:10.1177/1464700106069040

34. Knapp, L. G., Kelly-Reid, J. E., & Ginder, S. A. (2012). *Enrollment in postsecondary institutions, fall 2010; financial statistics, fiscal year 2010; and graduation rates, selected cohorts, 2002-07 (NCES 2012-280)*. U.S. Department of Education. Washington, DC: National Center for Education Statistics. Retrieved from http://nces.ed.gov/pubs2012/2012280.pdf

35. Williams, M. J., Paluck, E. L., & Spencer-Rodgers, J. (2010). The masculinity of money: Automatic stereotypes predict gender differences in estimated salaries. *Psychology of Women Quarterly, 34*(1), 7–20.

36. McRobbie, A. (2008). Young women and consumer culture: An intervention. *Cultural Studies, 22*, 531–550. doi:10.1080/09502380802245803

37. Keller, J. (2011). Feminist editors and the new girl glossies: Fashionable feminism or just another sexist rag? *Women's Studies International Forum, 34*(1), 1–12. doi:10.1016/j.wsif.2010.07.004

38. Brown, K. D., & Brown, A. L. (2010). Silenced memories: A examination of the sociocultural knowledge on race and racial violence in official school curriculum. *Equity & Excellence in Education, 43*, 139–154. doi:10.1080/10665681003719590

39. Brown, K. D., & Brown, A. L. (2010). Silenced memories: A examination of the sociocultural knowledge on race and racial violence in official school curriculum. *Equity & Excellence in Education, 43*, 139–154. doi:10.1080/10665681003719590

40. Twenge, J. M., & Foster, J. D. (2010). Birth cohort increases in narcissistic personality traits among American college students, 1982–2009. *Social Psychological and Personality Science, 1*, 99–106. doi:10.1177/1948550609355719

41. Twenge, J. M. (2009). Status and gender: The paradox of progress in an age of narcissism. *Sex Roles, 61*(5–6), 338–340. doi:10.1007/s11199-009-9617-5

42. DeWall, C., Pond, R. S., Campbell, W. K., & Twenge, J. M. (2011). Tuning in to psychological change: Linguistic markers of psychological traits and emotions over time in popular U.S. song lyrics. *Psychology of Aesthetics, Creativity, and the Arts, 5*(3), 200–207. doi:10.1037/a0023195

43. Budgeon, S. (2001). Emergent feminist(?) identities: Young women and the practice of micropolitics. *The European Journal of Women's Studies, 8*(1), 7–28. doi:10.1177/135050680100800102

44. Baker, J. (2010). Claiming volition and evading victimhood: Post-feminist obligations for young women. *Feminism & Psychology, 20*(2), 186–204. doi:10.1177/0959353509359142

45. Konrath, S. H., O'Brien, E. H., & Hsing, C. (2011). Changes in dispositional empathy in American college students over time: A meta-analysis. *Personality and Social Psychology Review, 15*(2), 180–198. doi:10.1177/1088868310377395

46. Redfern, C., & Aune, K. (2010). *Reclaiming the F word: The new feminist movement*. New York, NY: Zed Books.

47. Southard, B.A.S. (2008). Beyond the backlash: *Sex and the City* and three feminist struggles. *Communication Quarterly, 56*(2), 149–167. doi:10.1080/01463370802026943

48. McRobbie, A. (2009). *The aftermath of feminism: Gender, culture and social change.* London, UK: Sage.

49. McRobbie, A. (2009). *The aftermath of feminism: Gender, culture and social change.* London, UK: Sage.

50. Edley, N., & Wetherell, M. (2001). Jekyll and Hyde: Men's constructions of feminism and feminists. *Feminism & Psychology, 11,* 439–457.

51. Edley, N., & Wetherell, M. (2001). Jekyll and Hyde: Men's constructions of feminism and feminists. *Feminism & Psychology, 11,* 439–457.

52. Griffin, C. (1989). "I'm not a women's libber, but. . .": Feminism, consciousness and identity. In S. Skevington & D. Baker (Eds.), *The social identity of women* (pp. 173–193). London, UK: Sage.

53. Houvouras, S., & Carter, J. S. (2008). The F word: College students' definitions of a feminist. *Sociological Forum, 23,* 234–256. doi:10.1111/j.1573-7861.2008.00072.x

54. Liss, M., & Erchull, M. J. (2010). Everyone feels empowered: Understanding feminist self-labeling. *Psychology of Women Quarterly, 34,* 85–96.

55. Douglas, S. J. (2010). *Enlightened sexism: The seductive message that feminism's work is done.* New York, NY: Times Books.

56. Douglas, S. J. (2010). *Enlightened sexism: The seductive message that feminism's work is done.* New York, NY: Times Books.

57. McRobbie, A. (2009). *The aftermath of feminism: Gender, culture and social change.* London, UK: Sage.

58. McRobbie, A. (2009). *The aftermath of feminism: Gender, culture and social change.* London, UK: Sage.

59. Mager, J., & Helgeson, J. G. (2011). Fifty years of advertising images: Some changing perspectives on role portrayals along with enduring consistencies. *Sex Roles, 64,* 238–252.

60. Mager, J., & Helgeson, J. G. (2011). Fifty years of advertising images: Some changing perspectives on role portrayals along with enduring consistencies. *Sex Roles, 64,* 238–252.
This description reflects Goffman's advertisement category called, "Ritualization of Subordination." See:Goffman, E. (1976). *Gender advertisements.* New York, NY: Harper Torchbooks.

61. Mager, J., & Helgeson, J. G. (2011). Fifty years of advertising images: Some changing perspectives on role portrayals along with enduring consistencies. *Sex Roles, 64,* 238–252. doi:10.1007/s11199-010-9782-6
I'm describing Goffman's "Licensed Withdrawal." See:Goffman, E. (1976). *Gender advertisements.* New York, NY: Harper Torchbooks.

62. For a review, see: Zimmerman, A., & Dahlberg, J. (2008). The sexual objectification of women in advertising: A contemporary cultural perspective. *Journal of Advertising Research, 48*(1), 71–79. doi:10.2501/S0021849908080094

63. Walter, N. (2010). *Living dolls: The return of sexism.* London, UK: Virago.

64. Levy, A. (2005). *Female chauvinist pigs: Women and the rise of raunch culture.* New York, NY: Free Press.

65. Cited in: Heldman, C., & Wade, L. (2011). Sexualizing Sarah Palin: The social and political context of the sexual objectification of female candidates. *Sex Roles, 65,* 156–164. doi:10.1007/s11199-011-9984-6

66. Barron, M., & Kimmel, M. (2000). Sexual violence in three pornographic media: Toward a sociological explanation. *The Journal of Sex Research, 37,* 161–168.

67. Donnerstein, E. (1980). Aggressive erotica and violence against women. *Journal of Personality and Social Psychology, 39,* 269–277.

68. Jhally, S. (Writer, Narrator, & Editor). (2007). Dreamworlds 3 [Documentary film]. United States. Media Education Foundation.

69. Cady, J. (2009, August 10). Miley Cyrus pole dances at the Teen Choice Awards. Retrieved from http://www.eonline.com/news/miley_cyrus_pole_dances_teen_choice/138591

70. Schwartz, A. (2011, August 12). Britney Spears gives DJ Pauly D a lap dance. Retrieved from http://www.people.com/people/article/0,20517936,00.html

71. Pages 46–47 in: Moran, C. (2011). *How to be a woman.* New York, NY: Harper Perennial.

72. Pages 47–48 in: Moran, C. (2011). *How to be a woman.* New York, NY: Harper Perennial.

73. De Costa, A. (2013, May 22). 5 unintended consequences of America's war on pubic hair. Retrieved from http://www.alternet.org/print/sex-amp-relationships/5-unintended-consequences-americas-war-pubic-hair

74. For a discussion, see: Heldman, C., & Wade, L. (2011). Sexualizing Sarah Palin: The social and political context of the sexual objectification of female candidates. *Sex Roles, 65,* 156–164.

75. Walter, N. (2010). *Living dolls: The return of sexism.* London, UK: Virago.

76. McRobbie, A. (2008). Young women and consumer culture: An intervention. *Cultural Studies, 22,* 531–550. doi:10.1080/09502380802245803

77. See for example: http://www.juicycouture.com/accessories/little-luxuries/ Juicy Butt
http://itcantallbedior.blogspot.com/2011_08_01_archive.html 7/25/2012
http://www.hollywoodgrind.com/tag/juicy-couture/ 7/25/2012
http://buttercuppunch.wordpress.com/category/fashion/page/3/ 7/25/2012
Fun is back.
http://www.juicycouture.com/designer-handbags/canvas-bags/fun-is-back-tote-bag/098689292540,default,pd.html 07/25/2012

78. Walter, N. (2010). *Living dolls: The return of sexism*. London, UK: Virago.

79. Page 152: Carty, V. (2005). Textual portrayals of female athletes: Liberation or nuanced forms of patriarchy? *Frontiers, 26*(2), 132–155.

80. Carty, V. (2005). Textual portrayals of female athletes: Liberation or nuanced forms of patriarchy? *Frontiers, 26*(2), 132–155.

81. For a review of historic and contemporary stereotypes of African American women, see: Harris-Perry, M. V. (2011). *Sister citizen: Shame, stereotypes, and black women in America*. New Haven, CT: Yale University Press.

82. McRobbie, A. (2009). *The aftermath of feminism: Gender, culture and social change*. London, UK: Sage.

83. Emphasis added. Thomas Cobb, *An Inquiry into the Law of Negro Slavery*, 1858. Cited on page 157 in Accomando, C. (2001). *The regulations of robbers: Legal fictions of slavery and resistance*. Columbus, OH: The Ohio State University Press.

84. *George v. State*, Mississippi 1859. Cited on page 158 in Accomando, C. (2001). *The regulations of robbers: Legal fictions of slavery and resistance*. Columbus, OH: The Ohio State University Press.

85. Harris-Perry, M. V. (2011). *Sister citizen: Shame, stereotypes, and black women in America*. New Haven, CT: Yale University Press.

86. Smiley, T., & West, C. (2012). *The rich and the rest of us: A poverty manifesto*. New York, NY: Smiley Books.

87. McRobbie, A. (2009). *The aftermath of feminism: Gender, culture and social change*. London, UK: Sage.

88. McRobbie, A. (2009). *The aftermath of feminism: Gender, culture and social change*. London, UK: Sage.

89. Douglas, S. J. (2010). *Enlightened sexism: The seductive message that feminism's work is done*. New York, NY: Times Books.

90. Hanisch, C. (2011, Winter). Women's liberation: Looking back, looking forward. Retrieved from www.ontheissuesmagazine.com/2011/winter/2011_winter_Hanisch.php

91. McRobbie, A. (2009). *The aftermath of feminism: Gender, culture and social change*. London, UK: Sage.

92. Vavrus, M. D. (2012). Post-feminist redux? *The Review of Communication, 12*, 224–236.

93. Vavrus, M. D. (2012). Post-feminist redux? *The Review of Communication, 12*, 224–236.

94. Vavrus, M. D. (2012). Post-feminist redux? *The Review of Communication, 12*, 224–236.

95. Genz, S. (2006). Third way/ve: The politics of post-feminism. *Feminist Theory, 7*, 333–353. doi:10.1177/1464700106069040

96. McRobbie, A. (2009). *The aftermath of feminism: Gender, culture and social change*. London, UK: Sage.

97. Alam, J. (2012, November 28). Bangladesh factory fire: Disney, Sears used factory in blaze that killed more than 100 workers. Retrieved from: http://www.huffingtonpost.com/2012/11/28/bangladesh-factory-fire_n_2203614.html

98. Over 200 killed in Bangladesh factory collapse after workers forced to ignore building's dangers. (2013, April 25). Retrieved from http://www.democracynow.org/2013/4/25/over_200_killed_in_bangladesh_factory

2

POST-FEMINISM POST-9/11

I really believe that the pagans, and the abortionists, and the feminists, and the gays and the lesbians who are actively trying to make
that an alternative lifestyle, the ACLU, People for the American Way—
all of them who have tried to secularize America—I point the finger in
their face and say "you helped [9/11] happen."

—REVEREND JERRY FALWELL, *September 12, 2001*[1]

It is difficult to exaggerate the effect that the terror attacks of
September 11, 2001 had on nearly every aspect of American culture. Just as baby boomers recall where they were when President
Kennedy was assassinated, the present generation will remember
where they were when they heard of the 9/11 attacks. The short- and
medium-term impact of these attacks on the American people was
more than the wars in Iraq and Afghanistan. There was a war on progress that accelerated soon after the towers fell.

This chapter explores one set of consequences of the 9/11 terrorist attacks: the rolling back of progress on civil and human rights
and the retreat to traditional gender roles. We explore the post-9/11
trends that reflect the swiftness with which progress toward civil
rights and equality reverts to traditional patriarchal patterns of men
as breadwinners/protectors and women as homemakers/victims during times of crisis. The dust had not even settled after the fall of the
Twin Towers when many specific gains and the general progress of
the women's movement were swept away, leaving reinstitutionalized
"old-fashioned" patriarchal values.

This chapter is divided into two parts. First we look at the immediate aftermath of the 9/11 attacks and the emergence of a gendered
dominant narrative in the media. Social psychological theories such
as *terror management* join political and media analysis in an effort to
explain the reactions to the 9/11 attacks and the corresponding retreat
to traditional gender roles. Next, the post-9/11 retro trends such as
the media-reported "nesting" trend and popularity of "comfort food,"
the popularity of television shows that capture elements of a romantic
patriarchal past, and even the emergence of the purity ball as a way to

control young women's sexuality are examined. Finally, we explore these events and trends and their relationship to anti-feminist post-feminism.

September 11 and the Retreat to Traditional Gender Roles

It's probably a good thing they have blindfolds over the justice lady with the scales because if she could see what's going on she'd probably be pretty disgusted.

—DAVE GAUKROGER, 2013[2]

After the terror attacks on 9/11, President George W. Bush addressed the nation, and the joint session of Congress,[1] and characterized the attacks as "a world where freedom itself is under attack." President Bush specified that "America was targeted for attack because we're the brightest beacon for freedom and opportunity in the world." Those who committed the terrorist act were "enemies of freedom." Bush insisted that "they hate our freedoms—our freedom of religion, our freedom of speech, our freedom to vote and assemble and disagree with each other." In closing, President Bush declared "freedom and fear are at war."[3]

Apparently fear won because shortly after these declarations from the president, freedom, American or otherwise, was under attack. Not from Al Qaeda or Iraq but from within. By January of 2002, only four months after the attacks, a detention camp under U.S. military control at Guantánamo Bay in Cuba opened to imprison boys and men who were captured in Afghanistan—the planning center of the 9/11 attacks. Those detained were labeled "enemy combatants"—a vague military term that allowed the detainees to not be treated as prisoners of war, and thus without the rights guaranteed to those accused of crimes. Detainees were not afforded due process rights, the right to a speedy trial (or *any* trial), or the right to defend themselves; they were not even allowed to see the evidence against them. Only 8% of the boys and men imprisoned at Guantánamo were captured on a battlefield. Instead, they were captured in markets, taken from their homes, often turned in by neighbors or acquaintances who were enticed by flyers distributed by the U.S. military that advertised generous bounties for turning over people who might be "associated" with terrorists.[4] Many of the detainees were essentially kidnapped and turned over to the U.S. military. The hundreds of detainees at the detention camp were allowed no visits with family members,[5] no contact with the Red Cross,[6] heard no formal charges against them, were afforded no opportunity to answer to charges,[7] and offered no hope of ever leaving.

The Guantánamo disaster continued under President Obama, despite his promise to close the prison. By mid 2013, apparently having given up hope of ever being released despite being cleared of any terrorism charges by the U.S. Government, most of the remaining prisoners engaged in a prisonwide hunger strike. The U.S. military response was to push a tube through the detainees' noses and down their throats and force-feed them a liquid diet.[8]

This protracted international disappointment represents one of many victories of fear over freedom. Additional ongoing victories for fear are embodied in the form of the USA PATRIOT Act.[9] Hastily passed by a nervous Congress only 45 days after 9/11, the PATRIOT Act implied through its name that if you did not support and willingly comply with the repressive laws making up the Act, you did not love your country. The act was the first of many changes to surveillance laws that made it easier for the government to spy on any American citizen with newly expanded authority to monitor phone calls and email messages, collect bank and credit records, track Americans' usage of the Internet, obtain individual borrower library records, even search homes without telling the occupants. On May 26, 2011, the US Congress passed a four-year extension of the act and President Obama signed it.

How did we get here? How did optimism turn to fear, relative harmony in international relations to multiple wars, and relatively high regard by the international community to distrust? In her book *The Shock Doctrine: The Rise of Disaster Capitalism*, Naomi Klein[10] describes a process whereby a nation is so traumatized by a disaster—war, earthquake, market meltdown, terrorist attack—that the entire population finds itself in a state of collective shock. Government is increasingly influenced by *corporatists*—those who favor the transfer of public wealth to private companies—who seek to profit from the collective trauma of catastrophes and use the events to engage in radical economic and social engineering.[11] Klein argues that catastrophes in any part of the world constitute an "opportunity" for corporatists to enter the region for rebuilding and cleanup only to privatize nearly every aspect of the rebuilding: demolishing public schools for private, sometimes for-profit charter schools; creating private, for-profit prisons; even privatizing security by hiring firms such as *Blackwater*[12] to "keep order" in places like New Orleans after Hurricane Katrina. Peacekeeping and law enforcement that used to be carried out by local authorities has become contracted to private mercenary armies operating both within and outside of the United States. The "opportunity" here is for a huge transfer of public wealth into corporate hands. These trends representing movement from publicly owned entities to the private, for-profit sector is in line with the neoliberal corporatist trends described in Chapter 1.

Klein's description of the trauma after a catastrophe is useful to help us understand the state of collective shock experienced by Americans immediately after

9/11. People in a shocked state become weakened and beleaguered, Klein argues, and subsequently receptive to all kinds of tricks and takeovers they might otherwise resist. "The falling bombs, the bursts of terror, the pounding winds serve to soften up whole societies much as the blaring music and blows in the torture cells soften up prisoners. Like the terrorized prisoner who gives up the names of comrades and renounces his faith, shocked societies often give up things they would otherwise fiercely protect."[13] This is what happened to the United States after 9/11. With the help of a news media that hardly questioned the justification to invade Iraq in 2003,[14] or the rash passage of the PATRIOT Act,[15] we find that in the weeks and months after 9/11 Americans found themselves in a state in which the fear of another terrorist attack was greater than the fear of living in a society with restricted rights, hyper-surveillance, indefinite imprisonment, and drone killings of American citizens. Americans traditionally expect and cherish a right to privacy, freedom of speech, and freedom from intrusions from the federal government into private lives. In his many post-9/11 declarations, President George W. Bush linked these freedoms to American vulnerability to terrorist attack and in the name of the ongoing war on terror these freedoms were swiftly abridged. A New York Times/CBS News poll[16] in December of 2001, three months after the attacks, found that 80% of Americans supported indefinite detention for noncitizens who were deemed a threat to national security; 70% favored government monitoring of conversations between suspected terrorists and their lawyers; 64% favored allowing the president the authority to change rights guaranteed by the Constitution—tactics that many Americans would likely have opposed before 9/11. Tragically, indefinite detention, even of Americans, was codified into American law, not by President Bush but by President Obama when he signed the National Defense Authorization Act in January 2012.

Traditional Gender Roles: The New *Old* Normal

As the enormity of the attacks was unfolding, a narrative emerged in the media coverage of the event and aftermath that holds many years later. That narrative includes the heroic rescuer—men, mostly white, and heterosexual—who were police officers, firefighters, EMTs, and other first responders. The necessary contrast to the heroic rescuer were the victims—women—mostly in the form of widowed wives of the men who perished in the attacks. Of course, in reality, many first responders were women and many men were widowed as a result of the attacks. However, in the days after the attacks, the master narrative that emerged in the media was of women as damsels-in-distress and men as heroic protectors.[17]

And now, years after the attacks, the iconic images of 9/11 provided by media fit this same frame.

In this traditional narrative of the masculinization of first responders and the ignoring of the women firefighters, police officers, and medical personnel, we witnessed the revitalization of the gendered "firemen" rather than the professional term, "firefighters."[18] Using these outdated terms reflected the mass media gender narrative and at the same time reinforces and perpetuates this gendered arrangement. The graphic cartoon *Our Towering Heroes* likened the images of the twin towers of the World Trade Center to the bodies of two men—a firefighter and a police officer.[19]

In her book, *The Terror Dream: Myth and Misogyny in an Insecure America*, Susan Faludi describes the new gender role confines for women and men post-9/11.[20] As women were relegated to the role of victims, the widowed women became repositories of grief. The post-9/11 United States was a defensive country eager to demonstrate its toughness and masculinity. Barbara Berg writes of the "rush to defend and bolster an American manhood compromised and belittled by the attacks."[21] In the wake of the attacks, New York Mayor Rudolph Guiliani, Secretary of Defense Donald Rumsfeld, and President George W. Bush were represented as tough-guy super heroes, as were New York firefighters, or rather, fire*men*.[22]

The discourse of grief following the attacks suggests that it was mostly white, heterosexual families who had been torn apart by the attacks.[23] Hidden in the news reports of the hijackings was the story of a gay man who had left behind "friends" (and not "family") in San Francisco. The media did not show images of these friends; rather we saw only his grieving mother. Also forgotten in this picture of heroes and victims were the nonwhite, working class women and men—cooks, dishwashers, mail handlers, janitors, and immigrant workers—who died at the Pentagon and World Trade Center that day. These images would be incongruent with the image of the "real" American, an image of white masculinity that was easy for Americans to rally around.

Soon after the attacks, the widows of 9/11 could be seen on the evening news and talk shows, whereas widowed men were, for the most part, invisible. The women survivors were celebrated as grieving wives and mothers, with the country projecting their fears, sadness, and sympathies onto these women. But as Susan Faludi argues, the 9/11 widows were shown sympathetically as long as they did not deviate from the constructed damsel-in-distress script provided for them by the media. When a group of 9/11 widows who became known as the "Jersey Girls" began to question the script—by asking questions critical of the Bush Administration and its handling of the aftermath of the attacks—they were marginalized in the press in favor of more easily digestible traditional women.

Likewise, the documentary *Women at Ground Zero*, about women rescue workers, was criticized as anti-male and anti-American because it did not follow the script of men as rescuers/women as victims and dared to put women first-responders at the center for a moment.[24] Women firefighters and police officers not only battled the 9/11 attacks but also were under attack from a society that views them as trespassing men's domain. These women were under attack from some of their male coworkers who sabotaged them by draining their oxygen tanks and making death threats.[25] An article on the CNN website about its documentary, "Beyond Bravery: The Women of 9/11," generated hostile comments from readers on the CNN website. One reader writes, "*I find this article almost offensive, really. Fighting for recognition 'as women?' Seriously? Why is this about men and women?*" Another reader says, "*Are you kidding me? Come on, this is ridiculous, women always think they have it worse then[sic] men.*"[26] These comments reflect the notion of the *center-stage problem*[27] we will examine in Chapter 4. When attention is turned away from the majority (and thus legitimate) group, however briefly, the attention is interpreted as a takeover of the majority group by the encroaching minority group. These reader comments also reflect the fiction of a level playing field; a fiction that the playing field is equal and only becomes destabilized when women and minorities attempt to gain some ostensibly undeserved and unearned advantage.

Dealing with Dissent

Dissent was one of the first casualties of the war on terror. Shortly after the attacks commentators and celebrities who were critical of U.S. policies toward Arab and Muslim countries were shunned in the national press. Bill Maher lost his television show *Politically Incorrect* in 2002 after he questioned the script that prescribed the 9/11 terrorists as cowards. Like the treatment of the Jersey Girls—those 9/11 widows that questioned the gendered script—women critics seemed to have gotten the worst of it. According to Susan Faludi, a particular kind of fury was directed at women writers and commentators such as Susan Sontag, Katha Pollitt, and Fran Lebowitz, who dared question U.S. policy. They were labeled traitorous, idiotic, and haughty. Both Faludi and Barbara Berg note that the presence of women op-ed writers and broadcast pundits decreased shortly after September 11. Women who did appear were anti-feminist commentators such as Kate O'Beirne, Christina Hoff Sommers, Peggy Noonan, and Camille Paglia.[28]

The crushing of dissent continued through the invasion of Iraq. When country music stars the Dixie Chicks criticized President Bush in 2003, they faced boycotts from radio stations and even death threats in this new environment that was intolerant of dissent.[29] In the weeks before the U.S. invasion of Iraq—a time when our country should have been vigorously debating the merits of invading a country that had nothing to do with the 9/11 attacks—conservative pro-war voices were almost exclusively heard on TV. Fairness & Accuracy in Reporting (FAIR) conducted a study of nightly news stories about Iraq on ABC, CBS, NBC, and PBS in the weeks before the U.S. invasion of Iraq in 2003.[30] FAIR found that 76% percent of all sources on these programs were current or former government officials—no political scientists, historians, Iraqis, anti-war activists, religious leaders, or veterans not working for the government.[31] On the four major networks combined, just *one* of 267 U.S. sources was affiliated with antiwar activism—less than half a percent. This coverage occurred at a time when 61% of U.S. respondents were telling pollsters that an invasion of Iraq was premature and more time was needed for diplomacy with Iraq. Overall, only 17% of the total on-camera sources represented skeptical positions on the U.S. war policy.[32] Thus, even when a majority of Americans were skeptical of the invasion of Iraq, the media presented the invasion as justified and inevitable. There was virtually no space for alternative points of view.

Once the U.S. invasion of Afghanistan and Iraq began, the media had another type of woman to grapple with—one who did not fit the damsel-in-distress script: the woman soldier. How did the media fit women GIs into a master narrative of retrograde roles for women? To the extent that women fighting in Afghanistan and Iraq were covered by news media, their role as wives and mothers was emphasized.[33] Like the Jersey Girls, women who disturbed the script, when they weren't vilified or invisible, were reconceived and reconstructed into a traditional gender narrative: primarily wives and mothers. Like women firefighters, women in the military were fighting battles on two fronts: the wars in Iraq and Afghanistan and the war against them by men in the military who saw women not as comrades but as targets for sexual assault. Enlisted women face higher levels of sexual assault than non-enlisted women and most of the assaults are perpetrated by the men they work with. Rape occurs in the military nearly twice as often as in the civilian world, and rates of sexual assault are even higher during war. A 2013 Pentagon report estimated that 26,000 active duty soldiers (both women and men) were sexually assaulted the previous year—an average of about 70 assaults each day.[34] Women who reported such violence to their commanding officers were often forced to take a lie detector test and continue to work with the perpetrators when nothing further was done about the crime. The post 9/11 veneration of the American male soldier makes criticism of the military unacceptable.[35]

In the post-9/11 context, feminist discussions were denied and marginalized, placed on indeterminate hold, as other discussions such as killing terrorists were deemed more serious and of greater importance.[36] In this context, bringing up gender issues is seen as a sign of disloyalty.[37] Civil rights become an extravagance that the country cannot afford during wartime. These post-9/11 trends illustrate the quickness with which progress toward civil rights and equality became subverted as the country returned to traditional patriarchal patterns of men as breadwinners/heroes and women as homemakers/moms. It is almost as if in the amount of time it took the Twin Towers to fall, much of the progress from the women's movement was pushed aside for the safety, comfort, and reassuring veneer of "old-fashioned" patriarchal values. When the country is under siege and at war, progressive politics and civil rights are easily dismissed as capricious luxuries that distract from constructed core values of masculine protector and female victim.[38]

One constituency of women that was tolerated was the "security mom." By 2004 when President George W. Bush ran for reelection, "security moms"— women identified as mothers concerned about the safety of their children and the country—were constructed by the media as a serious constituency for presidential candidates to court.[39] And then by 2008, the "Mama Grizzly," inspired by Sarah Palin's vice-presidential run, served the same purpose.[40] Tough, fiercely protective women, but tough in a mommy way.

The atmosphere of war shapes voters' attitudes about women and men as candidates for political office. Military and foreign policy issues had not played much of a central role in recent U.S. political campaigns prior to 2001.[41] That changed after 9/11. In one sample, 80% of respondents reported that foreign policy was an "important" or "very important" issue determining vote choice. This view was the norm regardless of the gender, race, or political affiliation of the respondent. In peacetime, women are about as likely as men to win elections, but not during war. People tend to believe that men candidates are better at dealing with military issues than are women. In the time after 9/11 people tended to believe that men would be more competent at punishing those responsible for 9/11 and would be more able to protect the nation from future attacks.[42]

Since 1937 national random samples have answered the question, "If your political party nominated a woman for president, would you be willing to vote for her if she were qualified for the job?" The majority of Americans were unwilling to vote for a woman in the 1930s and 1940s, but levels of support increased throughout the next several decades. By the late 1990s, about 95% of those surveyed expressed willingness to vote for a woman candidate. In fact, because the question produced such a high percentage of agreement, it was dropped by the pollsters in 2000. A different survey in 2002, however, found that only 65% of respondents would be willing to vote for a woman for president. A political climate dominated by foreign policy and military concerns appears to account for part of the reason that overall willingness to elect a woman president in 2002 was as low as it was in the early 1970s.[43]

Recognition of the women heroes of 9/11 and its aftermath by feminists did little to shake up the pervasive imagery of masculine men in uniform storming up the stairs of the World Trade Center and construction crews (made up entirely of men) digging through dusty rubble in search of bodies. There was a parallel imagery of sorrowful widows, but that too turned out to be a false image of helplessness when the women became an aggressive activist group. Another activist group was the lesbian and gay partners of those who died on 9/11. They sued to be recognized as family members by the federal September 11 Victim Compensation Fund.[44] The conventional categories and familiar roles convey stability in times of crisis, so it looks as though "men fight and women weep." But the reality is that in this disaster, as in many others, women can be on the frontlines, and men cry—even if their tears are off camera.

Managing Mortality during Terror Attacks

In the aftermath of 9/11 political attitudes shifted to the right with Americans becoming significantly more conservative following the attacks. This shift occurred among self-identified liberals, moderates, and conservatives. The most pronounced shifts were seen when people were asked their opinion of George W. Bush and the military.[45] *Terror management theory* is based on the idea that individuals grapple with two human characteristics—the instinct for self-preservation and the knowledge that one's death is inevitable. Humans deal with this existential terror by developing cultural institutions and worldviews that provide them meaning and explanation of this conflict. Culture and institutions, such as the family, religion, and nation, provide security and the sense that membership in those institutions can transcend death. People are motivated to defend their culture, their values, and their worldview—against real and imagined challenges alike. Hundreds of studies on terror management find that when people are made aware of the inevitability of their own deaths, that is, when their *mortality is made salient*, they experience a need to reinforce strong attachment to faith in their beliefs.[46] Terror management theory then predicts that when people are faced with actual or symbolic mortality they cling tightly to their worldviews; they derogate those who are perceived to threaten their worldview; and in a leap from internal thought process to large-scale social and political practice, they support leaders that make them feel safe. The mere existence of differing points of view or diverse opinions raises the possibility that one's own views could be misguided or wrong. To avoid consciously recognizing that their own opinions could be wrong, people disparage the views of the others by questioning others' values, motives, integrity, and intelligence. In times of crisis, dissent is dealt with harshly.[47]

The terror attacks of 9/11 serve as a gigantic mortality salience experience. The deaths, the destruction of buildings, and the obliteration of perceived and actual cherished symbols (World Trade Center, American Airlines and United Airlines planes used in the attacks) severely destabilized the functional integrity of the psychological protection that usually enables us to feel protected and safe in a world where the only real certainty in life is death. If we look at the events in the days, weeks, and months after 9/11 in the context of terror management, we see a lot of clinging to the familiar and disparaging of the unfamiliar. Terror management theory explains in part why men, but not women, who were first responders were elevated as heroes and why women, but not men, were pictured in need of rescue. In times of crisis, this constructed gender arrangement feels comfortable and consistent with many individuals' values and worldviews. Terror management theory also explains why dissenters were harshly punished in media, and why those who criticized U.S. policy were quashed. Especially women dissenters. The post-9/11 conservative climate alongside traditional gender roles that call for women to be not too opinionated produced an intolerance of women critical of the U.S. government. In times of terror, people look for strong (male) leaders to help them feel safe. A 2005 study found that when thoughts of death were primed, support for President George W. Bush increased and support for the 2004 presidential candidate John Kerry decreased; in the control condition—when death thoughts were not primed—attitudes were the opposite.[48] Trust in the federal government (and state and local) increased immediately after the attacks. This change was especially likely for white women and men but it did occur to a lesser extent for African American women and men (other ethnicities were not examined). After about six months, attitudes returned to pre-9/11 opinions.[49]

The retreat to traditional gender roles is consistent with a nation reminded of its symbolic and literal mortality. One way people manage their anxiety about mortality is by identifying with and supporting those in power who make them feel like they are a valued part of something larger than themselves. When mortality is made salient, people adhere to values that give them comfort. One experiment[50] on the evaluation of leaders found that when men were made to think of death (compared to something less threatening), they preferred a male leader who was assertive, decisive, and independent, whereas women preferred a leader of either gender with those characteristics. Another study[51] found that mortality salience increased adherence to cultural gender stereotypes such that people favored women job candidates who were applying to be a fashion writer and men candidates who were applying for a sports writer position over applicants applying for the counterstereotype positions. When people are reminded of their mortality, they seek to confirm the validity of their cultural worldviews.

Correspondingly, mortality salience produces especially punitive reactions to perceived moral transgressions. For example, one study found that municipal court judges assigned far greater penalties to prostitutes after a brief reminder of their own deaths, compared to judges not reminded of death.[52] And when mortality salience is induced, men report more negative feelings toward a "seductive" woman versus a "wholesome" woman (same woman, just presented differently) and they recommended a more lenient sentence for a perpetrator of male to female violence compared to male-male violence.[53] Thus, in the post-9/11 context, women in the military, women firefighters, feisty widows, and "unwholesome" women present a problem for people. As we will explore in Chapter 5, nontraditional women are always a problem for people, but especially in times of crisis and uncertainty. Terror management theory allows us to understand why dissent was punished so harshly and why so many Americans, though certainly not all, seemed to tolerate the incursion on civil and human rights post-9/11.

Terror management would also predict the post-9/11 increases in hate crimes against Muslims, or those thought to be Muslim (or Arab or Middle Eastern).[54] People who are different from "us" are also dealt with harshly by the majority as a result of heightened concerns about death. Mortality salience leads to increased prejudice and stereotyping. The mere existence of those who are different from us is threatening in that the validity of our own death-transcending cultural worldview is or can be questioned. When people need protection from anxiety, which is the case when they have been reminded of their mortality, there is a tendency to stereotype and reject those who are different from themselves.[55] Interestingly, whereas the endorsement of violence in general did not increase after 9/11, the endorsement of violence through war, as well as endorsement of violence toward people who break the law, did increase after 9/11.[56] These attitudes began to return to the original baseline rates within a year after the attacks. Did these changes in attitudes make it easier to accept the invasions of Afghanistan and Iraq? Or perhaps the invasion of Afghanistan influenced these pro-war attitudes.

Post-9/11 Retro Trends

In the weeks and months after 9/11 reporters and pundits commented on the return to traditional values. There were articles, for instance, about single women who had placed careers ahead of matrimony but now were said to be looking for husbands.[57] Regardless of whether these reports reflected actual trends or simply anecdotes that resonated with the post-9/11 traditional gender frame, these reports circulated nonetheless. In support of these trends, women in the late 2000s were actually found to be more likely to change their names to their husband's last name after marriage than women in the 1990s.[58] Media reported on the post-9/11 "nesting" trend by which people stayed home and avoided travel[59]—taking "staycations" rather than vacations. There were even reports of a post-9/11 trend in American cooking: "comfort food"—traditional food characteristic of the 1950s such as meatloaf, macaroni and cheese, and mashed potatoes.[60] Of course, comfort food in this context is not universal but is raced and classed; it refers to the old timey food characteristics of middle-class whites. Collard greens, tamales, and pork buns are not included on the post-9/11 comfort food menu. Although there appeared to be no actual link between sales of meatloaf and mashed potatoes and 9/11,[61] many in the media made explicit the link between comfort food and 9/11, even if it was not real.[62] These reports are consistent with the prediction from a terror management perspective that in uncertain times Americans gravitate toward the familiar, a harkening back to a (supposedly) simpler time.[63] Even if the simpler times of the "good old days" of the 1950s didn't actually exist, and certainly did not exist for communities of color in the pre-civil-rights-movement era,[64] comfort food symbolizes this ostensibly simpler, familiar, more predictable time.

In the several years after 9/11 you still see retro trends. A 2009 article titled "Comfortably Yum: In Times of Uncertainty, Comfort Food Makes a Comeback"[65] still refers to 9/11 but also references job loss and recession as factors in the attraction of comfort food. Beginning with the 2005 revival of the Ford Mustang, there has been a resurgence of 1960s-era American-made muscle cars such as the Camaro, Challenger, GTO, and Charger. These vehicles represent an earlier time, a stronger and more masculine time, and an era that was also more profitable for the U.S. auto industry and the U.S. more generally. It is ironic that these low-gas-mileage muscle cars resurfaced while the debate about peak oil and global warming was occurring. Retro television shows became popular by the end of the first decade of the 21st century. In 2007, the television show *Mad Men*, about the white, heterosexual, male-dominated world of Madison Avenue "ad men" in the 1960s, became a hit. Riding the retro wave clothing company Banana Republic introduced their *Mad Men* collection in 2011. Inspired by the television show, the collection offered consumers sophisticated dressing from the early 1960s. The women's collection offered "ladylike pieces" such as "feminine lace shell blouses and chic coral cropped capris"[66] and tight dresses that accentuate the sexy secretary style so common in 1960s film (if not in real life). The styles for professional women stand in stark contrast to the more tailored men's styled business attire women wore in, say, the 1980s. Back by popular demand, Banana Republic debuted its second collection of *Mad Men* styles in time for the 2012 season premiere of the television show. The attire inspired by *Mad Men* has different implications for feminism and women than the actual television show. The TV show offered the viewer a critique of the sexism, racism, and homophobia of the advertising industry and the culture of the 1960s dealing with issues such as segregation, abortion, and rape. The ladylike pieces from Banana Republic offer the hyperfeminine looks of the time without the critique of how women were treated in the workplace and how women were limited in their choices between the bored housewife of *Mad Men's* Betty Draper or the vixen working woman Joan Holloway.

For the 2011 television season networks introduced retro shows such as *The Playboy Club* about the early days of Hugh Hefner's men's clubs in the 1960s, and *PanAm*, a retro look at flight attendants ("stewardesses") in the early days of Pan American Airlines. The actual Playboy clubs that were scattered about the United States in the 1960s that showcased bunny-eared, cotton-tailed, corseted young women as hosts and servers closed its remaining club in 1986 when the tenor of the times changed. However, by 2006, a Playboy club opened in Las Vegas, followed by openings in London and other cities. By 2011 there were plans to reopen the club in Chicago close to the original Playboy Club.[67] Apparently, in the post-9/11 world, the time was ripe to relaunch this gender throwback replete with its stylized retro trappings.

On the *Lifetime* television network, the program *Army Wives* premiered in 2007. Its sixth season began in 2012. This present-day drama follows the lives of four army wives and one army husband. It is different from *Mad Men, The Playboy Club*, and *PanAm*, in that it is based on the present, not on the past, when gender roles were more rigid and women's options were more limited than they are today. However, at a time when the United States was active in two wars and enlisted women's military service was relatively normalized, it is a revealing choice to create a show focused on the wives and families of enlisted *men*.

In her analysis of "chick-flick" films that came out after 9/11, Diane Negra[68] finds that women characters in these films are encouraged to find love over career, or to the extent that the main character keeps her career, it becomes privatized—she begins to work at home, for instance. Negra argues that these post-feminist qualities in chick flicks were already in play in the years immediately before 9/11; however, they were given new traction after 9/11 because they were consistent with the discourse that advocated traditionalism as the appropriate response to the new conservative national climate. Negra contends, "the post-9/11 cultural climate emphasized the re-essentialization of gender as a panacea for the doubt, confusion, sadness, and anger that marked national life."[69]

Another curious phenomenon of the post-9/11 era is the purity ball. Purity balls correspond to the popularity of abstinence-only education of the George W. Bush era. The first purity ball was held in 1998, but the phenomenon became popularized and prevalent in the United States in the early and mid 2000s. One source reports that 4,000 purity events took place in the United States in 2007.[70] The purity ball centers on maintaining the purity of girls and young women until marriage. Daughters pledge their virginity to their fathers at these ceremonies, which resemble something of a wedding, a prom, and a debutante ball. The website purity-ball.com sponsored by The Christian Center enthuses, "God thinks the protection of a woman's purity should be extravagant and so do we!"[71] These events usually include a formal dinner, dance, pictures with father and daughter(s), and some kind of ceremony during which the father pledges to his daughter, "I will be pure in my own life as a man, husband, and father." "I will be a man of integrity and accountability as I lead, guide and pray over my daughter and my family as the High Priest in my home."[72] Daughters in turn pledge their moral, physical, and sexual purity to their fathers until they are able to transfer the commitment from their fathers to the man they will marry. The ball usually culminates in prayer and the signing of a purity pledge or the presentation of a purity ring given by father to daughter (that she wears on her left hand). Many critics' reports of these events describe them as "creepy"—an article in *Maclean's* is titled, "Dad's your prom date."[73] That the girls and young women wear prom-like attire—spaghetti straps and heels—and their fathers wear suits or tuxedos is a confusing positioning of girls wearing feminine and even revealing attire—designed to attract suitors—at an event during which she pledges to her father her commitment to virginity until marriage.

There is much to criticize about purity events such as the reification of the father being in charge of a daughter's purity until he gives her away to another man. The father gives permission to the new man to have sex with her: women are first the property of fathers and then the property of husbands, and female honor rests with male protectors. There is also the extreme gender essentialism and absurd sexual double standard that says a young woman's "purity" is more important than a young man's. What about boys' and young men's purity? What are they up to while their same-aged female peers are pledging their purity to their fathers and God? Of course the assumption of heterosexuality as the only normal type of relationship option is implicit in these events. Where do young lesbians fit in to these events and this discourse? The websites showcasing these events appear to be events exclusively for white girls and their fathers. Do young women of color have a chance at purity as well? Probably not because, as discussed in Chapter 1, stereotypes about African American women, for example, have branded them as hypersexual and therefore their purity is impossible or irrelevant.[74]

On a more practical note, the message preached at these events is sexual abstinence. As we know after considerable study of abstinence-only education programs in schools, preaching abstinence has significant negative outcomes for its pupils. Analyses of abstinence-only programs demonstrate a profound disconnect between intention and practice on the part of young people. Abstinence-only education programs are associated with *higher* than average teenage pregnancy and birth rates in the United States. In contrast, the lowest teen pregnancy rates are from those programs that provide comprehensive sex education, covering abstinence alongside proper contraception, condom use, and HIV prevention.[75] What about the young women who take purity pledges? In a five-year longitudinal study of U.S. adolescents comparing those who took a virginity pledge and teens who did not, those who pledged virginity were just as likely to engage in premarital sex and had just as many sexually transmitted diseases as those teens who did not make a virginity pledge. However, those teens who took pledges were significantly less likely to use birth control and condoms than those who did not take a virginity pledge.[76] Unfortunately, the function of a virginity pledge seems to be to create an environment of ignorance and complacency that results in reckless behavior. And purity balls are certainly consistent with other retro trends that function to bring women back to an earlier and controlled time.

Conclusion

The previous chapter explored the features of anti-feminism in a post-feminist era. This chapter explores the role of 9/11 in a retreat to gender traditionalism that has occurred in the decade since 9/11, influenced by the reaction to the terror attacks of 9/11. The events of 9/11 did not introduce a brand new set of norms and agendas. Rather, 9/11 enhanced and accelerated a conservative agenda already in place in the United States. The attacks afforded an opportunity to make this post-feminist agenda palatable to more Americans. Like the post-feminist trends described in Chapter 1, this process began in the early 1980s, not on September 12, 2001. The neoliberal agenda ushered in by Ronald Reagan was allowed to flourish after the trauma of 9/11. Given the gravity of the event, no good American would question this new reality, or what Barbara Berg calls, the new *old* normal.[77]

The collective shock experienced by a nation during a crisis makes possible large movements of privatizing public institutions and curtailing constitutional rights—in the post-9/11 context these are seen as shared sacrifices for the good of winning the war on terror. Progressive politics become viewed as capricious extravagances that distract from killing terrorists. But the sacrifice is not shared equally. Women are relegated to the home and are punished for speaking out. Part of the corporatist agenda is to cut back and deregulate. The first responders of 9/11 were constructed as heroes in the news media. But when they got sick it took Congress nearly 10 years for the government to formally recognize that the toxins at Ground Zero of the World Trade Center caused illness and death in the workers and to pass a law that would cover health care costs for first responders. When the bill finally came to a vote in 2010, 41 of 42 Republican Senators voted against it. So politicians were quick to use 9/11 responders and their bravery when they were constructing a rationale to invade Iraq and Afghanistan and rolling back civil rights, but they then abandoned those same heroes when they became vulnerable and ill. This shameful paradox prompted *The Daily Show's* Jon Stewart to say, "You know what Republicans? You use 9/11 so much, if you don't owe 9/11 first responders health care, at least you owe them royalties."[78]

In Chapter 1, we explored some key aspects of post-feminism such as consumerism, neoliberalism, privatization, and hypersexualization under the auspices of choice and empowerment for women. The mainstreaming of pornography and the hypersexualization of girls and women might at first glance seem incongruous with the retrograde trends described in this chapter. In fact, both pressures on and constructions of women represented in these two chapters work in concert to marginalize women and to relegate them to traditional gender roles. In the case of "empowerment" through self-objectification described in Chapter 1, women are offered "choices" through their ability to purchase consumer goods with their own incomes (middle-class women, at least). However, the range of their choices is confined to being sexually appealing to others. There is little room for actual sexual pleasure and agency, unless agency is measured by your ability to make yourself look hot. One of the contributions of the feminist movement of the 1970s was women's control over their own bodies—to have sexual intercourse without coercion, without the fear of pregnancy, and for pleasure, to be able to terminate a pregnancy, and to be able to have children by choice. In post-feminism, women are encouraged to be sexually appealing, but there is little discourse of women's own sexual agency and pleasure. Being sexy is not the same as being sexual. And spinning on a pole for others' pleasure is not the same as choosing sexual partners for a woman's own sexual pleasure, on her own terms.

The post-9/11 retreat to traditionalism is similarly confining and retrograde. A crisis like 9/11 demonstrates how tenuous civil rights and progressive gender politics are and how they can be pushed back. The result is the claim that women are best suited for playing the role of the helpless victim and when they resist, when they get mouthy, they are punished publicly—even more so than mouthy men. Sassy women violate traditional gender roles that prescribe women as smiling and supportive and in the background. The focus on women as wives and mothers confines women into narrow, old-fashioned roles where agency and empowerment take the form of cooking comfort food and being a "mama grizzly."

The constructions of women in both chapters are retrograde and objectifying, just in different ways. There are always tensions in cultural tropes—seemingly contradictory stereotypes and roles, but they are roles that work together and help define each other: virgin/whore, mammy/jezebel, lotus blossom/dragon lady. These dimensions often undergird each other. They are two sides of the same sexist coin. Rather than women being divided into these two contradictory roles that we have seen historically, today's post-feminist woman is likely to feel pressure to be both. The post-feminist woman takes pole-dancing classes at the gym and gets home in time to make macaroni and cheese for her husband. That might seem doubly oppressive, but post-feminism tells women that these roles reflect freedom—she is "free" to put on an apron and cook mash potatoes and is "free" to take off that apron and twirl around a pole.

Notes

1. Falwell apologizes to gays, feminists, lesbians (2001, September 14). *CNN.com* Retrieved from http://articles.cnn.com/2001-09-14/us/Falwell.apology_1_thomas-road-baptist-church-jerry-falwell-feminists?_s=PM:US

2. Gaukroger, D., & Sear, J. (2013, April 25). The austerity of hope. *Something Wonky* [podcast]. See http://somethingwonky.com

3. Bush, G. W. (2001, September 20). Address to joint session of congress following 9/11 attacks. Retrieved at http://www.washingtonpost.com/wp-srv/nation/specials/attacked/transcripts/bushaddress_092001.html

4. For a more extensive discussion, see Chapter 1 in: Anderson, K. J. (2010). *Benign bigotry: the psychology of subtle prejudice.* Cambridge, UK: Cambridge University Press.

5. Margulies, J. (2006). *Guantánamo and the abuse of presidential power.* New York, NY: Simon & Schuster.

6. Glaberson, W. (2007, November 16). Red Cross monitors barred from Guantánamo. *The New York Times.* Retrieved from http://www.nytimes.com
See also: Soldz, S., & Assange, J. (2007, November 17). Guantanamo document confirms psychological torture. *Wikileaks.* Retrieved from www.wikileaks.org/wiki/Guantanamo_document_confirms_psychological_torture

7. Margulies, J. (2006). *Guantánamo and the abuse of presidential power.* New York, NY: Simon & Schuster.

8. Harris, P., McVeigh, T., & Townsend, M. (2013, May 4). How Guantánamo's horror forced inmates to hunger strike. Retrieved from http://www.guardian.co.uk/world/2013/may/04/guantanamo-hunger-strike

9. Whitehead, J. W., & Aden, S. H. (2002). Forfeiting "enduring freedom" for "homeland security": A constitutional analysis of the USA Patriot Act and the Justice Department's anti-terrorism initiatives. *American University Law Review, 51,* 1081–1133.

10. Klein, N. (2007). *The shock doctrine: The rise of disaster capitalism.* New York, NY: Picador.

11. Here I use Naomi Klein's definition and description of *corporatist*: "Its main characteristics are huge transfers of public wealth to private hands, often accompanied by exploding debt, an ever-widening chasm between the dazzling rich and the disposable poor and an aggressive nationalism that justifies bottomless spending on security" (p. 18). Klein, N. (2007). *The shock doctrine: The rise of disaster capitalism.* New York, NY: Picador.

12. Because of its tarnished reputation, *Blackwater* changed its name to *Xe Services*, and then changed its name again to *Academi*.

13. Page 20: Klein, N. (2007). *The shock doctrine: The rise of disaster capitalism.* New York, NY: Picador.

14. Rendall, S. (2003, April). In prelude to war, TV served as official megaphone. *Fairness & Accuracy in Reporting.* Retrieved from: http://www.fair.org/index.php?page=4292

15. Muted response to Aschcroft's sneak attack on liberties. (2003, February 2). *Fairness & Accuracy in Reporting.* Retrieved from http://fair.org/press-release/muted-response-to-ashcrofts-sneak-attack-on-liberties/

16. Toner, R., & Elder, J. (2001, December 12). A nation challenged: Attitudes; public is wary but supportive on rights curbs. *The New York Times.* Retrieved from: http://www.nytimes.com

17. Faludi, S. (2007). *The terror dream: Myth and misogyny in an insecure America.* New York, NY: Picador.

18. Dowler, L. (2002). Women on the frontlines: Rethinking war narratives post 9/11. *GeoJournal, 58,* 159–165.

19. Dowler, L. (2002). Women on the frontlines: Rethinking war narratives post 9/11. *GeoJournal, 58,* 159–165.

20. Faludi, S. (2007). *The terror dream: Myth and misogyny in an insecure America.* New York, NY: Picador.

21. Page 103: Berg, B. J. (2009). *Sexism in America: Alive, well, and ruining our future.* Chicago, IL: Lawrence Hill Books.

22. Faludi, S. (2007). *The terror dream: Myth and misogyny in an insecure America.* New York, NY: Picador.

23. Grewal, I. (2003). Transnational America: Race, gender and citizenship after 9/11. *Social Identities, 9,* 535–561. doi:10.1080/1350463032000174669

24. Faludi, S. (2007). *The terror dream: Myth and misogyny in an insecure America.* New York, NY: Picador.

25. Dowler, L. (2002). Women on the frontlines: Rethinking war narratives post 9/11. *GeoJournal, 58,* 159–165.

26. O'Brien, S. (2011, September 7). Reporter's notebook: Women of 9/11 still fighting for recognition, respect. *CNN.com.* Retrieved from http://www.cnn.com/2011/ US/09/05/beyond.bravery.soledad.notebook/index.html?iref=allsearch

27. Grillo, T., & Wildman, S. M. (1997). Obscuring the importance of race: The implication of making comparisons between racism and sexism (or other isms). In A. K. Wing (Ed.) *Critical race feminism: A reader* (pp 44–50). New York, NY: New York University Press.

28. Berg, B. J. (2009). *Sexism in America: Alive, well, and ruining our future.* Chicago, IL: Lawrence Hill Books.
Faludi, S. (2007). The terror dream: Myth and misogyny in an insecure America. New York, NY: Picador.

29. Dixie Chicks recall death threat. (2006, May 11). *NBCNews.com* Retrieved from: http:// www.today.com/id/12745436/ns/today-entertainment/t/dixie-chicks-recall-death-threat/

30. Rendall, S. (2003, March 18). In Iraq crisis, networks are megaphones for official views. *Fairness & Accuracy in Reporting.* Retrieved from http://www.fair.org/index. php?page=3158

31. Rendall, S. (2003, April). In prelude to war, TV served as official megaphone. *Fairness & Accuracy in Reporting.* Retrieved from http://www.fair.org/index. php?page=4292

32. Rendall, S. (2003, March 18). In Iraq crisis, networks are megaphones for official views. *Fairness & Accuracy in Reporting.* Retrieved from http://www.fair.org/index. php?page=3158

33. Dowler, L. (2002). Women on the frontlines: Rethinking war narratives post 9/11. *GeoJournal, 58,* 159–165.

34. Department of Defense. (2013, May 3). Department of Defense annual report on sexual assault in the military (Vol. 1): Fiscal year 2012. Retrieved from http:// www.sapr.mil/media/pdf/reports/FY12_DoD_SAPRO_Annual_Report_ on_Sexual_Assault-VOLUME_ONE.pdf

35. Wilson, N. (2010, Spring). Culture of rape. *Ms. Magazine, 20*(2), 32–35.

36. Dowler, L. (2002). Women on the frontlines: Rethinking war narratives post 9/11. *GeoJournal, 58,* 159–165.

37. Dowler, L. (2002). Women on the frontlines: Rethinking war narratives post 9/11. *GeoJournal, 58,* 159–165.

38. Faludi, S. (2007). *The terror dream: Myth and misogyny in an insecure America.* New York, NY: Picador.

39. Elder, L., & Greene, S. (2007). The myth of the "security moms" and "NASCAR dads": Parenthood, political stereotypes, and the 2004 election. *Social Science Quarterly, 88,* 1–19.

40. McCabe, J. (2012). States of confusion: Sarah Palin and the politics of US mothering. *Feminist Media Studies, 12,* 149–153.

41. Lawless, J. L. (2004). Women, war, and winning elections: Gender stereotyping in the post-September 11 era. *Political Research Quarterly, 57,* 479–490.

42. Lawless, J. L. (2004). Women, war, and winning elections: Gender stereotyping in the post-September 11 era. *Political Research Quarterly, 57,* 479–490.

43. Lawless, J. L. (2004). Women, war, and winning elections: Gender stereotyping in the post-September 11 era. *Political Research Quarterly, 57,* 479–490.

44. Knauer, N. J. (2005). The September 11 relief efforts and surviving same-sex partners: Reflections on relationships in the absence of uniform legal recognition. *Women's Rights Law Reporter, 26,* 101–116.

45. Nail, P. R., & McGregor, I. (2009). Conservative shift among liberals and conservatives following 9/11/01. *Social Justice Research, 22,* 231–240. doi:10.1007/s11211-009-0098-z

46. Pyszczynski, T., Solomon, S., & Greenberg, J. (2003). *In the wake of 9/11: The psychology of terror.* Washington, DC: American Psychological Association.

47. Pyszczynski, T., Solomon, S., & Greenberg, J. (2003). *In the wake of 9/11: The psychology of terror.* Washington, DC: American Psychological Association.

48. Cohen, F., Ogilvie, D. M., Solomon, S., Greenberg, J., & Pyszczynski, T. (2005). American roulette: The effect of reminders of death on support for George W. Bush in the 2004 presidential election. *Analyses of Social Issues and Public Policy, 5*(1), 177–187.

49. Perrin, A. J., & Smolek, S. J. (2009). Who trusts? Race, gender and the September 11 rally effect among young adults. *Social Science Research, 38,* 134–145. doi:10.1016/j.ssresearch.2008.09.001

50. Hoyt, C. L., Simon, S., & Reid, L. (2009). Choosing the best (wo)man for the job: The effects of mortality salience, sex, and gender stereotypes on leader evaluations. *The Leadership Quarterly, 20,* 233–246. doi:10.1016/j.leaqua.2009.01.016

51. Schimel, J., Simon, L., Greenberg, J., Pyszczynski, T., Solomon, S., Waxmonsky, J., & Arndt, J. (1999). Stereotypes and terror management: Evidence that mortality salience enhances stereotypic thinking and preferences. *Journal of Personality and Social Psychology, 77,* 905–926. doi:10.1037/0022-3514.77.5.905

52. Pyszczynski, T., Solomon, S., & Greenberg, J. (2003). *In the wake of 9/11: The psychology of terror.* Washington, DC: American Psychological Association.

53. Landau, M. J., Goldenberg, J., Greenberg, J., Gillath, O., Solomon, S., Cox, C.,...Pyszczynski, T. (2006). The siren's call: Terror management and the threat of men's sexual attraction to women. *Journal of Personality and Social Psychology, 90*(1), 129–146. doi:10.1037/0022-3514.90.1.129

54. Singh, A. (2002, November). "We are not the enemy": Hate crimes against Arabs, Muslims, and those perceived to be Arab or Muslim after September 11. *Human Rights Watch, 14*(6). Retrieved from http://www.hrw.org

55. Pyszczynski, T., Solomon, S., & Greenberg, J. (2003). *In the wake of 9/11: The psychology of terror*. Washington, DC: American Psychological Association.

56. Carnagey, N. L., & Anderson, C. A. (2007). Changes in attitudes toward war and violence after September 11, 2001. *Aggressive Behavior, 33*, 118–129. doi:10.1002/ab

57. Faludi, S. (2007). *The terror dream: Myth and misogyny in an insecure America*. New York, NY: Picador.

58. Bindley, K. (2011, August 16). Should women change their last names after marriage? *The Huffington Post*. Retrieved from http://www.huffingtonpost.com/2011/08/15/women-changing-name-after-marriage_n_927707.html

59. Faludi, S. (2007). *The terror dream: Myth and misogyny in an insecure America*. New York, NY: Picador.

60. Faludi, S. (2007). *The terror dream: Myth and misogyny in an insecure America*. New York, NY: Picador.

61. Reyes, S., & Sperber, B. (2002, September 9). Comfort eating versus comfort food. *Brandweek, 43*(32), 6.

62. Balon, R. (2002, September 16). Dine-out customers in post-9/11 world value affordable comfort food in a family setting. *Nations Restaurant News*. Retrieved from http://www.nrn.com

63. Wolf, B. (2005, October 23). Dishing up comfort food for hard times. *National Public Radio, Weekend Edition*. Retrieved from http://www.wgbh.org/News/Articles/index2.cfm?ID=4970452

64. Coontz, S. (1992). *The way we never were: American families and the nostalgia trap*. New York, NY: Basic Books.

65. Mikles, N. (2009, March 18). Comfortably yum: In times of uncertainty, comfort food makes a comeback. *Tulsa World*. Retrieved from http://www.tulsaworld.com/

66. Ginsberg, M. (2012, February 2). Banana Republic's Mad Men collection renewed for next season. *The Hollywood Reporter*. Retrieved at http://www.hollywoodreporter.com/fash-track/banana-republic-mad-men-collection-amc-286713

67. Channick, R. (2011, August 29). Playboy Club to reopen in Chicago. Retrieved from http://articles.chicagotribune.com/2011-08-29/news/chi-playboy-club-to-reopen-in-chicago-20110829_1_playboy-clubs-chicago-club-new-club

68. Negra, D. (2008). Structural integrity, historical reversion, and the post-9/11 chick flick. *Feminist Media Studies, 8*(1), 51–68. doi:10.1080/14680770701824902

69. Page 57: Negra, D. (2008). Structural integrity, historical reversion, and the post-9/11 chick flick. *Feminist Media Studies, 8*(1), 51–68.

70. Gibbs, N. (2008, July 17). The pursuit of teen girl purity. *Time, 172*, 36. Retrieved from http://www.time/time/printout/8,8816,182393,00.html

71. Welcome to the purity ball (2012). Retrieved from http://www.purityball.com/

72. Gillis, C. (2007, October 8). Dad's your prom date: Wedding-like purity balls celebrate men as father-protectors. *Macleans, 120*(39), 66–68. Retrieved from

http://www.macleans.ca/culture/lifestyle/article.jsp?content=20071008_110113_110113

73. Gillis, C. (2007, October 8). Dad's your prom date: Wedding-like purity balls celebrate men as father-protectors. *Macleans, 120*(39), 66–68. Retrieved from http://www.macleans.ca/culture/lifestyle/article.jsp?content=20071008_110113_110113

74. Davis, A. (2002, Spring). Joan Little: The dialectics of rape (1975). *Ms. Magazine.* Retrieved from http://www.msmagazine.com/spring2002/davis.asp

75. Abstinence-only education does not lead to abstinent behavior, researchers find. (2011, November 29). *Science Daily.* Retrieved from http://www.sciencedaily.com

76. Rosenbaum, J. E. (2008). Patient teenagers? A comparison of the sexual behavior of virginity pledgers and matched nonpledgers. *Pediatrics, 123,* 110–120. doi:10.1542/peds.2008-0407

77. Page 102: Berg, B. J. (2009). *Sexism in America: Alive, well, and ruining our future.* Chicago, IL: Lawrence Hill Books.

78. [No author]. December 15, 2010. Railing against failure of 9/11 health bill, Fox News analyst doesn't mention Republicans. *The Raw Story.* Retrieved from http://www.rawstory.com/rs/2010/12/15/fox-news-analyst-omits-gop-opposition-911-rescue-workers-bill/

3

MANUFACTURING MAN-HATING FEMINISM

One swims against the feminist tide at one's peril.

—*Kathleen Parker*[1]

A key feature of modern anti-feminism is the cornerstone belief that the work of the feminist movement is done and that feminism itself has become obsolete—an antique piece of 20th-century ideology. The belief is that women have, more or less, achieved equality through legislative changes in sexual harassment and antidiscrimination laws, Title IX in education, and changes in norms that now accept women in the military and in the workplace. Thus, women have little to complain about. Those women who *do* insist on being feminists and favor a continued feminist movement must want to get *ahead* of men, or believe they are superior to men. Modern anti-feminism tells us that those who still complain about inequality just don't like men.

This chapter explores a pervasive and surprisingly durable belief about feminists—that they dislike men. The "man-hating feminist" is not a new trope. Feminists have been accused of man-hating at least as far back as the first wave of the women's movement in the United States and Europe in the late 1800s. The man-hating allegation works in the post-feminist era of the early 21st century because, assuming the goals of feminism have been met, those women who continue to call themselves feminists, or insist on a feminist movement, are either innocuously passé or simply trying to gain the upper hand. Only isolated individual cases of overt gender discrimination against women are recognized. Consequently, today's feminists who talk about gender inequality as a *system* face allegations of man-hating. In fact, according to this view, the real victims of gender discrimination today are boys and men. We address the "boy crisis" of recent years in the next chapter. This chapter begins by describing beliefs about feminists—both media representations and beliefs of respondents in research studies. Next, we examine the empirical research on feminists' and nonfeminists' actual attitudes toward men. Do feminists have more negative attitudes toward men compared to nonfeminists? Finally, we explore the functions and implications of the man-hating-feminist myth. What are the implications of this myth for gender roles, lesbians and lesbian-baiting, and heterosexual relationships, and what further implications are there for marginalizing and silencing women's progress and the women's movement?

Views of Feminists

A major theme in politics and popular culture is the belief that feminism has achieved its goals and a feminist movement is no longer necessary. There's an assumption that the goals of the second-wave feminist movement, from the late 1960s through the 1970s, have largely been achieved.[2] The claim of this argument is that there has been sufficient progress toward equality manifesting in improvements to access to education, paid employment, and a few legislative remedies. Some commentators insist that feminism was a failure—it only brought women childlessness, a man-shortage, burnout, and loneliness.[3] Many of the more high-profiled anti-feminists, however, argue that feminism did what it was supposed to do and those who now hang on to a feminist movement are only trying to surpass men. Christina Hoff Sommers, one of the main purveyors of this point of view, valorizes first-wave feminists such as Elizabeth Cady Stanton and Susan B. Anthony but regards present-day "gender feminists"[4] as chronic complainers and male bashers. Sommers insists that there is no need for modern feminism because discrimination against women is largely in the past; those women who are left complaining about gender discrimination just don't like men. Roy Baumeister, author of the book, *Is There Anything Good About Men?*, characterizes the evolution of the feminist movement in a similar way:

> The early feminists wanted equality, and it served their goal to deny that there were any real gender differences. But female chauvinists were among them, those who resented and disliked men, and they gradually took control of the feminist movement. Hence, they embraced any findings of women being better than men, even if it went against the equality theme. Gradually the feminists in gender studies abandoned the idea of equality. Why settle for a tie when you can be sure of winning?[5]

Baumeister's argument is that early feminists favored gender equality but today's feminists favor superiority of women over men—feminism has been hijacked by man-haters. Baumeister never mentions a single feminist by name who represents this viewpoint, yet he is confident they exist. Note that it is *feminists* who are against equality in this worldview, not men and not patriarchy. From Baumeister's perspective, if it weren't for feminists trying to get ahead of men, the playing field would be level and there would be equality between the sexes.

Feminism, as a movement to end sexism, sexist exploitation, and oppression,[6] has always faced resistance. Feminists of the late 1800s and early 1900s who fought for women's right to vote were described as "drabs," "hangdog dowdies," and "monsters in bloomers."[7] Women who step out of their traditional role as quiet caregivers or hyperorganized über-moms face significant hostility and resistance. We discuss backlash against nontraditional women in Chapter 5.

Anti-feminists blame feminists for a variety of social problems: for young men entering college at a lower rate than that of young women;[8] for the decline in "manliness" in American culture;[9] for gangs[10] and even for the terrorist attacks of September 11, 2001.[11] Anti-feminist Kate O'Beirne describes feminists as "humorless" and "prickly"; they are "angry women,"[12] with "persecution fantasies,"[13] who are "chronically dissatisfied."[14] In his book, *Manliness*, Harvey Mansfield describes feminists as "anti-male."[15] In 2005, the Pentagon established the Office of the Victim Advocate to handle hundreds of sexual assault claims made by women soldiers against men soldiers. Elaine Donnelly, the president of the Center for Military Readiness, an anti-feminist and antigay lobbying group,[16] described the effort as establishing an "Office of Male-Bashing."[17] The office, designed to investigate rape and harassment, as well as to support victims, was predicted by Donnelly to "create a new job market for 'women's studies' graduates schooled in man-hating ideology."[18] With characterizations like these, it's understandable why relatively few women (and fewer men) call themselves feminists. For instance, in surveys of university women, the percentage who identify as feminists range from 8%[19] to 44%,[20] depending on the demographic makeup of the students. What accounts for these low rates? One factor is race/ethnicity. Some women of color have felt or do feel alienated by the mainstream feminist movement because feminism in the 1960s and 1970s was dominated by a white middle-class woman's perspective. For instance, in the 1960s and 1970s abortion rights were at the center of the American women's rights movements, but forced sterilization was a concern for poor women.[21] Likewise, African American women and men are more likely to describe themselves as "black feminists," "womanists," or "Africana womanists" than "feminists."[22] Many women who hold feminist beliefs report being hesitant to describe themselves as feminists because they know that feminism is viewed negatively.[23] But descriptions of feminists aren't all bad. When college students, as opposed to anti-feminist political pundits, are asked about feminism, we find that feminists are described in neutral-to-positive ways.[24] Surveys of college students find that feminists are seen as confident and "willing to take a stand;"[25] they are perceived as logical, knowledgeable, realistic, intelligent, caring, flexible, and comforting;[26] feminists are also viewed as productive, responsible, and secure.[27] On the other hand, feminists are described as aggressive and "manly,"[28] also as "going overboard,"[29] stubborn, tense, and egotistical.[30] Men tend to view women who identify as feminists more negatively than women who do not.[31] And, in general, feminists are evaluated less favorably than the average woman.[32]

Recall the interviews conducted by Nigel Edley and Margaret Wetherell[33] described in Chapter 1. Edley and Wetherell interviewed men from the United Kingdom about their views of feminism and feminists. The interviews provide some insight into the ambivalence people feel toward feminists. From the interviews, two versions of feminists emerged. One version might be described as a "liberal feminist," who simply desires equality. The second version of feminist is more complicated and threatening. This more elaborated feminist is a highly theatrical character who neglects her appearance, dislikes men, and is probably a lesbian. Edley and Wetherell describe these two versions of feminists as working in a "Jekyll and Hyde" fashion. Like fictional Dr. Jekyll, feminists and feminism in the liberal version have a rational and sane character. Feminist desires for gender equality were reported as simple, ordinary, reasonable matters of fact. Yet when feminists become Hyde, she becomes monstrous. Thus, there's a polarization of discourse about feminism and feminists set up between "the extremist" and the more palatable liberal feminist. Dr. Jekyll is the ordinary woman who simply desires equality while Ms. Hyde is the extreme political activist, ugly and unfeminine. Ms. Hyde is impatient and demands that equality be achieved more quickly than what society has in mind. As an activist, Ms. Hyde fights for equality, and dislikes men. Correspondingly, surveys find more support for the relatively neutral terms such as "women's movement" and even the "women's liberation movement" compared to the more loaded terms, "feminism" and "feminists."[34]

One factor that separates feminists from those who believe in equality but don't describe themselves as feminists is *activism*. Feminists, more than women who simply believe in equality, believe that there are problems facing women in society and that women need to work together to fix them.[35] But many people do not like agitators.[36] Agitators disrupt the status quo. And as we saw in Chapter 2, women agitators are particularly disliked because activist women are acting outside their gender role. Activists are complainers. They are noncompliant and inconvenient. And feminists tend to be activists. One study looked at whether complaints about discrimination are taken more or less seriously depending on whether a feminist or nonfeminist makes the claim. An experiment conducted by Robin Roy and her colleagues[37] provides a window into people's hostility and suspicion of feminists. Roy presented white women college students with a scenario in which a woman named "Jill" alleges that gender discrimination was the reason she was passed over for a promotion. In one version of the scenario, Jill was described as a feminist and in another version she was not. Otherwise the details of the event were identical. Did people interpret the events differently depending on whether or not they believed that Jill was a feminist? Indeed. Feminist Jill was viewed as more of a complainer and less credible as a reporter of discrimination than nonfeminist Jill. Feminists are stereotyped as being hypersensitive to gender discrimination—even by women college students. People may not know whether a feminist's claim of discrimination results from actual discrimination or from a predisposition to interpret events as discrimination. Interestingly, although feminist Jill was perceived as more of a complainer than the nonfeminist Jill, neither woman was rated very positively. Women who challenge the status quo, as well as those who complain about discrimination, tend to be disliked and derogated, but especially if they are identified as feminist.

There are important implications of the Edley and Wetherell study and the Roy study. First, people tend to believe that feminists are not rational and objective but nonfeminists are. Second, those who call out discrimination force people to look at their own mistreatment or their own complicity in discrimination. If people admit that discrimination exists they should feel obligated to do something about it; however, that recognition can be threatening and overwhelming, making it easier to deny credibility to the messenger. And feminists are just such a messenger.

Are Feminists Man-Haters? What Is the Evidence?

In the context of the belief that feminism's work is done and the goals of feminism have been met, those women who continue to call themselves feminists or insist on a feminist movement are judged as trying to prove their superiority and thus as antimale.[38] Because there is nothing left for women to complain about, the remaining feminists must dislike men. In her book, *Save the Males: Why Men Matter and Why Women Should Care*, Kathleen Parker states, "The same feminist movement that encouraged women to use their critical faculties also gave them the green light to be hostile and demeaning toward men."[39]

It is surprising that the strength of the man-hating feminist stereotype is not in direct proportion to the evidence that feminists dislike men. There is a miniscule number of empirical studies on the subject. Anthony Iazzo's[40] 1983 study is an early study that links feminists with positive and negative attitudes toward men. Iazzo's Attitudes Toward Men Scale measured the degree to which women agreed with 32 statements about *Marriage/Parenthood* (e.g. "Men consider marriage a trap."); *Sexuality* (e.g., "A man cannot get enough sex."); *Work* (e.g., "A man's job is the most important thing in his life."); and *Physical/Personality Attributes* (e.g., "An athletic man is to be admired."). Women expressed their agreement on a 1 to 4 scale ranging from *Agree Strongly* (most negative attitude) to *Disagree Strongly* (most positive attitude). A score of 80 would indicate a neutral attitude toward men.

The "control group" in Iazzo's sample was 104 mostly white women recruited from a university, department stores, and other places of business. They were compared with battered wives, rape victims, lesbians, and feminists recruited from a local chapter of the National Organization for Women. The control group mean score was 89.93, above the neutral midpoint of 80.00, suggesting slightly positive attitudes toward men. The average score of feminists was 79.54, statistically indistinguishable from the 80.00 midpoint, indicating neutral attitudes toward men. So feminists did not hold negative attitudes toward men. What about lesbians, a group often stereotyped as disliking men and an identity often conflated with feminists?[41] Lesbians scored, on average, 70.97, so somewhat lower than neutral but hardly a score indicative of man-hating. Why were lesbians' scores somewhat lower than the "control group" of women and than feminists? Further inspection of the statements that make up the Attitudes Toward Men survey may account for these slight negative attitudes. Some of the statements may not be relevant to lesbians. For instance, some of the items are "Male sex organs are attractive," "The male body is visually unappealing," and "The sight of a penis is repulsive." These are questions from the *Sexuality* subscale. It would have been more informative to have analyzed how feminists and lesbians scored on each separate subscale. For instance, perhaps lesbians had relatively "antimale" attitudes on the seven items that made up the *Sexuality* scale because they do not find men's body parts attractive. Conversely, their scores on the other subscales could have been neutral or even positive. A significant limitation of surveys used to measure attitudes toward men is that statements might be irrelevant to lesbians as the statements assume that women have had, or desire to have, romantic and sexual relationships with men.

John Maltby and Liza Day[42] examined various psychological characteristics that correlate with attitudes toward women and men among British college students. For women, a feminine-stereotyped gender role orientation—the degree to which individuals see themselves in terms of feminine stereotypes—was correlated with negative attitudes toward men. In other words, the more feminine a woman is, the less she likes men. Maltby and Day did not measure *feminists'* attitudes toward men, but their results may shed light on the question. Their findings imply that perhaps it is *non*feminists who do not like men because feminists tend to have relatively more masculine-stereotyped and androgynous gender role orientations than nonfeminists. Put another way, women with traditional gender role orientations (who tend to be nonfeminists) had more negative attitudes toward men than did women with nontraditional gender role orientations (who are more likely to be feminists).

Another study,[43] with an ethnically diverse sample of women university students, found that women who perceived large value and belief differences between women and men tended to like men less than women who did not perceive large value and belief differences. Again, this study did not examine feminists' attitudes specifically; however, we can extrapolate from the data. Other studies find that feminists tend to think women and men are more similar than different,[44] whereas nonfeminists are more likely to think that women and men are fundamentally different (e.g., that men are from Mars and women are from Venus).[45] These data suggest that nonfeminists view women and men as fundamentally different and also have more negative attitudes toward men than do feminists.

Susan Condor's[46] interviews with women reveal the apparent paradox that women with traditional views about gender might have more negative attitudes about men than would feminists. Her interviews with French-Canadian women with traditional gender role attitudes revealed some intriguing patterns. First, traditional women were not only more likely to view women and men in terms of a dichotomy but also in terms of complementarity and interdependence than were nontraditional women. In other words, traditional women believed that women and men have different roles to play but those roles complement one another. Second, whereas feminist women might find the traditional world of women in the domestic sphere as oppressive and narrow, traditional women reported that their domestic role was preferable (even superior) to roles available to men. In fact traditional women viewed *men's* roles as restrictive. Third, and most relevant for this discussion, the traditional women tended to view women as superior (e.g., more civilized, more responsible) to men. These women had positive attitudes toward feminine characteristics and negative attitudes toward masculine characteristics. In fact, traditional women articulated a high level of antipathy towards men and male characteristics. So whereas traditional women are predictably antifeminist, they also were pro-woman in that they held traditional feminine characteristics in high regard. These same women also tended to hold men and masculine characteristics in low regard. Condor's interviews, along with the other studies presented in this section, demonstrate the lack of support the feminist-man-hater notion has in empirical research.

Ambivalence Toward Men: Explaining Traditional and Nontraditional Women's Attitudes Toward Men

A more recent method of measuring people's attitudes toward men is Peter Glick and Susan Fiske's Ambivalence toward Men Inventory.[47] Glick and Fiske find that there are two aspects of women's (and to a somewhat lesser extent men's) attitudes toward men. The first aspect, *Hostility Toward Men*, represents overtly negative attitudes toward men. Hostility toward men taps into resentment about men's power relative to women, men's aggressiveness, cultural attitudes that dictate men as superior, and the way men exert control within heterosexual intimate relationships. It characterizes men as inferior in ways that are safe to criticize, such as that men are babies when they are sick. Individuals with high levels of hostility toward men tend to agree with statements such as, "When men act to 'help' women, they are often trying to prove they are better than women," and "Most men pay lip service to equality for women, but can't handle having a woman as an equal." The second aspect of attitudes toward men is *Benevolence Toward Men*. Benevolence toward men represents overtly positive or affectionate attitudes toward men. Similar to the traditional women in Susan Condor's interviews, benevolence toward men comprises a set of beliefs that includes the idea that just as women are dependent on men, so too are men dependent on women. Benevolence toward men suggests that a woman's role is to take care of a man in the domestic context. Experiencing subjectively positive feelings of admiration, affectionate protectiveness, and connection with men in intimate heterosexual relationships represents benevolence toward men. Those who score high on benevolence toward men agree with statements such as, "Women are incomplete without men," and "Even if both members of a couple work, the woman ought to be more attentive to taking care of her man at home."

Hostility and benevolence toward men are distinct concepts, although they tend to be correlated. That is, women who have high scores on hostility toward men tend to also have high scores on benevolence toward men. They simultaneously hold beliefs that actively support and justify male dominance (benevolence toward men) at the same time they resent the consequences of this dominance (hostility toward men). Thus, women may resent men's power even as they subscribe to beliefs that bolster it. So a question relevant to this chapter is, If some women resent men, which women are resentful? Feminists or nonfeminists? Glick and Fiske speculate that the more a woman is dependent on men, the more she is likely to hold both benevolent and hostile attitudes toward men; the former because of her recognition of her investment in men and the latter because of resentment over her dependence.

Glick and Fiske do not directly answer the question of where feminists fall in terms of their benevolent or hostile attitudes toward men, but they do explore the relationship between gender inequality and hostility toward men and benevolence toward men. This, in turn, has implications for feminism and attitudes toward men. In a massive study of 16 nations, Glick and Fiske,[48] along with several colleagues around the world, gathered individual responses to the Ambivalence toward Men Inventory. In addition, they utilized two United Nations indices of gender inequality: the Gender Empowerment Measure, which is a measure of women's representation in powerful occupational roles and government; and the Gender Development Index, which measures how women fare on development measures such as life expectancy, literacy rates, schooling, and standard of living. Glick and Fiske found that in most nations, hostility toward men was higher among women than among men. In addition, hostility toward men scores correlated with the national measures of gender inequality. Specifically, hostility toward men was higher in traditional than in egalitarian nations. At the same time, benevolence toward men was also higher in traditional than in egalitarian nations. Glick and Fiske reason that women in traditional nations may be more resentful toward men for what they view as abuses of power, but because this resentment coexists with benevolent beliefs about men's roles as protectors and providers, it is not necessarily a challenge to the gender hierarchy. The more hostile men are toward women, the more women resent and show hostility toward men. Heightened resentment of men's hostility may explain why women's hostility toward men scores increasingly exceed men's in more traditional cultures.

It is worth noting that there were many more gender similarities than differences across nations—women and men in the 16 nations tended to have similar attitudes toward women and men. In terms of addressing the myth of feminists and man-hating, Glick and Fiske's study on attitudes toward men suggests that man-hating is linked more to *anti*-feminism and gender *in*equality than it is to feminism and gender equality.

Glick and Fiske's 16-nation study illuminates some relevant patterns about what underpins women's hostility toward men, but it does not answer the question about feminists' hostility toward men. Another study[49] does directly examine feminists' and nonfeminists' attitudes toward men. An ethnically diverse sample of U.S. college students were asked to respond to statements about gender roles including the items from the Ambivalence toward Men Inventory measuring benevolence and hostility towards men. Students were also asked whether or not they were feminists. Women overall did tend to have higher levels of hostility toward men than did men, but did feminists? Contrary to popular stereotypes, self-identified feminists had *lower* levels of hostility toward men than nonfeminists. Feminists also tended to have lower levels of benevolence toward men. Low levels of benevolence toward men does not mean one has malevolence toward men, it just means that the respondent does not agree with traditional gender roles—for instance that women should take care of men in the home, while men should be the main wage earners. Thus, it appears that feminists, compared to nonfeminists, do not have negative attitudes toward men. Feminists do tend to reject traditional gender roles that put women in less powerful positions than men. Feminists also tend to reject the notion that women's and men's gender roles are inherent and complementary.

Taken together, systematic empirical studies do not find evidence that feminists dislike men. In contrast, there is some suggestion than *nonfeminists,* those women who adhere to traditional gender stereotypes, dislike, or at least, resent, men. We must ask then, why does the myth of the man-hating feminist persist?

The Persistence of the Man-Hater Myth

In Chapter 5 we explore people's attitudes toward nontraditional women. That discussion merits an entire chapter because, in fact, most women are nontraditional but perhaps not always recognized as such. People respond negatively to women who violate traditional gender roles. Feminists tend to reject traditional gender roles and are more likely than nonfeminists to believe that women and men are more alike than different. The suggestion that women can do much of what men do (and vice versa) threatens the traditional gender order prescribing certain specific characteristics and behaviors to women and different specific characteristics and behaviors to men. If women can do what men can do, then the justification for excluding women from certain activities (e.g., fighting fires, combat) crumbles.

Lesbian-Baiting

The false link between feminism and lesbianism is a good place to explore the function and implications of the myth of the man-hating feminist. Understanding the link between perceptions of feminism and lesbianism reveals some of the fundamental sources of the discomfort and antagonism toward feminism we have explored thus far. Indeed, in casual contexts and in mass media, *lesbian* is often erroneously portrayed as interchangeable with *feminist,* with the presumption that lesbians are probably feminists, and feminists are presumed to be lesbians.[50] Both lesbians and feminists are understood as women who disrupt and threaten gender, and both terms describe nontraditional women. Like feminists, lesbians are viewed as unladylike, assertive, and outspoken, and women like this threaten the gender status quo.[51]

Homophobia, in addition to anti-feminism and sexism, creates a set of tactical opportunities to discredit and marginalize feminism's efforts to achieve comprehensive equality for women. Like the accusation of male-bashing, the framing of lesbianism as the inevitable result of feminism or as a necessary dimension of feminism is a scare tactic designed to frighten people away from associating with feminism and feminist activism. The very positioning of lesbianism as a source of discredit reveals the underlying layer of homophobia that often joins sexism to maintain systems of oppression and privilege. For example, women who have worked actively against sexual assault and rape are often the targets of lesbian-baiting. Accusations of lesbianism, framed as insults and debasement, work alongside descriptions of feminists as angry, unladylike, and unfeminine to make feminists, and by extension, the goals of feminism, unattractive and repellent. Ali Grant,[52] who studied community responses to antiviolence activists, observes that these insults are the result of people feeling as though women are acting out of their place by complaining too much about men's violence against women. It's as though it is okay to believe that rape is wrong, but that women should not complain—or at least if they complain, they should be ladylike about it. Battered women's shelters and rape crisis centers have been vandalized with graffiti such as "No Means Dyke," or "No Means Tie Her Up."[53] Rape crisis centers have been charged with "turning women into lesbians" or "being man-hating."[54] As we have seen in this chapter, women's activism threatens male dominance. In addition, focusing on "male-bashing" by women obscures the fact that victims of men's violence can be other men and boys.[55]

Lesbian functions as a regulatory term as much as it does an expression of sexual identity.[56] In addition to its definition of women who are romantically affiliated with women, *lesbian* refers to women who are independent from men. That is why it can be used against a woman who refuses sexual advances from a man. Since *lesbian* is often conflated with *feminist*, and because of widespread heterosexism and homophobia, feminists are often required to prove they are not lesbians. It's no wonder that many women do not identify as feminists because they are afraid of a potential allegation of lesbianism.[57]

Lesbian-baiting can also be a form of sexual extortion, especially in the military. Kelly Corbett, a staff attorney at Servicemembers Legal Defense Network, has written about lesbian-baiting during the time when homosexuals were banned from military service in the U.S.[58] According to Corbett, accusations of lesbianism are a threat to all military women, regardless of their sexual orientation. The military's antigay policy gave harassers and rapists tools of sexual extortion, as allegations of lesbianism could ruin a woman's career. It didn't matter whether or not the allegations were true. Women soldiers who refused sexual advances from men could be accused of being lesbians and subjected to investigation for homosexual conduct. Thus, the ban against homosexuals in the military was used as a weapon of retaliation against women who report sexual harassment or rape, against those who rebuff sexual advances, or against those who succeed in their careers. Now that lesbians and gay men can serve openly in the military, lesbian-baiting should be a somewhat less effective weapon against women service members.

Although lesbians, like feminists, are seen as man-haters, there is no empirical evidence suggesting they are. Judy Markey begins an article in the magazine, *Redbook*, "Male Bashing," with, "I used to be a rather accomplished male-basher. After all, I was married to a man. . ."[59] Magazines from the popular press indicate that "male-bashers" are actually heterosexual women writing about traditional gender roles: women complain about men's infidelity,[60] inept husbands,[61] and men who are not "domesticable."[62] In her book, *Save the Males*, anti-feminist Kathleen Parker epitomizes the heterosexual wife's and mother's frustration with "men":

> Despite my admiration for the other sex, I confess to occasional ambivalence. As I researched this book, I often thought to myself: What am I doing? I hate men! I told my best male friends this. They laughed. That's because men hate women, too. Sort of. But not really. Every few days, I told my husband and sometimes my sons: 'You have to shape up or I can't write this book.' As usual, they laughed at me. As usual, I was furious. It may be the particular dilemma of men and women that they are doomed to suffer a love/hate relationship—and why not? It is hard not to despise something that has such a hold on your heart, even if you give that heart freely.[63]

Lesbians are likely to have different relationships with men and therefore do not have the complaints, disappointments, and frustrations that some heterosexual women have. Ali Grant interviewed lesbian feminist activists who reported that, rather than disliking men, they felt that men were either neutral individuals (e.g., male relatives) or just not relevant to their lives. Perhaps it is that men play a less significant role in some lesbians' (and feminists') lives that make lesbians and feminists so threatening. Women who do not put men at the center of their lives may be the threat. When you combine women with a rather neutral approach to men with women who are activists fighting against patriarchy and male privilege, it can make people who support the status quo uncomfortable.

Fighting Patriarchy or Particular Men?

Feminists are accused of man-hating when they object to gender discrimination because some interpret the complaint as being anti-man (whether about *particular, individual* men, or even *all* men) rather than as a protest against the patriarchal system that grants unearned power and privilege to men relative to women. Other people may be more deliberate and cynical in their attempts to demonize feminists and feminism, and they may seek to use those efforts to drive a wedge between feminist and nonfeminist women. Feminists see sexism as part of a *system* of inequality.[64] In his book, *Manliness*, Harvey Mansfield describes feminism as women being "none too pleased with men and not shy about letting them know it."[65] Those who do not understand the systemic nature of gender inequality translate feminists' activism as complaints directed at particular men or at men as a *category*, as if feminists dislike each man or all men. In fact, a recent empirical study demonstrates the distinction between hating gender inequality and hating men. When African American, Latina, and white women were asked about their attitudes toward men and toward male dominance, those women who identified as feminists were shown to resent structural-level gender inequality more than nonfeminists, but not individual men.[66]

One manifestation of the focus on individual men versus the focus on systemic gender discrimination and male privilege is the "battle-of-the-sexes"[67] rhetoric that is prevalent in popular culture. Kathleen Parker's statement, quoted earlier, represents this battle-of-the-sexes dynamic. Heterosexual romantic relationships are often pitched in a he-said-she-said frame that produces a false parallelism implying that women and men are equally advantaged and disadvantaged—just in different ways.[68] For instance, in a *Time* magazine article, "Men, Are They Really That Bad?," Lance Morrow[69] takes on what he describes as the "overt man bashing of recent years."[70] He says, "both men and women have been oppressed by the other sex, in different ways,"[71] and, "American men and women should face the fact that they are hopelessly at odds."[72] Judy Markey[73] says in a *Redbook* article entitled, "Male-Bashing," "How can we gripe that they put us down as a group, if we do the same to them?"[74] and, "We'll wind up sounding like squabbling children crying, 'He started it!' 'No, she did!' "[75] In his book, *Is There Anything Good About Men?* Roy Baumeister blames feminism for this dynamic: "From reading feminist accounts of gender politics one gets the impression that men and women have been collective enemies throughout history (and still are)."[76] Baumeister provides no citations of these unnamed feminists, so the reader doesn't know what "feminist accounts" he is referring to, but his personal opinion is at odds with the empirical research studies we have examined here. This battle-of-the-sexes popular discourse suggests that women's and men's complaints are parallel and equal. The "sex wars"[77] rhetoric trivializes genuine critiques about patriarchy and male privilege and reduces discrimination to a he-said-she-said dynamic in which there are no real winners and no real losers, but merely miscommunication between the sexes. This rhetoric also conveys the idea that complaints about sexism are about individual women and men fighting with each other. However, like other "isms" (e.g., racism, heterosexism) sexism is a *system* of inequality based on the belief that men are superior to women.

This view of individual-based gender debates can reduce things such as sexual harassment and even sexual assault to simple miscommunication between women and men, but the supposed miscommunication can actually leave *men* victims. For instance, in his book *The Myth of Male Power*, Warren Farrell[78] writes, "Feminism has taught women to sue men for creating a 'hostile environment' or date rape when men initiate with the wrong person or with the wrong timing."[79] Similarly, Lance Morrow claims that a successful approach to a woman is *romance* and *courtship*. Sexual harassment, according to Morrow, is simply an unsuccessful approach, and, in his view, is unfairly treated as a crime.[80] Following this argument to it's illogical conclusion, we could find that the *real* victims of sexual harassment and rape are not women but men who are victimized by women's flirtations and mixed messages. Women are teases who "elaborately manipulate and exploit men's natural sexual attraction to the female body, and then deny the manipulation and prosecute men for the attraction—if the attraction draws in the wrong man."[81] So the problem lays with individual women who cannot take a joke or who tease men. Or the problem lies with individual men who misread women's signals, rather than considering a system that sexualizes women and girls and creates an environment in which women are meant to be sexual objects and subordinate to men.[82]

These writers imply that male chivalry should be highly valued in our culture, but this kindly chivalry is misinterpreted by overly sensitive, humorless feminists. These writers would have us regress to a time of "knightly solicitude for the sake of women's safety. . .and men's honor"[83] because, "Male chivalry protected women far better than feminist lawsuits over girlie calendars and dirty jokes."[84] But is male chivalry really better for women than feminism? Should a woman be flattered when a man opens a door for her? We will see in Chapter 5 that attitudes of male chivalry entail patronizing and condescending attitudes toward women that imply that women are suited only for the domestic role of wife and mother. We will see that chivalrous attitudes toward women are correlated with hostile sexism, a social dominance orientation, and even victim-blame.

Who Is Bashing Whom?

Kathleen Parker, author of *Save the Males*, thinks she has found concrete evidence of the widespread male bashing in our culture. "Male bashing is among America's favorite sports and is a popular bonding agent among women. If you

Google 'male bashing,' you get eleven times more hits than for 'female bashing.' The reason: Men are easy."[85] It's hard to tell which part of this Orwellian statement is the most bizarre—the idea that "men" as a group are easily victimized? That "America" is actively "bashing" males? That counting Google hits represents some sort of empirical test of women's attitudes toward men? The most important harm that comes out of such rhetoric is the obfuscating of actual violence. What is the significance of using the term "bashing" in this discourse? What is "male bashing" and why is that particular term deployed to stifle feminism? Sue Cataldi[86] discusses the ugly irony of the term "male bashing." To *bash* means to violently strike with a heavy, crushing blow. "Bash" connotes an indiscriminate, random, and violent lashing out. "Bashing" suggests that the striking of the blow is extreme, unfair, and undeserved. Consider how the term *gay-bashing* is used to denote violently beating or killing someone because of their presumed homosexuality. Cataldi reminds us that women (in general) are not bashers, they are *bashees*.

Take homicide. Men are nearly four times more likely than women to be murdered but men are also seven times more likely than women to commit murder.[87] Sixty-eight percent of homicides occur among a male offender and male victim, 21% among male offender and female victim, and only 9% among a female offender and male victim.[88] Women are more likely than men to be victimized by someone they know than by a stranger for all measured violent crimes except robbery.[89] Specifically, female murder victims are far more likely to be killed by an intimate partner than are men. For instance, in 2010, 39% of female homicide victims were killed by an intimate whereas only 3% of male homicide victims were killed by an intimate.[90] In the United States, one study of more than 5,000 American women college students found that 28.5% had experienced an attempted or completed sexual assault either before or since entering college.[91] Sexual assault of women is also common in already physically abusive relationships. Sixty-eight percent of physically-abused women are also sexually assaulted by their intimate partners.[92] And finally, women are more than twice as likely to be stalked as men.[93] One out of every 14 American women will be stalked at some point in their lives, and 87% of the stalkers will be men. And, according to the U.S. Department of Justice, four out of five stalking victims are women.[94]

Isn't it curious that physical assaults on women by men are not characterized as "female bashing?" Sue Cataldi[95] argues that conjuring up images of abused men bashed by women and casting women in the role of bash*ers* obviously reverses what actually happens. This reversal functions as a means of victim-blame, minimizing what some men do to women and exaggerating any verbal harm done to men by women. Another function of co-opting the term *bashing* and its brutality is to lead us into thinking that the "male bashing" women supposedly engage in is equivalent to what men do to women. Those who use the expression may also be attempting to siphon attention and support away from women and from those who are physically harmed by men.

Calling feminists "male-bashers" shifts the focus from the systemic problem of men's literal violence against women to a focus on men who have gotten their feelings hurt by feminists and feminism. The feminist critique of sexism may be disconcerting to some men and some women. It might hurt their feelings, it might seem unfair, and it might seem to disregard men's good intentions. This may make men feel uncomfortable, but it's not male bashing. Feminists are not critical of men simply for being men. The target of feminist critique is sexism in a male-dominated society.

When we reexamine Parker's statement in the context of men's violence against women we begin to understand why a Google search of "male bashing" produces higher results than "female bashing"—and how this contorts the true reality of bashing. Perhaps the smaller number of references to "female bashing" is due in part to the way that violent crimes are often reported. In newspaper accounts of rape, the crime tends to be written in the passive voice (e.g., "On the evening of March 6, a woman was raped near. . .") rather than an active voice (e.g., "On the evening of March 6, a man raped a woman near. . ."). Notice that in the first version of the event, there is no perpetrator. The focus of the crime is on the victim. Research finds that when readers are exposed to a description of sexual violence constructed in the passive versus active voice, readers tend to belittle the amount of harm suffered by the victim and to lessen the perpetrator's responsibility for the violence.[96]

There even seems to be a slight trend in newspaper coverage of domestic violence toward using the active voice to describe woman-against-man violence but the passive voice to describe man-against-woman violence.[97] Research participants tend to view male-to-female violence in the passive rather than active voice in comparison to female-to-male violence. For instance, Alexandra Frazer and Michelle Miller supplied research participants with information about domestic violence scenarios that varied according to the perpetrator, the victim, weapon used, date of the incident, and so forth. Participants were asked to summarize the incident in a 50 to 100 word narrative description. Frazer and Miller found that both women and men participants produced a higher number of passive voice sentences to describe male-to-female violence than female-to-male violence. These different sentence constructions suggest that, perhaps unconsciously, people tend to highlight women's responsibility for violence, perhaps due to the novelty of it, and deemphasize men's responsibility for violence. The reality of some men's violence against women reveals how ludicrous it is to describe feminists as male-bashers.

Conclusion

This chapter addressed a key piece of modern misogyny—the belief that feminism's work is done and those women who continue to press for equality just don't like men. This chapter and the next address the idea that feminism is out of control, that it has become extreme. Women have attained equality, so they should stop whining. The false belief that women have achieved equality is troubling for at least two reasons. First, the individualism discourse discussed in Chapter 1 encourages young women to believe that they were born into a free society, so if they experience discrimination, it must be their fault—they haven't worked hard enough. Second, the claim that feminism has accomplished its goals and now women can focus on choice through consumer goods denies the reality of many women's and girls' lives—particularly poor women, women of color, and women who live in developing nations.[98] Wages have gone down in the past two decades and households that were previously middle class are now closer to poverty, and working class and poor households are even worse off under neoliberal corporatist capitalism. The U.S. Federal Reserve reported that an American family in 2010 has no more wealth than in the early 1990s, erasing almost two decades of accumulated prosperity.[99]

This false but persistent view of feminists as man-haters is so strong, in fact, that it actually prevents people from correctly identifying themselves as feminists. Individuals surveyed about feminism and feminists reveal that they actually hold neutral-to-positive attitudes about both feminist ideals and the people who identify with these ideals. We have seen that there is no empirical evidence whatsoever to support the notion that feminists' attitudes toward men are more negative than nonfeminists'. In fact, empirical studies on the topic, find that feminists report lower levels of hostility toward men than nonfeminists.

Anti-feminists accuse feminists of gender oppositionality, of fighting a gender war. But anti-feminists, not feminists, are the ones who believe that women and men are fundamentally different and that their difference is grounded in nature—suggesting that this is normal or even ideal. Feminists tend to see women and men as not very different from each other, and this is threatening to the gender status quo. If, as feminism argues, women can do what previously only men were thought to be able to do, then you can see how some would perceive manhood as under assault and the perpetrator of the assault as feminism. Manhood is exclusionary and, to the extent that men's activities can be performed by women, it is no longer a special role, no longer male. If women can perform the men's role, it must mean neither the qualities nor the role are so special after all.[100] Tom Digby observes that the mutual hostility between women and men—rooted in exaggerated gender differences, often oppressive social and economic roles, and the systematic domination of women by men—is the established context that *predated* and gave rise to feminism, so feminism can hardly be responsible for it. In fact, many feminists argue that generalized antimale sentiment is contrary to feminism precisely because it replicates the bipolar gender oppositionality that has been crucial to male domination.[101]

The incorrect notion that feminists hate men (rather than feminism being a critique of patriarchy) does more than make women afraid to call themselves feminists. It also makes invisible the roles that women play in contributing to gender inequality. I review hundreds of studies on gender discrimination in this book and most studies find that men *and* women participants discriminate against women.[102] Sexism and gender discrimination is not just something men do to women. Everyone participates in a sexist system, unless you actively work against it. It is certainly true that men benefit because of sexism through the male privilege inherent in a sexist system that has constructed maleness as superior to femaleness. Ignoring the systemic nature of gender inequality also leads men to feel stuck in a defensive response rather than being able to see that men, too, are confined and controlled by gender expectations. Jackson Katz argues that anti-sexist men's voices are crucial in the struggle for gender equality. They can change the conversation because men can say things about men's violence that most women cannot say. Men cannot kill the messenger as easily with other men. Men will not accuse other men of male-bashing.[103] Trivializing feminists' resistance to inequality as anger at men insults the women's liberation movement that fights for the right to vote, for equal pay, for educational equity, and for reproductive freedom—efforts focused on changing the system, not on "bashing" anyone.

Notes

1. Page 72: Parker, K. (2008). *Save the males: Why men matter, why women should care.* New York, NY: Random House.
2. Dube, K. (2004). What feminism means to today's undergraduates. *Chronicle of Higher Education, 50*(41), b5.
3. For a review of the supposed failures of feminism, see: Faludi, S. (1991, September/October). Blame it on feminism. *Mother Jones, 16*, 24–29.
4. Page 16: Sommers, C. H. (1994). *Who stole feminism? How women have betrayed women.* New York, NY: Touchstone.
5. Page 28: Baumeister, R. F. (2010). *Is there anything good about men? How cultures flourish by exploiting men.* New York, NY: Oxford University Press.
6. See page viii in: hooks, B. (2000). *Feminism is for everybody.* Cambridge, MA: South End Press.
7. Wolf, N. (1992, March 16). Feminist fatale. *The New Republic, 206*(11), 23–25.

8. Sommers, C. H. (2000). The war against boys. New York, NY: Simon & Schuster.

9. Mansfield, H. C. (2006). Manliness. New Haven, CT: Yale University Press.

10. Page 39: Parker, K. (2008). Save the males: Why men matter, why women should care. New York, NY: Random House.

11. Falwell apologizes to gays, feminists, lesbians (2001, September 14). CNN.com Retrieved from http://articles.cnn.com/2001-09-14/us/Falwell.apology_1_thomas-road-baptist-church-jerry-falwell-feminists?_s=PM:US

12. Pages xiv, xiv, and xviii, respectively, in: O'Beirne, K. (2006). Women who make the world worse: And how their radical feminist assault is ruining our schools, families, military, and sports. New York, NY: Sentinel.

13. Page xvi in: O'Beirne, K. (2006). Women who make the world worse: And how their radical feminist assault is ruining our schools, families, military, and sports. New York, NY: Sentinel.

14. Page xv: in: O'Beirne, K. (2006). Women who make the world worse: And how their radical feminist assault is ruining our schools, families, military, and sports. New York, NY: Sentinel.

15. Page 5: Mansfield, H. C. (2006). Manliness. New Haven, CT: Yale University Press.

16. Stone, A. (2011, September 18). Center for Military Readiness criticized for lax oversight. Retrieved from http://www.huffingtonpost.com/2011/07/19/elaine-donnelly-lobbyist-_n_903494.html

17. Page 7: Donnelly, E. (2005, December 5). Pentagon doesn't need an office of male-bashing. Human Events, 61, 7.

18. Page 7: Donnelly, E. (2005, Week of December 5). Pentagon doesn't need an office of male-bashing. Human Events, 61(41), 7.

19. Myaskovsky, L., & Wittig, M. A. (1997). Predictors of feminist social identity among college women. Sex Roles, 37, 861–883.

20. Bullock, H. E., & Fernald, J. L. (2003). "Feminism lite?" Feminist identification, speaker appearance, and perceptions of feminist and anti-feminist messengers. Psychology of Women Quarterly, 27, 291–299.

21. Kane, E. W. (2000). Racial and ethnic variations in gender-related attitudes. Annual Review of Sociology, 26, 419–439.

22. Harnois, C. E. (2009). Generational difference in feminist identities? Exploring gender conscious identities among African American women and men. Sociation Today, 7(2), 3.

23. For instance see: Alexander, S., & Megan, R. (1997). Social constructs of feminism: A study of undergraduates at a women's college. College Student Journal, 31, 555–567.
And see: Aronson, P. (2003). Feminists or "post-feminists"? Young women's attitudes toward feminism and gender relations. Gender & Society, 17, 903–922. doi:10.1177/0891243203257145 and Scharff, C. (2011). "It is a colour thing and a

status thing, rather than a gender thing": Negotiating difference in talk about feminism. *Feminism & Psychology, 21*, 458–476. doi:10.1177/0959353511419816

24. Twenge, J. M., & Zucker, A. N. (1999). What is a feminist? Evaluations and stereotypes in closed- and open-ended responses. *Psychology of Women Quarterly, 23*, 591–605.

25. Alexander, S., & Ryan, M. (1997). Social constructs of feminism: A study of undergraduates at a women's college. *College Student Journal, 31*, 555–567.

26. Berryman-Fink, C., & Verderber, K. S. (1985). Attributions of the term *feminist*: A factor analytic development of a measuring instrument. *Psychology of Women Quarterly, 9*, 51–64.

27. Twenge, J. M., & Zucker, A. N. (1999). What is a feminist? Evaluations and stereotypes in closed- and open-ended responses. *Psychology of Women Quarterly, 23*, 591–605.

28. Scharff, C. (2011). "It is a colour thing and a status thing, rather than a gender thing": Negotiating difference in talk about feminism. *Feminism & Psychology, 21*, 458–476. doi:10.1177/0959353511419816

29. Alexander, S., & Ryan, M. (1997). Social constructs of feminism: A study of undergraduates at a women's college. *College Student Journal, 31*, 555–567.

30. Twenge, J. M., & Zucker, A. N. (1999). What is a feminist? Evaluations and stereotypes in closed- and open-ended responses. *Psychology of Women Quarterly, 23*, 591–605.

31. Anderson, V. N. (2009). What's in a label? Judgments of feminist men and feminist women. *Psychology of Women Quarterly, 33*, 206–215.

32. Twenge, J. M., & Zucker, A. N. (1999). What is a feminist? Evaluations and stereotypes in closed- and open-ended responses. *Psychology of Women Quarterly, 23*, 591–605.

33. Edley, N., & Wetherell, M. (2001). Jekyll and Hyde: Men's constructions of feminism and feminists. *Feminism & Psychology, 11*, 439–457.

34. Hall, E. J., & Rodriguez, M. S. (2003). The myth of post-feminism. *Gender & Society, 17*, 878–902. doi:10.1177/0891243203257639

Huddy, L., Neely, F. K., & Lafay, M. R. (2000). The polls—trends: Support for the women's movement. *Public Opinion Quarterly, 64*, 309–350.

Alexander, S., & Ryan, M. (1997). Social constructs of feminism: A study of undergraduates at a women's college. *College Student Journal, 31*, 555–568.

35. Yoder, J. D., Tobias, A., & Snell, A. F. (2011). When declaring "I am a feminist" matters: Labeling is linked to activism. *Sex Roles, 64*, 9–18. doi:10.1007/s11199-010-9890-3

36. Roy, R. E., Weibust, K. S., & Miller, C. T. (2009). If she's a feminist it must not be discrimination: The power of the feminist label on observers' attributions about a sexist event. *Sex Roles, 60*, 422–431. doi:10.1007/s11199-008-9556-6

37. Roy, R. E., Weibust, K. S., & Miller, C. T. (2009). If she's a feminist it must not be discrimination: The power of the feminist label on observers' attributions about a sexist event. *Sex Roles, 60*, 422–431. doi:10.1007/s11199-008-9556-6

38. Bloom, L. R. (1997). A feminist reading of *Men's Health*: Or, when Paglia speaks, the media listens. *Journal of Medical Humanities, 18*(1), 59–73.

Vint, S. (2007). The new backlash: Popular culture's "marriage" with feminism, or love is all you need. *Journal of Popular Film & Television, 34,* 160–169.

39. Page xi: Parker, K. (2008). *Save the males: Why men matter why women should care.* New York, NY: Random House.

40. Iazzo, A. N. (1983). The construction and validation of Attitudes Toward Men Scale. *The Psychological Record, 33,* 371–378.

41. Scharff, C. (2011). "It is a colour thing and a status thing, rather than a gender thing": Negotiating difference in talk about feminism. *Feminism & Psychology, 21,* 458–476. doi:10.1177/0959353511419816

42. Maltby, J., & Day, L. (2001). Psychological correlates of attitudes toward men. *The Journal of Psychology, 135,* 335–351.

43. Stephan, C. W., Stephan, W. G., Demitrakis, K. M., Yamada, A. M., & Clason, D. L. (2000). Women's attitudes toward men: An integrated threat theory approach. *Psychology of Women Quarterly, 24,* 63–73.

44. Liss, M., Hoffner, C., Crawford, M. (2000). What do feminists believe? *Psychology of Women Quarterly, 24,* 279–284.

Liss, M., O'Connor, C., Morosky, E., & Crawford, M. (2001). What makes a feminist? Predictors and correlates of feminist social identity in college women. *Psychology of Women Quarterly, 25,* 124–133.

45. Yoder, J. D., Fischer, A. R., Kahn, A. S., & Groden, J. (2007). Changes in students' explanations for gender differences after taking a psychology of women class: More constructionist and less essentialist. *Psychology of Women Quarterly, 31,* 415–425.

46. Condor, S. (1986). Sex role beliefs and 'traditional' women: Feminist and inter-group perspectives. In S. Wilkinson (Ed.) *Feminist social psychology: Developing theory and practice* (pp. 97–118). Philadelphia, PA: Open University Press.

47. Glick, P., & Fiske, S. T. (1999). The Ambivalence toward Men Inventory: Differentiating hostile and benevolent beliefs about men. *Psychology of Women Quarterly, 23,* 519–536.

48. Glick, P., Lameiras, M., Fiske, S. T., Eckes, T., Masser, B., Volpato, C.,…Wells, R.(2004). Bad but bold: Ambivalent attitudes toward men predict gender inequality in 16 nations. *Journal of Personality and Social Psychology, 86,* 713–728.

49. Anderson, K. J., Kanner, M., & Elsayegh, N. (2009). Are feminists man-haters? Feminists' and non-feminists' attitudes toward men. *Psychology of Women Quarterly, 33,* 216–224.

50. Scharff, C. (2011). 'It is a colour thing and a status thing, rather than a gender thing': Negotiating difference in talk about feminism. *Feminism & Psychology, 21,* 458–476. doi:10.1177/0959353511419816

51. Alexander, S., & Megan, R. (1997). Social constructs of feminism: A study of undergraduates at a women's college. *College Student Journal, 31,* 555–567.

52. Ali Grant critiques the notion that feminist activists are accused of man-hating: Grant, A. (2000). And still, the lesbian threat: Or, how to keep a good woman a woman. *Journal of Lesbian Studies, 4*(1), 61–80.

Elaine Donnelly's article is an example of women activists being called man-haters: Donnelly, E. (2005, December 5). Pentagon doesn't need an office of male-bashing. *Human Events, 61*(41), 7.

53. See pages 67–68 in: Grant, A. (2000). And still, the lesbian threat: Or, how to keep a good woman a woman. *Journal of Lesbian Studies, 4*(1), 61–80.

54. See page 66 in: Grant, A. (2000). And still, the lesbian threat: Or, how to keep a good woman a woman. *Journal of Lesbian Studies, 4*(1), 61–80.

55. Katz, J. (2006). *The macho paradox: Why some men hurt women and how all men can help.* Naperville, IL: Sourcebooks.

56. See page 71 in: Grant, A. (2000). And still, the lesbian threat: Or, how to keep a good woman a woman. *Journal of Lesbian Studies, 4*(1), 61–80.

57. Liss, M., O'Connor, C., Morosky, E., & Crawford, M. (2001). What makes a feminist? Predictors and correlates of feminist social identity in college women. *Psychology of Women Quarterly, 25*, 124–133.

58. Corbett, K. M. (1997, November). Lesbian-baiting: A threat to all military women. *Lesbian News, 23*(4), 16–18.

59. Page 104: Markey, J. (1993, May). Male-bashing. *Redbook, 181*, 104–107.

60. Lego, S. (1999). Monicagate and male bashing. *Perspectives in Psychiatric Care, 35*(1), 3–4.

61. Heckard, I. R. (1998, January/February). Male bashing: Is it trash talk or harmless humor? *Today's Christian Woman, 20*(1), 46–48.

62. Heard, A. (1989, August). Stop blaming men for everything! *Mademoiselle, 95*, 232–234.

63. Page viii: Parker, K. (2008). *Save the males: Why men matter, why women should care.* New York, NY: Random House.

64. Kane, E. W. (2000). Racial and ethnic variations in gender-related attitudes. *Annual Review of Sociology, 26*, 419–439.

McCabe, J. (2005). What's in a label? The relationship between feminist self-identification and "feminist" attitudes among U.S. women and men. *Gender & Society, 19*, 480–505. doi:10.1177/0891243204273498

65. Page 4 in: Mansfield, H. C. (2006). *Manliness.* New Haven, CT: Yale University Press.

66. Robnett, R. D., Anderson, K. J., & Hunter, L. E. (2012). Predicting feminist identity: Associations between gender-traditional attitudes, feminist stereotyping, and ethnicity. *Sex Roles, 67*, 143–157. doi:10.1007/s11199-012-0170-2

67. See for instance: Heard, A. (1989, August). Stop blaming men for everything! *Mademoiselle, 95*, 232–234.

68. Page xi in: O'Beirne, K. (2006). *Women who make the world worse: And how their radical feminist assault is ruining our schools, families, military, and sports.* New York: Sentinel.

69. Morrow, L. (1994, February 14). Men: Are they really that bad? *Time*, *143*, 53–59.

70. Page 54 in: Morrow, L. (1994, February 14). Men: Are they really that bad? *Time*, *143*, 53–59.

71. Page 56 in: Morrow, L. (1994, February 14). Men: Are they really that bad? *Time*, *143*, 53–59.

72. Page 59 in: Morrow, L. (1994, February 14). Men: Are they really that bad? *Time*, *143*, 53–59.

73. Markey, J. (1993, May). Male-bashing. *Redbook*, *181*, 104–108.

74. Page 105 in: Markey, J. (1993, May). Male-bashing. *Redbook*, *181*, 104–107.

75. Page 105 in: Markey, J. (1993, May). Male-bashing. *Redbook*, *181*, 104–107.

76. Page 8: Baumeister, R. F. (2010). *Is there anything good about men? How cultures flourish by exploiting men*. New York, NY: Oxford University Press.

77. See, for instance: Heard, A. (1989, August). Stop blaming men for everything! *Mademoiselle*, *95*, 232–234.

78. Farrell, W. (1993). *The myth of male power: Why men are the disposable sex.* New York, NY: Berkley Books.

79. Page 18 in: Farrell, W. (1993). *The myth of male power: Why men are the disposable sex*. New York, NY: Berkley Books.

80. Morrow, L. (1994, February 14). Men: Are they really that bad? *Time*, *143*, 53–59.

81. Page 57 in: Morrow, L. (1994, February 14). Men: Are they really that bad? *Time*, *143*, 53–59.

82. For an examination of popular culture's perpetuation of women-as-teases, see: Anderson, K. J., & Accomando, C. (1999). Madcap misogyny and romanticized victim-blaming: Discourses of stalking in "There's Something About Mary." *Women & Language*, *22*, 24–28.

83. Page 58 in: Morrow, L. (1994, February 14). Men: Are they really that bad? *Time*, *143*, 53–59.

84. Page xx in: O'Beirne, K. (2006). *Women who make the world worse: And how their radical feminist assault is ruining our schools, families, military, and sports*. New York, NY: Sentinel.

85. Page 16: Parker, K. (2008). *Save the males: Why men matter, why women should care*. New York, NY: Random House.

86. Cataldi, S. L. (1995). Reflections on "male bashing." *NWSA Journal*, *7*(2), 76–85.

87. Cooper, A., & Smith, E. L. (2011, November). Homicide trends in the U.S., 1980–2008. U.S. Department of Justice. Retrieved from http://bjs.ojp.usdoj.gov/content/pub/pdf/htus8008.pdf

88. Cooper, A., & Smith, E. L. (2011, November). Homicide trends in the U.S., 1980–2008. U.S. Department of Justice. Retrieved from http://bjs.ojp.usdoj.gov/content/pub/pdf/htus8008.pdf

89. Truman, J. L. (2011, September). National crime victimization survey: Criminal victimization, 2010. U.S. Department of Justice. Retrieved from http://bjs.ojp. usdojgov/content/pub/pdf/cv10.pdf.

90. Catalano, S. (2012). Stalking victims in the United States: Revised. The U.S. Department of Justice. Retrieved from http://www.bjs.gov/content/pub/pdf/ svus_rev.pdf

91. Krebs, C. P., Lindquist, C. H., Warner, T. D., Fisher, B. S., & Martin, S. L. (2007, December). *The campus sexual assault (CSA) study: Final report.* Prepared for National Institute of Justice (NIJ Grant No. 2004-WG-BX-0010).

92. McFarlane, J., & Malecha, A. (2005, October). Sexual assault among intimates: Frequency, consequences, and treatments. Prepared for National Institute of Justice (Award No. 2002-WG-BX-0003). Retrieved September 24, 2008, from www.ncjrs.gov/pdffiles1/nij/grants/211678.pdf

93. Catalano, S. (2012). Stalking victims in the United States: Revised. The U.S. Department of Justice. Retrieved from http://www.bjs.gov/content/pub/pdf/ svus_rev.pdf

94. U.S. Department of Justice Office on Violence Against Women (2005–2006). Report to congress on stalking and domestic violence, 2005 through 2006. Retrieved September 24, 2008, from http://www.ncjrs.gov/pdffiles1/ ovw/220827.pdf

95. Cataldi, S. L. (1995). Reflections on "male bashing". *NWSA Journal, 7*(2), 76–85.

96. Henley, N. M., Miller, M., & Beazley, J. A. (1995). Syntax semantics, and sexual violence: Agency and the passive voice. *Journal of Language and Social Psychology, 14*(1–2), 60–84.

97. Frazer, A. K., & Miller, M. D. (2009). Double standards in sentence structure: Passive voice in narratives describing domestic violence. *Journal of Language and Social Psychology, 28*(1), 62–71. doi:10.1177/0261927X08325883

98. Bloom, L. R. (1997). A feminist reading of *Men's Health*: Or, when Paglia speaks, the media listens. *Journal of Medical Humanities, 18*(1), 59–73.

99. Appelbaum, B. (2012, June 11). Family net worth drops to level of early '90s, Fed says. Retrieved from http://www.nytimes.com/2012/06/12/business/economy/ family-net-worth-drops-to-level-of-early-90s-fed-says.html?_r=1

100. Digby, T. (1998). Do feminists hate men?: Feminism, anti-feminism, and gender oppositionality. *Journal of Social Philosophy, 29*(2), 15–31.

101. Digby, T. (1998). Do feminists hate men?: Feminism, anti-feminism, and gender oppositionality. *Journal of Social Philosophy, 29*(2), 15–31.

102. Rudman, L. A., & Phelan, J. E. (2008). Backlash effects for disconfirming gender stereotypes in organizations. *Research in Organizational Behavior, 28*, 61–79. doi:10.1016/j.riob.2008.04.003

103. Katz, J. (2006). *The macho paradox: Why some men hurt women and how all men can help.* Naperville, IL: Sourcebooks.

THE END OF MEN AND THE BOY CRISIS

This whole sort of war on women thing, I'm scratching my head,
because if there was a war on women, I think they won... In fact,
I worry about our young men sometimes, because I think the women
really are outcompeting men in our world.

—U.S. Senator Rand Paul, 2014[1]

In 1982 feminist psychologist Carol Gilligan published her land-mark book *In a Different Voice: Psychological Theory and Women's Development*.[2] The 1980s and early 1990s were marked by a surge of scholarship and activism related to girls' and women's development and educational opportunities. A 1992 report from the American Association of University Women entitled *How Schools Shortchange Girls*, and Myra and David Sadker's *Failing at Fairness: How Our Schools Cheat Girls*,[3] critiqued the decades and centuries-long focus on boys and men in the educational domain. Mary Pipher's 1994 *Reviving Ophelia: Saving the Selves of Adolescent Girls*[4] looked at the marginalization of girls relative to boys in a variety of domains. Almost immediately this brief and still intermittent attention paid to girls' and women's needs was met with resistance. These works on girls and women were and continue to be viewed as a takeover, an emblem of feminism having gone too far. By the 1990s, the anti-feminist response constituted a massive recovery effort to bring boys and men back to the center, and this effort has not relented since. These "boy crisis" books are represented by, for instance, the well-intentioned *Real Boys: Rescuing Our Sons from the Myths of Boyhood*,[5] by William Pollack in 1998, and Dan Kindlon and Michael Thompson's 1999 *Raising Cain: Protecting the Emotional Life of Boys*.[6] Anti-feminist Michael Gurian produced book after book on the subject, beginning with *The Wonder of Boys*[7] in 1996. Anti-feminist boy-crisis trailblazer Christina Hoff Sommers helped solidify the industry with her 2000 *The War Against Boys: How Misguided Feminism Is Harming Our Young Men*.[8] The main claim of these works is that feminism has gone too far and now boys and men are paying for it.

In the last chapter, we addressed the anti-feminist fiction that feminists are man-haters and male bashers. In this chapter, we examine another claim reflecting the belief that feminism has gone too far: that feminism has so empowered girls and women that they are now taking over and getting ahead of boys and men. Kathleen Parker is one of the anti-feminist conservative columnists at the center of this moral panic launching arguments that begin with, "America is a dangerous place for males these days."[9] In her 2008 book, *Save the Males: Why Men Matter, Why Women Should Care*, Parker writes, "today's world is hostile toward men, who are no longer considered necessary for much of anything,"[10] and the first chapter of Parker's book is entitled, "Women Good, Men Bad." And while the United States ranks a miserable 47th in the world on gender equality[11]—meaning there are 46 other countries in which men's advantage over women is less dramatic—we still see headlines claiming that women are surpassing men in all areas of society.

In this chapter we first address the claim that mass media and society have become antimale. Next, we address the supposed "boy crisis" in American schools—the belief that schools have become hostile to boys and biased in favor of girls. Finally, we consider the issue of male privilege and entitlement as one explanation of why boys and men tend to earn lower grades and pursue university studies in fewer numbers than girls and women.

Mass Media and the Marginalization of Men?

Is the Media Mean to Men?

Media scholars have documented the near invisibility of women and people of color in television and film for decades. But the feminism-gone-too-far wave has imagined a mass media that marginalizes men and boys. For example, Steve Biddulph, author of *Raising Boys: Why Boys Are Different—and How to Help Them Become Happy and Well-Balanced Men,* says "The media continually portrays males as rapists, murderers, or inadequate fools. So a boy may easily feel quite bad about himself as a masculine being."[12] These claims stand in stark contrast to the actual media representations of men that children encounter. It is true that men can be seen playing violent predators or incompetent buffoons. However, claims that there are uniformly negative representations of men are erroneous. In fact, there are many more representations of men and they are depicted in a wider range of behavior than are women characters.[13] And in terms of negative portrayals of men, there are just as many men who play heroes as villains.[14] In other words, because there is such a diversity of positive and negative roles, especially for white men, the negative portrayals of men are simply one way in which they are portrayed. As researchers of one study concluded: "male characters did more of almost *everything* than did the female characters, simply because they appeared more often."[15]

Let's take a look at various genres of mass media to address the panic over the belief that women are taking over all the major institutions in society. Are women truly taking over mass media? In prime-time television women make up 45% of the regular characters.[16] Patterns are more exaggerated in film. Major male characters in top-grossing films outnumber female characters by a huge 73% to 27%.[17] When you consider the age of actors and characters, the representations of women are even bleaker. In both prime-time television[18] and in popular films[19] women are most frequently seen in the age range of 20 to 30, whereas men are more likely to be in their 30s and 40s. When you get into the 50s and 60s, women virtually disappear. This latter fact is particularly interesting because the largest percentage of women in the population is in the 51+ group.[20] So the largest age demographic of women in real life is the least likely to be seen in celluloid life. There is another reason that the erasure of older women in television and film is significant in addition to the mismatch between representation in media and representation in real life. Typically, older adults on TV and in film have more power, status, and leadership, but this is true for men, not women. For example, in TV and film, men in their 40s and 50s are more likely to play leaders than younger men, and women in the same age range. Men in their 50s have greater occupational power than women in their 50s.[21] So for men, as they get older they gain status and power; as women get older, they disappear—women disappear in terms of being shown on TV and film and they disappear in terms of their status, power, and significance as characters.

In terms of important and influential genres of TV and film there is a lot of work that still needs to be done regarding gender equality. Roles for men and stories about men continue to be the norm. As evidence, consider the use of the term *chick flicks*—those films dominated by women characters with storylines supposedly of interest to women more than men. Movies dominated by men, on the other hand, with characters and plots telling men's stories, are considered the norm and thus are not gender marked due to their supposed universal appeal. However, films that are thought to be of interest to women get the gender marking of "chick flick." This is similar to when films about heterosexuals are simply called films—they should resonate with everyone—but films with gay characters are marked, described as "gay films."

Disparity also exists in terms of occupational roles on television. Men are more likely than women to play criminals, but they are also more likely to be in professional roles, law enforcement roles, and in blue collar jobs. In contrast, women are more likely to not work, or their work is not known,[22] conveying the message that being professionals with meaningful work outside the home is not a significant aspect of women's identity. This same pattern holds for both white and African American women[23] (there are so few other people of color on TV, calculations are not available). Women characters on television continue to enact interpersonal roles involved with romance, family, and friends (emphasizing communal/expressive traits), whereas men characters are more likely to enact work-related roles (emphasizing the instrumental/agentic traits of ambition and desire for success).[24]

Is the picture so positive for all men, or only for white men? Anti-feminist writers and commentators who support this masculine recovery effort do not address race in their concerns about portrayals of men in the media. Their concerns lie with the disruption of the status quo, the supposed loss of status and influence of white heterosexual men. In fact, there is something to be concerned about when we do take into account how men of color are portrayed in the media: African American men continue to be portrayed as dangerous thugs. For instance, in television news African American men are *overrepresented* as criminal suspects and *underestimated* as victims of crime compared to actual crime statistics. The opposite is true of white men: they are *underrepresented* as perpetrators and *overrepresented* as victims.[25] Thus, in their eagerness to keep white, heterosexual men at the center of society, the end-of-men/boy-crisis authors miss an opportunity to address a group that is actually marginalized and actually negatively portrayed in media representations—men of color.

In music videos women are worse than marginal. Even though women have made progress in terms of their numbers as pop stars and musicians, the roles they play in music videos are as sexual objects used by men.[26] Men outnumber women in music videos nearly three to one.[27] Worse than the sheer lack of representation of women is the role they play when they do appear in videos. Women's chief role in music videos is as sexual objects that are denigrated and debased. They are pushed, grabbed, and slapped by men in videos. African American women are even more sexualized and abused than white women.[28] What explains the lack of creativity and range in the roles that women play in music videos? One answer is the intertwining of pornography and music videos. Former pornographic film directors now can be found directing music videos and former porn stars can be found starring in them.[29] This trend corresponds to the increased mainstreaming of pornography and hypersexual representations of girls and women described in Chapter 1.

There have been some changes in the representations of women and men in advertisements. In terms of role portrayals, women and men are more equal than in the 1960s. One study[30] looked at 50 years of advertisements in popular U.S. magazines. The findings indicated that the traditional patterns of ads showing that a woman's place is in the home, and that women do not do important things or make important decisions, is less true than in previous decades. However, ads still show men as leaders and protectors, whereas women are shown in roles that are dependent on men. And in the area of sexual objectification, portrayals are actually worse than they were in the 1960s. Women are more likely to be portrayed as sexual objects than they were previously. The female body and women's dismembered body parts are used much more often than the male body as a visual element in ads. In this way, one can see how advertising has co-opted the feminist desire for sexual freedom described in Chapter 1. In print ads today men are still more likely to be shown in authoritative, superior, and more powerful positions than women, and women are depicted in more deferential positions to men.[31] Even more puzzling and alarming, women are also more likely to be positioned in weakened psychological states, looking away, disoriented, and even looking dead or passed out—and these depictions have actually *increased* over the 50-year period.[32] Magazines show ads depicting dead women from Marc Jacobs, Gucci, Lanvin, Jimmy Choo, and Louis Vuitton and ads depicting gang rape by Calvin Klein, Dolce & Gabbana, and Tom Ford. It is difficult to imagine what the end-of-men/boy-crisis authors have in mind when you see how women are depicted in advertisements.

In terms of television commercials men comprise 39% of the main characters in prime-time ads, whereas women make up 30% (about 1/3 contain both women and men). Roles played by women and men in U.S. television commercials are still highly gender-stereotyped. For example, 32% of women's roles are as homemaker, but only 1% of men's roles are as homemaker; 14% of the men in commercials are professionals (doctor, lawyer), but only 5% of women play these roles.[33] Television voiceovers are an important feature of many commercials, as a narrator conveys authority, gravity, and wisdom. Women's voices make up only 27% of commercial voiceovers compared to men's 73%.[34] Like most of the other media genres, television commercials convey the message that men are out in the world doing important things, and they are experts who should be listened to, whereas women tend to be relegated to the domestic sphere.

In newspaper comics, 61% of the characters are male and 28% of the characters are female (11% of the characters are animals, and male animals outnumber female animals 6 to 1). Women characters in comics are more than twice as likely to appear in the home and men characters are twice as likely to appear at work. Women characters are less likely to be identified as having a job, more likely to be married, and more likely to be taking care of children.[35]

Even in clipart—those graphics that enhance workplace PowerPoint presentations—women characters are invisible or relegated to silly roles. Middle-aged white men are the most common characters in clipart. Like TV and film roles, men are depicted in a wider range of activities than women. Women are more likely to be portrayed as younger (e.g., teenagers) rather than older. Clipart images of men show them as more physically mobile and producing some product, whereas images depict women in passive positions such as sitting, reclining, or accompanying a man. When women are engaged in activity, they are more likely than men to be cleaning and taking care of children.[36] The analysis of clipart images might, at first glance, appear to be trivial and of little consequence. However, if you consider where and when these images are used—in office and business settings—it becomes clear that these images are important. Professional women already have to battle gender discrimination in the form of pay inequality, sexual harassment, and the glass ceiling. Clipart images reinforce the notion that men are the professional norm, whereas women do not quite belong in the workplace the way that men do.

Men even dominate media coverage of "women's issues." In an analysis of 2012 election coverage, men were more likely to be quoted on their opinions in newspapers and on television. For example, in front page articles about the 2012 election that mention abortion, men were 81% of those quoted; on birth control, they were 75% of those quoted; even on women's rights, they were 52% of those quoted (women were only 31% of those quoted and organizations were 17%).[37] Can you imagine the media seeking out women as the main experts on issues pertaining to men?

As this review of mass media portrayals of women and men demonstrates, women are hardly in the position of threatening the traditional domains of men. In every aspect of the mass media they are underrepresented compared to their actual numbers in the population. When women are seen, they are more likely to be portrayed as homemakers, as sexual objects, and as young. Men, on the other hand, are more likely to be portrayed in a range of professional fields; they are more active, and they are older and portrayed with more power and influence.

Is the Media Mean to Boys?

Authors of end-of-men/boy-crisis books claim that the world is now geared toward girls. For instance, Christina Hoff Sommers, author of *The War Against Boys*, writes that feminists see boys' masculinity as "politically incorrect."[38] Kathleen Parker, author of *Save the Males,* says "boys learn early that they belong to the 'bad' sex and their female counterparts to the 'good.'"[39] Parents even have been accused of leaping on the antiboy bandwagon, according to *The Atlantic* writer, Hannah Rosin. In her 2010 article "The End of Men," Rosin reports that American couples are now preferring girls to boys when contemplating pregnancy.[40] The belief in a preference for girls resonates with those who believe that feminism has gone too far, but that belief is false. American couples still prefer sons over daughters. When presented with the question, "Suppose you could only have one child. Would you prefer that it be a boy or a girl?" 37% of the respondents express a preference for a boy, and 28% for a girl.[41]

Parents may still prefer boys, but does the mass media? Let's begin with children's television cartoons. Consistent with empirical studies over several decades, male cartoon characters continue to outnumber female characters.[42] Some cartoon genres are extreme. For instance, in the traditional adventure genre (e.g., *Batman, Aladdin*) male characters outnumber female characters more than 4 to 1. In comedy cartoons (e.g., *Animaniacs*), males outnumber females 2 to 1. In nontraditional adventure series (e.g., *Sailor Moon, Reboot*), there is equal representation. *How* are females and males represented in TV cartoons? Anti-feminists are concerned that boys are being feminized and girlified, but this is not the case in TV cartoons. Male characters are portrayed in highly masculinized ways. They are more likely to engage in physical aggression and less likely to show fear than female characters. They are less likely to be supportive and polite, and less likely to be romantic, than female characters.[43] Overall, despite Christina Hoff Sommers' and Kathleen Parker's concerns about traditional male gender roles being undermined by feminism and feminizing, cartoons are still rigidly gender stereotyped.

Has the content of cartoons changed over time? One study[44] examined cartoons over a 60-year period. The representations of female and male characters have actually changed little. Females account for only 16% of all characters. Physical attractiveness was more important for female characters, whereas intelligence was more important for males. Male characters were 50% more likely to engage in antisocial behaviors, females were twice as likely as males to be considered "good." Over time, cartoons have contained fewer and fewer African Americans, Latinos, Native Americans, and Asians, relative to their population numbers. Even in educational programs such as *Mr. Wizard's World, Beakman's World, Bill Nye the Science Guy,* and *Newton's Apple,* twice as many adult male scientists as female scientists were shown. Fully 79% of the female characters that did appear were relegated to secondary roles such as helpers.[45]

When the content of children's picture books has been examined, we find nearly twice as many male as female main characters, and female characters are more likely to be portrayed inside the home and without a paid occupation. Furthermore, these representations have not changed over time.[46] Males are even more common in children's coloring books. A study of 56 coloring books found that 59% of the characters were male and 41% were female. Children were more likely to be females (58%) than males (42%), adults were more likely to be male (78%) than female (22%).[47]

Toy commercials on television reinforce these patterns. Although content analysis[48] of 455 commercials appearing on the network *Nickelodeon* found that commercials were more likely to be oriented toward girls (34%) than boys (27%), this hardly represents a girl takeover. Boys in commercials are shown in a wider range of interactions (e.g., competitive, cooperative, independent) than girls. And like other media genres featuring both adults and children, girls were once again more likely to be located inside the home. That commercials depicting boys showed them in a variety of settings implies that they have more opportunities and are involved in more action. So boys are doing stuff. One commercial for Silly 6 Pins has boys bowling and girls cheering them on, laying on the ground watching.[49] Can you imagine the roles in reverse? Girls bowling while boys lay on the ground cheering them on the sidelines?

You even see unequal gender representations on cereal boxes. In an analysis[50] of 217 cereal boxes, male characters outnumbered female characters by more than 2 to 1. Similar to other genres, animal characters are more likely to be male than female. Like children's coloring books, authority figures (e.g., adults) were more likely to be men than women and children were more likely to be girls than boys, thus suggesting that females are more dependent on others and are less powerful. Unlike research in other areas of media representation, there were no gender differences in activity level and passivity.

It is clear from this exhaustive (and exhausting) review of the literature on media representation that boys are not marginal, nor are they denigrated. Boys are portrayed as the gender that matters, that gets things done; boys are the default, the norm. These patterns from empirical research studies contradict what the boy-crisis authors say about society's view of boys. Let's take a look at what Steve Biddulph, author of the 1998 book *Raising Boys*[51] says:

> In an era when men are often targets of ridicule in the media, it's important to remember (and to show boys) that men built the planes, fought the wars, laid the railroad tracks, invented the cars, built the hospitals, invented the medicines and sailed the ships that made it all happen. There's an African saying, 'Women hold up half the sky.' But, clearly, men hold up the other half.

This statement reflects the upside down world of men-are-marginalized rhetoric you see from the boy-crisis authors. From Biddulph's perspective, men have been so erased from history and the present that we actually need to remind boys of men's accomplishments. His invented "era" of male erasure gives him permission to gratuitously reassert male dominance (men are the ones, after all, "who made it all happen") while pretending to apply a much-needed remedy to a perceived girl takeover.

Are Schools Antiboy?

Authors and commentators who claim a boy crisis argue that, even more than the media, schools are the main repositories of antiboy elements. Their focus on education is, in part, a response to the progress of Title IX—the 1972 statute prohibiting gender discrimination in educational institutions—and to the deliberate efforts of feminist educators to make schools hospitable to girls.

Content and Curricula: Are Boys Invisible?

William Pollack in his book *Real Boys* writes, "Our schools, in general, are not sufficiently hospitable environments for boys and are not doing what they could to address boys' unique social, academic, and emotional needs" because "they use curricula, classroom materials, and teaching methods that do not respond to how boys learn."[52] Kathleen Parker, author of *Save the Males*, also claims that classes and curricula "favor girl interests."[53] She says, "Elementary grade textbooks and literature rarely feature strong, active male roles or tales of valor, high adventure, or heaven forbid, gallantry, which feminists view as implying that men and women aren't equal. Biographies of presidents and inventors have been replaced by stories of brave and adventurous women."[54] Christina Hoff Sommers says that boys are forced to learn about Jane Eyre, when instead they should learn about Silas Marner and the war poets.[55]

Do classroom materials privilege girls and marginalize boys? Let's take the content of textbooks. There are more male (54%) than female (46%) characters in first and third grade children's developmental reading texts. Males are more likely to be portrayed as aggressive, argumentative, and competitive. Females are more likely to be described as affectionate, emotionally expressive, passive, and tender.[56] These gender-stereotyped depictions should please Sommers and Parker for their total lack of creativity and their strict adherence to traditional gender roles.

Much has been made in the last two decades about getting girls more interested in math and science. Unfortunately, school materials do little to encourage girls' interest in these fields. Like most materials, life science textbooks show pictures of males more often than females, males are positioned in active roles more frequently than females, and the accomplishments of women are less likely to be featured.[57] High school chemistry textbooks also show more pictures of males than females.[58] These depictions offer few role models for girls aspiring to be scientists. When early and more recent editions of high school chemistry texts have been examined, we find that most maintain a gender imbalance favoring representations of boys and men compared to girls and women, and a few have even increased the imbalance in recent years.[59] The patterns found in science textbooks send the message to readers that boys and men are engaged in the scientific endeavor, whereas girls and women are on the sidelines—they are not doing science so much as watching and observing those who are.

Even educational software favors boys and men. In a study of 43 popular educational software programs, 20 programs contained only male main characters but only 5 programs contained only female characters.[60] These numbers also reveal the gender-segregated nature of these software programs, which sends the message to young people that male and female characters inhabit different lives and gender cultures. Male characters were more likely to be shown as aggressive but also more athletic, more likely to rescue, and more likely to take risks than female characters.[61] Once again, educational software depicts boys and men as active, involved, and mattering more than girls and women.

Even teaching materials are gender biased in favor of boys. In an analysis of teacher education texts (texts used by those studying to become teachers), the content focuses mostly on males, although unlike the findings from other studies reviewed in this chapter, photos depict more females than males. The presence of females compared to males might suggest progress but the photos tended to show women as teachers and men as principals and administrators which only solidifies traditional gender roles. If there is any field in which women have made significant contributions, it would be education. Yet the pioneers of education shown in these texts are nearly all male.[62]

In this exhaustive review of educational materials, the only literature found with some gender balance or counter-stereotyped content was one study of 15 popular educational psychology textbooks.[63] The study analyzed student characters in classroom scenarios depicted in the texts. Girl and boy characters were presented at roughly the same frequency. Surprisingly, there were no gender differences found in portrayals of positive masculine traits (e.g., courage, confidence) or positive (e.g., nurturing, caring) or negative (submissiveness, emotionality) feminine traits. However, boys were portrayed as engaging in more negative masculine activities (e.g., aggression, bullying).

In contrast to the concerns of anti-feminist authors, an avalanche of research studies demonstrates that school materials overwhelmingly present males as the typical, normal student by portraying them more frequently than females. The content of materials caters to traditional boys' interests; boys are the active characters in these materials and girls provide marginal, largely supportive roles; and gender roles are traditional.

Are Teachers Mean to Boys?

Several writers express concern about the overinfluence of women in boys' lives. In her book *Women Who Make the World Worse*, anti-feminist Kate O'Beirne[64] argues that "Classrooms have been turned into feminist reeducation camps. . ." Most often women teachers are presented as the ones to blame for boys losing interest in school, boys not doing well, and even boys feeling marginalized *as* boys. In *Raising Cain*, Dan Kindlon and Michael Thompson lament: "a boy's experience of school is as a thorn among roses; he is a different, lesser, and sometimes frowned-upon presence, and he knows it,"[65] and "Grade school is largely a feminine environment, populated predominantly by women teachers and authority figures, that seems rigged against boys, against the higher activity level and lower level of impulse control that is normal for boys."[66] In *Save the Males*, Kathleen Parker says, "[Boys'] interests aren't valued, and their behavior isn't tolerated."[67] Parker describes the school day for boys as being "steeped in estrogen" during which boys are told of "how many 'bad choices' they've made."[68]

It is true that elementary and middle school teachers are much more likely to be women than men. Remarkably, the boy-crisis authors do not account for *why* there are not more teachers who are men and, conversely, why many talented, educated young women view teaching as one of the few careers available to them. Elementary school teaching is a low-status job and is considered "women's work." The median salary for an elementary school teacher in the United States in 2012 was $40,000.[69] So even though men who are elementary school teachers are paid more than women, it is not surprising that only 13% of them are men.[70] Those men who do choose woman-dominated fields tend to be treated differently, which in this case, means *better*. Men in woman-dominated careers benefit from what been called the "glass escalator"[71]—the phenomenon whereby men, at least white men,[72] in woman-dominated jobs such as nursing and elementary teaching, are given preferential treatment in terms of hiring and promotions. They are promoted into administrative and managerial positions at a faster rate than are women.

What does actual research find on teachers' treatment of girl and boy students? Is the classroom rigged against boys? Is boys' behavior not tolerated as the boy-crisis authors suggest? Are boys thorns among girls, who are roses? In 1988 Alison Kelly published a comprehensive meta-analysis on teacher-pupil interactions that examined the attention teachers give to girl and boy students. She compiled the data from 81 previously conducted studies. Here's a summary of what Kelly found:

> It is now beyond dispute that girls receive less of the teacher's attention in class, and that this is true across a wide range of different conditions. It applies to all age groups (although more in some than in others), in several different countries, in various socio-economic and ethnic groupings, across all subjects in the curriculum, and with both male and female

teachers (although more with males). Boys get more of all kinds of classroom interaction. This discrepancy is most marked for behavioral criticism, but this does not explain the overall imbalance. Boys also get more instructional contacts, more high-level questions, more academic criticism and slightly more praise than girls.[73]

Kelly's study is comprehensive but her work is dated. Does more recent research reveal different patterns of teacher treatment of girls and boys? One study found that the attention to boys was more likely to be negative than positive.[74] And some studies say that boys are given more attention because they take more initiative than do girls.[75] However, most studies find that boys receive more negative *and* more positive attention from teachers[76] and that boys' initiating interaction does not account for this differential treatment. In other words, boys may raise their hands or call out to the teacher more often than girls, but above and beyond this difference, teachers attend to them more than they attend to girls. What does the attention look like? One study found that boys receive more criticism of their behavior than girls, but they also receive more intellectual criticism and intellectual acceptance than do girls.[77] The positive and negative intellectual-related interactions boys have with teachers reveal that teachers take boys seriously as intellectual beings and encourage them to think critically. This differential treatment also reveals that more intellectual advances are expected of boys than girls, and that boys are more valued than girls for their intellect.

Boys get more of *all* kinds of classroom attention. These interactions do not amount to a "toxic" environment for the white middle class boys who are the focus of boy-crisis writers. A useful endeavor would be to examine the degree to which schools might be toxic to ethnic minority students—both boys and girls. For example, in their meta-analysis on teachers' expectations of students, Harriet Tenenbaum and Martin Ruck[78] found that teachers held more positive expectations for white and Asian American students than African American and Latino students. Teachers also made more positive comments to white students than to African American and Latino students. African American boys might be particularly targeted by teachers because teachers rate their behavior as more antisocial, and they have lower academic expectations for them than they do for African American girls.[79] African American students, African American boys especially, are more likely to receive disciplinary office referrals than students of other ethnicities.[80] There is a warehouse of studies finding that African American men are perceived as more dangerous and aggressive than white men who engage in the same behavior.[81] For authors who are so concerned with the plight of boys, it is unfortunate that Parker, Sommers, Pollack, Gurian, Kindlon and Thompson, and Biddulph do not address the challenges that ethnic minority boys and men have in school and in the mass media representations of them.

Center Stealing and Perceptions of Male Marginalization

How can books, articles, pundits, and politicians over the past 15 to 20 years have such a warped view of the regard and treatment of girls and women compared with boys and men? Trina Grillo and Stephanie Wildman[82] describe this blindness to inequality as the *center stage problem*. When those who are used to being at the center of everything important in society are moved from the center, however briefly, group members experience a threat and therefore are motivated to re-assert their privilege. The center stage problem occurs because dominant group members are already accustomed to being center stage; they have been treated that way by society; it feels natural, comfortable, and the natural order of things. Members of dominant groups assume that their perceptions are the pertinent ones, that their problems are the ones that need to be addressed, and that in discourse they should be the speaker rather than the listener. Part of being a member of a privileged group is being the center and the subject of all inquiry in which nonprivileged groups are the objects or pushed to the sidelines. So strong is this expectation of holding center stage that even when a time and place is specifically designated for members of a nonprivileged group to be central, members of the dominant group will often attempt to take back the focus. They are stealing the center—often with a complete lack of self-consciousness. As Grillo and Wildman argue, when people who are not regarded as entitled to the center move into it, even momentarily, they are viewed as usurpers. In other words, members of the privileged group experience a threat when attention even temporarily and briefly turns away from them and toward members of a marginalized group. Feelings of personal entitlement can lead members of dominant groups to be blind to seeing when they are unfairly overbenefiting, and their unearned and unjust privilege leads them to regard efforts to "level the playing field" as fundamentally unfair.[83]

Entitlement and the Privilege to Underperform

We do a great disservice to boys in how we raise them. We stifle the humanity of boys. We define masculinity in a very narrow way. Masculinity becomes this hard small cage and we put boys inside the cage. We teach boys to be afraid of fear. We teach boys to be afraid of weakness, of vulnerability.

—CHIMAMANDA NGOZI ADICHIE, 2012[84]

So if boys are getting plenty of teacher attention and the curriculum is geared toward them, why do boys tend to earn lower grades and go to college in fewer numbers than girls? There may be several reasons but two are presented here. First, school is considered a feminine environment, doing well in schools is inconsistent with masculinity. A second reason is the problem of male entitlement.

School Is for Sissies

Research on girls' and boys' interactions with teachers and peers finds that boys are more likely to be influenced by other boys—not teachers and not girls. If a boy peer responds positively to a behavior, boys are more likely to continue the behavior than if the peer criticizes the behavior. The reactions of teachers and girls to a boys' behavior tend to be irrelevant.[85] In her book *Save the Males,* Kathleen Parker states that boys prefer the company of men. "That is because a woman is perceived as just another mother, while a man is a *Man*."[86] Precisely. Just as our review of the literature indicates, women matter less than men in society, and, not surprisingly, boys internalize this message. Women, even women teachers who are in positions of authority, are perceived as just "moms," so who cares what they think? Men are more interesting, are higher in status, and worthy of boys' attention. But this pattern goes beyond simply finding women teachers boring. For boys as young as elementary school years, defying teachers' authority—and in the elementary years most teachers are women—is a means by which to gain popularity with other boys.[87]

Like boys, girls are also influenced by same-gender peers, but in contrast to boys, they are also influenced by teachers.[88] Boys are more concerned than girls about looking cool to their main social group—other boys. School achievement is incompatible with this goal.[89] The social dominance goals of having power over peers are negatively correlated with academic achievement for boys.[90] So the extent to which a student thinks that being powerful over others and seeming tough is important, that student will perform worse academically. Research finds that boys' culture is less study-oriented than girls' culture and that this study culture influences achievement.[91] In other words, one reason girls tend to outperform boys is because boys are concerned about conforming to gender stereotypes that say that school is for girls. Boys are worried about looking weak (i.e., feminine),[92] so boys will avoid academic achievement to the extent that it is viewed as feminine.[93] Stereotypically masculine traits (for example, competitiveness, assertiveness) are more valued in U.S. and western European cultures.[94] In fact, attributes arbitrarily labeled "male" are more valued than the exact same characteristics that are labeled "female."[95] So to the extent that school achievement is seen as feminine, even when curricula and teacher behavior are male-centered, some boys and young men will dismiss or discount school activities and academic achievement. Therefore, it's not the school experience that feminizes boys but rather the ideology of traditional masculinity that keeps boys from wanting to succeed. Unfortunately, some boys see academic success itself as a disconfirmation of their masculinity.[96]

In their book, *Raising Cain*, Dan Kindlon and Michael Thompson say, "Today many boys face a steady diet of shame and anxiety throughout their elementary school years. From it they learn only to feel bad about themselves and to hate the place that makes them feel that way."[97] Since boys are favored by curriculum *and* teachers, it is difficult to imagine too many boys feeling bad about themselves after a day at school.

The end-of-men/boy-crisis authors would have us believe that the world has become too female-centered, and that schools in particular are too female-focused thanks to feminism. We have already established this argument as baseless. Therefore, let's consider an alternative view.

In addition to the issue of school success as indicative of girliness, one way to help us understand and explain the data that boys are performing less well in school is to examine the role of entitlement and privilege. Psychological or personal entitlement refers to one's sense of deservingness. Entitlement reflects the belief that a person deserves a set of outcomes because of who they are or what they have done. Social psychologists tend to define entitlement as deservingness based less on what someone has accomplished (an *achieved* characteristic) and more on *who* the person is (an *ascribed* characteristic).[98] Individuals with a strong sense of entitlement believe they deserve good things to come to them. Not surprising, entitled people are fairly self-centered. They have the tendency to take credit for positive events and to blame others for negative ones.[99] Entitled people tend to shy away from information that contradicts their worldview and avoid situations that do not reinforce their positive self-image.[100] Studies consistently find that men have a stronger sense of entitlement than do women. (Unfortunately, most of the research on gender and entitlement has examined white respondents, therefore we know little about the interaction of gender and ethnicity.) Men also tend to score higher than women on the related concept of narcissism.[101] How does entitlement manifest? One way is in overconfidence. Men give higher estimates of their ability than do women, and men's self-estimates tend to be independent of their actual ability.[102] On cognitive tests, for instance, men give themselves higher ratings than their actual performance merits, whereas women tend to have a more realistic appraisal of their own performance.[103]

Entitlement is difficult to measure because individuals who are entitled tend not to recognize their own sense of it, just as individuals who experience and benefit from privilege (e.g., white people, men, heterosexuals) do not recognize their unearned privilege. Social psychologists typically measure entitlement through pay expectations; they assign individuals to a task and ask them how much they would expect to be paid. In study after study, we find that women's wage entitlement is lower than men's.[104] In a representative study, Lisa Barron[105] conducted simulated job interviews with MBA students. Men's initial salary requests were higher than women's, even though women and men did not differ in GPA, age, previous salary, and negotiation training. Men were more likely to have a strong sense of what they are worth, and they also expected the company to pay them what they believed they are worth. Men were more likely to believe that they could prove their value in the negotiation. In contrast, women were less likely to have a sense of what they are worth, and they expected the company to determine their worth. Women were also more likely to think that they could prove their value only once they got on the job. Men also reported that they were entitled to a higher salary than their similarly situated peers, whereas women were more likely to believe that they were entitled to the same salary as their peers.[106] In another study, researchers gave college students a task to complete, followed by instructions to pay themselves what they thought their work was worth. Although independent raters who judged the work perceived no differences in the quality of the work, self-ratings indicated that women and men evaluated and paid themselves differently. Men paid themselves 18% more than did women for the same amount and quality of work.[107]

Do men think they deserve more because they actually do better work? They might think they do better work, but they do not perform better in these studies. And even if they know they did not perform well, they think they should be paid as much as if they had performed well. This is entitlement. In one classic experiment, Brenda Major[108] and her colleagues had college students complete a task. When they were finished they could pay themselves what they considered fair for the work they completed, and leave any remaining money behind. Like most studies, women paid themselves significantly less than what men paid themselves. In a second experiment, Major and her colleagues[109] paid students a fixed amount of money to perform a task in which the students could work for as long as they thought was fair. When women and men cannot choose how much they deserve because the salary is fixed, do the usual gender differences in entitlement disappear? No, entitlement just takes a different form. In experiments in which pay is fixed, women (1) worked longer than men did, (2) completed more of the work than men, (3) did so more accurately, and (4) even worked more efficiently than men. After the main part of the study, participants were asked to provide evaluations of their own performances. Despite the fact that women worked longer than men, completed more work, and worked more accurately and efficiently, women and men did not differ in their self-rated performance evaluations. These experiments suggest important differences between women's and men's sense of entitlement.

Major's findings of gender differences in entitlement tend to be framed in terms of women having "depressed" entitlement, whereas men have a normal, healthy sense of entitlement. It is true that in these kinds of studies, women tend to pay themselves less than men for the same or better quality work, and believe the pay allocation to be fair.[110] However, a more recent experiment finds that the issue does not seem to be that women's entitlement is *deflated*, but rather that men's entitlement is *inflated*. Brett Pelham and John Hetts[111] asked American college students to solve easy, moderate, or difficult anagrams of scrambled words. Participants were asked to evaluate their own performance and then paid themselves for their work. You might guess that those who performed poorly would pay themselves less than those who performed well. This was the case for women, but not for men. Specifically, women paid themselves less when they had performed poorly—when they had solved fewer anagrams. However, men paid themselves well even when they had performed poorly. Pelham and Hetts speculate that men seem to think that their personal feelings of worth entitle them to a certain level of payment, regardless of the quality of their performance. The women in these studies based their level of self-pay on their evaluations of their *work* (performance, an *achieved* status) rather than their evaluations of their *worth* (who they are, an *ascribed* status).

Perhaps it is not surprising that men believe they are worth more than do women. Society rewards them accordingly. In experiments, participants tend to pay men more than women for the same job. For instance, Melissa Williams[112] and her colleagues presented Asian American and white participants with a description of an employee and job and were asked how much the employee should be paid. Participants allocated higher salaries to men than to women. Even in experiments when jobs are simply labeled as "male" they are viewed as higher valued and therefore meriting a higher salary than jobs with the exact same characteristics labeled "female."[113] So people think that men should be paid more than women for doing the same work and that "men's" jobs deserve more pay than "women's" jobs.

When women and men have been asked about what they deserve, how they compare to others, and what information should be used in hiring and salary decisions, there are interesting differences there too. One study found that women's investment in work is not determined by the financial rewards they receive: they invest as much as they can in work regardless of pay. Men, on the other hand, admit to doing more work when pay is higher and less work when pay is lower.[114] Mary Hogue[115] and her colleagues asked individuals about the characteristics important in determining pay. The following characteristics are

typically cited: *work output* (quality and quantity of work), *specific status charac-*
teristics (worker education, job experience*), job attributes* (responsibility, working conditions, impact of job, complexity), and *ascribed status characteristics* (age,
race, gender). When setting a salary, men placed greater importance on ascribed
status characteristics than women. Women placed greater importance on work
output, specific status characteristics, and job attributes. In terms of determinants
of salary, men feel comfortable relying on *who they are*, whereas women rely on
what they have done.

Both women and men seem to go along with men's overconfidence and
inflated entitlement, consequently men are led to see their level of deservingness as fair and equal even when, objectively, it is not. For example, one
study[116] asked people to play a bargaining game in which one person offers an
amount of money to another and the responder decides whether or not the
offered amount is acceptable. Of course each side in the negotiation is motivated to obtain the most amount of money—the proposer is motivated to give
up as little as possible and the responder is motivated to obtain as much as
possible. Women made higher offers overall than did men. Men were offered
more than women and less was demanded from men than women. So more
was offered to men even when they did not demand more. It is not surprising
that some men feel entitled to things they have not earned. How could they
not? People reward them accordingly.

What are the repercussions of these gendered patterns of entitlement and
salaries? Obviously, if women ask for less and are offered less, they will earn less
than men who ask for more and are offered more. Pay raises are often based on
a percentage of the worker's salary. If men start out earning more than women,
they will get higher and higher raises over their careers. Also, the mere recognition of a pay difference associated with group membership is enough to make
people believe that the higher-paid group is more competent and worthy than a
lower-paid group.[117] In other words, if people notice that men make more money
than women, they infer that men deserve more and are worth more; therefore,
the pay inequity is perceived as justified when it is not.

Academic Entitlement

Much of this chapter has examined the "boy crisis" in education. How do feelings of entitlement influence the school experience? Some research has examined
the concept of *academic entitlement*. In their research on academic entitlement,
Karolyn Chowning[118] and her colleagues find that on some dimensions of academic entitlement women and men score similarly. For instance, women and
men tend to agree with statements such as "Professors must be entertaining to

be good" and "My professors should curve my grade if I am close to the next grade." However, on a measure of *externalized responsibility*, men are more likely to agree with statements such as "It is unnecessary for me to participate in class when the professor is paid for teaching, not for asking questions" and "For group assignments, it is acceptable to take a back seat and let others do most of the work if I am busy." Men more than women are likely to agree with statements such as "Instructors should bend the rules for me" and "If I felt I deserved a higher grade, I would tell the instructor."[119] The authors conclude that students who attribute their performance to their courses or instructors may fail to self-correct or develop adaptive strategies for success in college.

As we mentioned earlier, men are more likely to be narcissists than are women. One particular type of narcissism, *exploitativeness/entitlement* is more common among men than women. Individuals with high levels of exploitativeness/entitlement narcissism would agree with statements such as "I find it easy to manipulate people" and "I will never be satisfied until I get all that I deserve." Interestingly, this particular aspect of narcissism is associated with academic disengagement, such as not attending class.[120] The implication here is that inflated self-importance may lead to shirking academic obligations and lower academic performance.

Unfortunately, parents contribute to some boys' overconfidence. Both parents of boys, as well as boys themselves, *overestimate* their intelligence relative to their actual intelligence. Parents of daughters, and girls themselves, tend to *underestimate* their intelligence.[121] Boys tend to view themselves as *more* competent than how teachers view them, whereas girls tend to view themselves as *less* competent than how teachers view them.[122] These differences, most evident in the lack of agreement between boys and their teachers on competence and the work cited previously indicating that boys are more likely to listen to other boys than they are to teachers, suggest that boys may be less attentive to expectations from others than girls, and therefore they also may be affected less by evaluations from others.[123] Boys' inflated sense of entitlement and their privileged status as males allows them to be insensitive to others' evaluations. Boys' and men's sense of entitlement, coupled with the perception that school performance and academic commitment is incompatible with masculinity, may account for boys and men's disengagement with school.

The Gender Gap in College Attendance

A key piece of the argument that there is a war against boys and men is that women now outnumber men in college and university attendance and graduation rates. Women make up 57% of the students at U.S. universities.[124] So they do make up the majority of college students, but this number hardly represents a female take-over and male demise. There are important caveats to even these fairly modest numbers. First, men continue to outnumber women in the attendance at most elite colleges and universities. Harvard has a 50/50 split of their undergraduate enrollment, but Princeton and Yale's men represent 51% of the student body; the University of Chicago has 56% men; Stanford has 52% men, Caltech has 65% men, and MIT has 63% men.[125] Second, men are still more likely to graduate with degrees that lead to higher-paying jobs. For example, in 2014 the average starting salary of a person with a degree in Education was $40,590, Humanities and Social Sciences majors earned $38,045, but Math/Sciences and Engineering majors earned $42,596 and $62,564, respectively.[126] Of course, women could choose to major in male-dominated fields such as math, sciences, and engineering, but they will still make lower salaries than men with the same majors.[127] Third, men make more money than women in every education category from high school dropouts to those with high school diplomas to college graduates.[128] In terms of earning power, then, men as a whole do not need as much education as do women for higher pay—simply because they are men. Surely, girls and boys alike should be encouraged to seek higher education, but end-of-men/boy-crisis authors fail to consider the causes other than a supposedly antimale climate that may account for the increase in young women attending college relative to men.

Another frequently cited gender difference used as evidence that schools are systematically harmful for boys is that girls generally excel at reading and writing relative to boys. Concerns about boys' reading and writing difficulties are valid; however, as noted earlier, the stereotypically male careers of math, science, and technology are much more prestigious and lucrative than stereotypically female careers in reading and writing. Support for boys' success in the more lucrative math and technology fields comes from parents, teachers, and boys themselves. Teachers and parents reinforce gender-segregated career categories. For instance, teachers overrate male students' mathematics capability and believe boys to be more interested, more confident, and to have higher achievement in science and math than girls.[129] Teachers also call on boys more often in science classes (although boys also more often volunteer questions and comments).[130] Parents perceive sons as more competent in science, and they expect better performance from them compared to daughters.[131] Again, pointing to boys' deficits in reading and writing as indicative of schools shortchanging boys does not take into account boys' achievements and the different value and compensation for those achievements. Parents encourage their children to take gender-stereotyped courses: they select fewer foreign language courses for their sons and fewer science courses for their daughters.[132] Across all academic domains parents' underestimate daughters' compared to sons' abilities, and this underestimation is reflected in their talk to their children. Even when girls and boys earn equivalent grades, when parents talk with daughters and sons about academics, they use more discouraging talk with their daughters than sons.[133] Parents tend to overestimate their sons' science ability relative to daughters' and believe that their sons like science more than their daughters. It's hardly a surprise then that boys tend to be more confident in their science ability than girls—but this gender difference is not reflective of their actual science ability because there tends to be no gender difference in actual science grades of kids.[134]

Conclusion

The end-of-men/boy-crisis rhetoric says that feminism brought attention to girls' and women's needs in education but, in doing so, feminists subordinated boys' needs to the point that girls and women got ahead of boys and men. Contrary to the inflamed rhetoric about the end-of-men, boys and men continue to be at the center of popular culture and education. Male characters continue to dominate television shows, television cartoons, children's television shows, television commercials, commercial voiceovers, films, music videos, magazine advertisements, newspaper comics, and even cereal boxes and clipart. Boys and men are portrayed as doing things—they take risks, they adventure, they are leaders, they work, and they take care of business. They matter. Boys and men continue to be portrayed as the regular, normal, natural human. Girls and women largely operate in a service capacity to boys and men. What girls and women do matters less.

Nonetheless, books continue to be written and sold that argue that the education system is "rigged against boys." A systematic review of school materials and teacher behavior demonstrates just the opposite. Just as mass media in general put men at the center, so do teaching materials. Teachers continue to focus most of their attention—both positive and negative—on boys. Teachers and parents expect more intellectually from boys than from girls. Even when teachers attempt to be "gender-blind" in their interactions with students, as well as their choices in curricula and lesson plans, they tend to use male-centered curricula without realizing what they are doing.[135] However, teachers who have been trained in gender equity tend to distribute their attention more equitably between girls and boys than those who have not.[136] The problem of course is that if teachers believe that it is *boys*, not girls who are short-changed, they are not prepared to notice their own behavior when it is directed to keep boys at the center.

The end-of-men/boy-crisis authors attack the relatively brief moment of academic, educational, and popular focus on the inhospitable nature of classrooms and educational institutions for girls and women and demand a focus not just broadened to include boys but redirected once again to exclude girls. William Pollack, author of *Real Boys,* even declares, "Boys' poor performance is a global issue."[137] He ignores the fact that in many countries girls are denied access to formal education simply because they are girls and, in some cultures, when a family has resources for only one child to attend school, it is the boy who is allowed to attend. According to UNESCO, women account for two-thirds of the global illiterate population and that number has remained virtually the same over the past twenty years.[138]

Feelings of personal entitlement can lead members of dominant groups to be blind to seeing when they are unfairly over-benefiting, and their unearned and unjust privilege leads them to regard efforts to "level the playing field" as fundamentally unfair to them.[139] Grillo and Wildman's center stage problem[140] helps us understand how those who are accustomed to being at the center of everything important in society are threatened when a spotlight is shone on a marginalized group even for a brief moment. When people who are not regarded as entitled to the center move into it, they are viewed as usurpers. The reaction is a backlash and a re-assertion of privilege.

Girls and women are usurpers. Jean Twenge[141] notes that in recent decades girls and women earn better grades and obtain college degrees because of an increased emphasis on instrumentality (e.g., assertiveness, competitiveness—characteristics traditionally associated with men) for women. Twenge argues that society has done a good job of encouraging girls to be instrumental, and now girls are prepared to compete with boys. Women regard achievement-related status enhancements (e.g., education, experience) as more important to employee pay decisions than men do, whereas men suggest that ascribed status (who a person is) should be utilized in pay decisions.[142] Trends in society suggest that women are taking the steps necessary to enhance their achievement-related status through education and training.[143] For some men, their sense of entitlement does not always match their actual achievement. Rather than blaming feminism for the supposed end of men, we should focus on patriarchy and male dominance as producing gender rules that dictate that school, and anything else coded as feminine, is viewed as weakness; that women teachers have nothing useful to say to boys and men; and that simply being a man should be good enough for success without hard work, education, and training.

Notes

1. Sledge, M. (2014, January 26). Rand Paul: "If there was a war on women, I think they won." Retrieved from http://www.huffingtonpost.com/2014/01/26/rand-paul-war-on-women_n_4669464.html

2. Gilligan, C. (1982). *In a different voice: Psychological theory and women's development.* Cambridge, MA: Harvard University Press.
3. Sadker, M., & Sadker, D. (1994). *Failing at fairness: How our schools cheat girls.* New York, NY: Touchstone.
4. Pipher, M. (1994). *Reviving Ophelia: Saving the selves of adolescent girls.* New York, NY: Ballantine Books.
5. Pollack, W. (1998). *Real boys: Rescuing our sons from the myths of boyhood.* New York, NY: Random House.
6. Kindlon, D., & Thompson, M. (1999). *Raising Cain: Protecting the emotional life of boys.* New York, NY: Ballantine.
7. Gurian, M. (1996). *The wonder of boys.* New York, NY: Putnam.
8. Sommers, C. H. (2000). *The war against boys: How misguided feminism is harming our young men.* New York, NY: Simon & Schuster.
9. Page 4: Parker, K. (2008). *Save the males: Why men matter, why women should care.* New York, NY: Random House.
10. Page 71: Parker, K. (2008). *Save the males: Why men matter, why women should care.* New York, NY: Random House.
11. Human Development Reports: United Nations Development Programme (UNDP). (2011). Gender Inequality Index and related indicators. Retrieved from http://hdr.undp.org/en/statistics/gii/
12. Page 106: Biddulph, S. (1998). *Raising boys: Why boys are different—and how to help them become happy and well-balanced men.* Berkeley, CA: Celestial Arts.
13. Signorielli, N. (2009). Race and sex in prime time: A look at occupations and occupational prestige. *Mass Communication and Society, 12,* 332–352. doi:10.1080/15205430802478693
14. Gerbner, G. (1998). Casting the American scene: A look at the characters on prime time and daytime television from 1994–1997. Retrieved from http://www.asc.upenn.edu/gerbner/Asset.aspx?assetID=1614
15. Page 668, emphasis in original: Thompson, T. L., & Zerbinos, E. (1995). Gender roles in animated cartoons: Has the picture changed in 20 years? *Sex Roles, 32,* 651–673.
16. Gay & Lesbian Alliance Against Defamation. (2012, October 5). GLAAD study records highest percentage ever of LGBT series regulars on broadcast television, cable LGBT character count also rises. Retrieved from http://www.glaad.org/releases/glaad-study-records-highest-percentage-ever-lgbt-series-regulars-broadcast-television-cable
17. Lauzen, M. M., & Dozier, D. M. (2005). Maintaining the double standard: Portrayals of age and gender in popular films. *Sex Roles, 52,* 437–446. doi:10.1007/s11199-005-3710-1
18. Lauzen, M. M., & Dozier, D. M. (2005). Recognition and respect revisited: Portrayals of age and gender in prime-time television. *Mass Communication & Society, 8,* 241–256.

19. Lauzen, M. M., & Dozier, D. M. (2005). Maintaining the double standard: Portrayals of age and gender in popular films. *Sex Roles*, 52, 437–446. doi:10.1007/s11199-005-3710-1

20. Greenberg, B. S., & Worrell, T. R. (2007). New faces on television: A 12-season replication. *The Howard Journal of Communications*, 18, 277–290. doi:10.1080/10646170701653651

21. Lauzen, M. M., & Dozier, D. M. (2005). Maintaining the double standard: Portrayals of age and gender in popular films. *Sex Roles*, 52, 437–446. doi:10.1007/s11199-005-3710-1

Lauzen, M. M., & Dozier, D. M. (2005). Recognition and respect revisited: Portrayals of age and gender in prime-time television. *Mass Communication & Society*, 8, 241–256.

22. Signorielli, N. (2009). Race and sex in prime time: A look at occupations and occupational prestige. *Mass Communication and Society*, 12, 332–352. doi:10.1080/15205430802478693

23. Signorielli, N. (2009). Race and sex in prime time: A look at occupations and occupational prestige. *Mass Communication and Society*, 12, 332–352. doi:10.1080/15205430802478693

24. Lauzen, M. M., Dozier, D. M., & Horan, N. (2008). Constructing gender stereotypes through social roles in prime-time television. *Journal of Broadcasting & Electronic Media*, 52, 200–214. doi:10.1080/08838150801991971

25. Oliver, M. B. (2003). African American men as "criminal and dangerous": Implications of media portrayals of crime on the "criminalization" of African American men. *Journal of African American Studies*, 7(2), 3–18.

26. Jhally, Sut. (Writer). (2007). *Dreamworlds 3: Desire, sex, & power in music videos* [DVD]. Available from http://www.mediaed.org/cgi-bin/commerce.cgi?preadd=action&key=223

27. Turner, J. S. (2011). Sex and the spectacle of music videos: An examination of the portrayal of race and sexuality in music videos. *Sex Roles*, 64, 173–191. doi:10.1007/s11199-010-9766-6

28. Turner, J. S. (2011). Sex and the spectacle of music videos: An examination of the portrayal of race and sexuality in music videos. *Sex Roles*, 64, 173–191. doi:10.1007/s11199-010-9766-6

29. Jhally, Sut. (Writer). (2007). *Dreamworlds 3: Desire, sex, & power in music videos* [DVD]. Available from http://www.mediaed.org/cgi-bin/commerce.cgi?preadd=action&key=223

30. Mager, J., & Helgeson, J. G. (2011). Fifty years of advertising images: Some changing perspectives on role portrayals along with enduring consistencies. *Sex Roles*, 64, 238–252. doi:10.1007/s11199-010-9782-6

31. Mager, J., & Helgeson, J. G. (2011). Fifty years of advertising images: Some changing perspectives on role portrayals along with enduring consistencies. *Sex Roles*, 64, 238–252. doi:10.1007/s11199-010-9782-6

This description reflects Goffman's advertisement category called, "Ritualization of Subordination." See:Goffman, E. (1976). *Gender advertisements*. New York, NY: Harper Torchbooks.

32. Mager, J., & Helgeson, J. G. (2011). Fifty years of advertising images: Some changing perspectives on role portrayals along with enduring consistencies. *Sex Roles, 64*, 238–252. doi:10.1007/s11199-010-9782-6

   I'm describing Goffman's "Licensed Withdrawal." See:Goffman, E. (1976). *Gender advertisements*. New York, NY: Harper Torchbooks.

33. Paek, H.-J., Nelson, M. R., & Vilela, A. M. (2011). Examination of gender-role portrayals in television advertising across seven countries. *Sex Roles, 64*, 192–207. doi:10.1007/s11199-010-9850-y

34. Paek, H.-J., Nelson, M. R., & Vilela, A. M. (2011). Examination of gender-role portrayals in television advertising across seven countries. *Sex Roles, 64*, 192–207. doi:10.1007/s11199-010-9850-y

35. Glascock, J., & Preston-Schreck, C. (2004). Gender and racial stereotypes in daily newspaper comics: A time-honored tradition? *Sex Roles, 51*, 423–431.

36. Milburn, S.S., Carney, D. R., & Ramirez, A. M. (2001). Even in modern media, the picture is still the same: A content analysis of clipart images. *Sex Roles, 44*, 277–294. doi:10.1023/A:1010977515933.

37. Silenced: Gender gap in election coverage. (2012). *4thEstate.net*. Retrieved from http://www.4thEstate.net/female-voices-in-media-infographic/

38. Page 21: Sommers, C. H. (2000). Victims of androgyny: How feminist schooling harms boys. *American Enterprise, 11*, 20–25.

39. Page 3: Parker, K. (2008). *Save the males: Why men matter, why women should care.* New York, NY: Random House.

40. Rosin, H. (2010, July/August). The end of men. *The Atlantic, 306*, 56–62.

41. Newport, F. (2007, July 5). Americans continue to express slight preference for boys: Little changed since 1941. *Gallup.com*. Retrieved from http://www.gallup.com/poll/28045/Americans-Continue-Express-Slight-Preference-Boys.aspx

42. Leaper, C., Breed, L., Hoffman, L., & Perlman, C. A. (2002). Variations in the gender-stereotyped content of children's television cartoons across genres. *Journal of Applied Social Psychology, 32*, 1653–1662.

43. Leaper, C., Breed, L., Hoffman, L., & Perlman, C. A. (2002). Variations in the gender-stereotyped content of children's television cartoons across genres. *Journal of Applied Social Psychology, 32*, 1653–1662.

44. Klein, H., & Shiffman, K. S. (2009). Underrepresentation and symbolic annihilation of socially disenfranchised groups ("out groups") in animated cartoons. *The Howard Journal of Communications, 20*, 55–72. doi:10.1080/10646170802665208

45. Steinke, J., and Long, M. (1996). A lab of her own? Portrayals of female characters on children's educational science programs. *Science Communication, 18*(2), 91–115.

46. Hamilton, M. C., Anderson, D., Broaddus, M., & Young, K. (2006). Gender stereotyping and under-representation of female characters in 200 popular children's picture books: A twenty-first century update. *Sex Roles, 55*, 757–765. doi:10.1007/s11199-006-9128-6

47. Fitzpatrick, M. J., & McPherson, B. J. (2010). Coloring within the lines: Gender stereotypes in contemporary coloring books. *Sex Roles, 62*, 127–137. doi:10.1007/s11199-009-9703-8

48. Kahlenberg, S. G., & Hein, M. M. (2010). Progression on Nickelodeon? Gender-role stereotypes in toy commercials. *Sex Roles, 62*, 830–847. doi:10.1007/s11199-009-9653-1

49. Kahlenburg, S. G., & Hein, M. M. (2010). Progression on Nickelodeon? Gender-role stereotypes in toy commercials. *Sex Roles, 62*, 830–847. doi:10.1007/s11199-009-9653-1

50. Black, K. A., Marola, J. A., Littman, A. I., Chrisler, J. C., & Neace, W. P. (2009). Gender and form of cereal box characters: Different medium, same disparity. *Sex Roles, 60*, 882–889. doi:10.1007/s11199-008-9579-z

51. Page 70: Biddulph, S. (1998) *Raising Boys*. Berkeley, CA: Celestial Arts.

52. Page 231: Pollack, W. (1998) *Real Boys: Rescuing Our Sons from the Myths of Boyhood*. New York, NY: Random House.

53. Page 13: Parker, K. (2008). *Save the males: Why men matter, why women should care*. New York, NY: Random House.

54. Page 15: Parker, K. (2008). *Save the males: Why men matter, why women should care*. New York, NY: Random House.

55. Sommers, C. H. (2000). Victims of androgyny: How feminist schooling harms boys. *American Enterprise, 11*, 20–25.

56. Evans, L., & Davis, K. (2000). No sissy boys here: A content analysis of the representation of masculinity in elementary school reading textbooks. *Sex Roles, 42*, 255–270.

57. Potter, E. F., & Rosser, S. V. (1992). Factors in life science textbooks that may deter girls' interest in science. *Journal of Research in Science Teaching, 29*, 669–686.

58. Bazler, J. A., & Simonis, D. A. (1991). Are high school chemistry textbooks gender fair? *Journal of Research in Science Teaching, 28*, 353–362. doi:10.1002/tea.3660280408

59. Bazler, J. A., & Simonis, D. A. (1991). Are high school chemistry textbooks gender fair? *Journal of Research in Science Teaching, 28*, 353–362. doi:10.1002/tea.3660280408

60. Sheldon, J. P. (2004). Gender stereotypes in educational software for young children. *Sex Roles, 51*, 433–444.

61. Sheldon, J. P. (2004). Gender stereotypes in educational software for young children. *Sex Roles, 51*, 433–444.

62. For a review, see: Zittleman, K., & Sadker, D. (2002). Gender bias in teacher education texts: New (and old) lessons. *Journal of Teacher Education, 53*, 168–180.

63. Yanowitz, K. L., & Weathers, K. J. (2004). Do boys and girls act differently in the classroom? A content analysis of student characters in educational psychology textbooks. *Sex Roles, 51*, 101–107.

64. Page 67: O'Beirne, K. (2006). *Women who make the world worse and how their radical feminist assault is ruining our schools, families, military, and sports.* New York, NY: Sentinel.

65. Page 24: Kindlon, D., & Thompson, M. (1999). *Raising Cain: Protecting the emotional life of boys.* New York, NY: Ballantine.

66. Page 23: Kindlon, D., & Thompson, M. (1999). *Raising Cain: Protecting the emotional life of boys.* New York, NY: Ballantine.

67. Page 15: Parker, K. (2008). *Save the males: Why men matter, why women should care.* New York, NY: Random House.

68. Page 12: Parker, K. (2008). *Save the males: Why men matter, why women should care.* New York, NY: Random House.

69. PayScale. (2012, March 17). Salary for all K-12 teachers. Retrieved from http://www.payscale.com/research/US/ALL_K-12_Teachers/Salary

70. PayScale. (2012, October 5). Elementary school teacher salary. Retrieved from http://www.payscale.com/research/US/Job=Elementary_School_Teacher/Salary

71. Williams, C. L. (1992). The glass escalator: Hidden advantages for men in the "female" professions. *Social Problems, 39*, 253–267. doi:10.1525/sp.1992.39.3.03x0034h

72. Wingfield finds that the "glass escalator" effect is not relevant to African American men working in women-dominated fields: Wingfield, A. (2009). Racializing the glass escalator: Reconsidering men's experiences with women's work. *Gender & Society, 23*(1), 5–26. doi:10.1177/0891243208323054

73. Page 20: Kelly, A. (1988). Gender differences in teacher-pupil interactions: A meta-analytic review. *Research in Education, 39*, 1–23.

74. Jones, S. M., & Dindia, K. (2004). A meta-analytic perspective on sex equity in the classroom. *Review of Educational Research, 74*, 443–471.

75. For instance, see: Einarsson, C., & Granström, K. (2002). Gender-biased interaction in the classroom: The influence of gender and age in the relationship between teacher and pupil. *Scandinavian Journal of Educational Research, 46*, 117–127. doi:10.1080/00313830220142155

76. Swinson, J., & Harrop, L. (2009). Teacher talk directed to boys and girls and its relationship to their behaviour. *Educational Studies, 35*, 515–524. doi:10.1080/03055690902883913

Duffy, J., Warren, K., & Walsh, M. (2001). Classroom interactions: Gender of teacher, gender of student, and classroom subject. *Sex Roles, 45*, 579–593.

Jones, M. G., & Wheatley, J. (1990). Gender differences in teacher-student interactions in science classrooms. *Journal of Research in Science Teaching, 27*, 861–874.

Kelly, A. (1988). Gender differences in teacher-pupil interactions: A meta-analytic review, *Research in Education, 39*, 1–23.

77. Jones, M. G., & Wheatley, J. (1990). Gender differences in teacher-student interactions in science classrooms. *Journal of Research in Science Teaching, 27*, 861–874.

78. Tenenbaum, H. R., & Ruck, M. D. (2007). Are teachers' expectations different for racial minority than for European American students? A meta-analysis. *Journal of Educational Psychology, 99*, 253–273. doi:10.1037/0022-0663.99.2.253

79. Ross, S. I., & Jackson, J. M. (1991). Teachers' expectations for Black males' and Black females' academic achievement. *Personality and Social Psychology Bulletin, 17*(1), 78–82. doi:10.1177/0146167291171012

80. Kaufman, J. S., Jaser, S. S., Vaughan, E. L., Reynolds, J. S., Di Donato, J., Bernard, S. N., & Hernandez-Brereton, M. (2010). Patterns in office referral data by grade, race/ethnicity, and gender. *Journal of Positive Behavior Interventions, 12*(1), 44–54. doi:10.1177/1098300708329710

81. For a review of studies on racial bias in the criminal justice system, see Chapters 1 and 2 in: Anderson, K. J. (2010). *Benign bigotry: The psychology of subtle prejudice.* Cambridge, UK: Cambridge University Press.

82. Grillo, T., & Wildman, S. M. (1997). Obscuring the importance of race: The implication of making comparisons between racism and sexism (or other isms). In A. K. Wing (Ed.) *Critical race feminism: a reader* (pp 44–50). New York, NY: New York University Press.

83. O'Brien, L. T., & Major, B. (2009). Group status and feelings of personal entitlement: The roles of social comparison and system-justifying beliefs. *Social and psychological bases of ideology and system justification.* (pp. 427–443). Oxford University Press.

84. Adichie, C. N. (2012, December 1). Challenging conventional wisdom. TEDxEuston. Retrieved from https://www.youtube.com/watch?feature=player_embedded&v=hg3umXU_qWc

85. Fagot, B. I. (1985). Beyond the reinforcement principle: Another step toward understanding sex role development. *Developmental Psychology, 21*, 1097–1104.

86. Page 11, emphasis in original: Parker, K. (2008). *Save the males: Why men matter, why women should care.* New York, NY: Random House.

87. Adler, P. A., Kless, S. J., & Adler, P. (1992). Socialization to gender roles: Popularity among elementary school boys and girls. *Sociology of Education, 65*,169–187.

88. Fagot, B. I. (1985). Beyond the reinforcement principle: Another step toward understanding sex role development. *Developmental Psychology, 21*, 1097–1104.

89. Adler, P. A., Kless, S. J., & Adler, P. (1992). Socialization to gender roles: Popularity among elementary school boys and girls. *Sociology of Education, 65*, 169–187.

90. This study included African American and white boys but this pattern holds only for white boys. Kiefer, S. M., & Ryan, A. M. (2008). Striving for social dominance over

peers: The implications for academic adjustment during early adolescence. *Journal of Educational Psychology, 100,* 417–428. doi:10.1037/0022-0663.100.2.417

91. Houtte, M. V. (2004). Why boys achieve less at school than girls: The difference between boys' and girls' academic culture. *Educational Studies, 30,* 159–173. doi:10/1080.0305569032000159804

92. Tyre, P. (2006, January 30). The trouble with boys. Newsweek. Retrieved from: http://www.newsweek.com/2006/01/29/the-trouble-with-boys.html

93. Adler, P. A., Kless, S. J., & Adler, P. (1992). Socialization to gender roles: Popularity among elementary school boys and girls. *Sociology of Education, 65,* 169–187.

94. Leaper, C. (1995). The use of *masculine* and *feminine* to describe women's and men's behavior. *Journal of Social Psychology, 135,* 359–369.

Twenge, J. M. (2009). Status and gender: The paradox of progress in an age of narcissism. *Sex Roles, 61,* 338–340. doi:10.1007/s11199-009-9617-5

95. Alksnis, C., Desmarais, S., & Curtis, J. (2008). Workforce segregation and the gender wage gap: Is "women's" work valued as highly as "men's"? *Journal of Applied Social Psychology, 38,* 1416–1441.

96. Kimmel, M. (2006). *Manhood in America: A cultural history* (2nd Ed.) New York, NY: Oxford University Press.

97. Page 26: Kindlon, D., & Thompson, M. (1999). *Raising Cain: Protecting the emotional life of boys.* New York, NY: Ballantine.

98. For a review of definitions of entitlement, see: Major, B. (1994). From social inequality to personal entitlement: the role of social comparisons, legitimacy appraisals, and group membership. In M. P. Zanna (Ed.), *Advances in experimental social psychology* (pp. 293–355). New York, NY: Academic Press.

99. Harvey, P., & Martinko, M. J. (2009). An empirical examination of the role of attributions in psychological entitlement and its outcomes. *Journal of Organizational Behavior, 30,* 459–476. doi:10.1002/job.549

100. Harvey, P., & Martinko, M. J. (2009). An empirical examination of the role of attributions in psychological entitlement and its outcomes. *Journal of Organizational Behavior, 30,* 459–476. doi:10.1002/job.549

101. Lessard, J., Greenberger, E., Chen, C., & Farruggia, S. (2011). Are youths' feelings of entitlement always "bad"?: Evidence for a distinction between exploitive and non-exploitive dimensions of entitlement. *Journal of Adolescence, 34,* 521–529. doi:10.1016/j.adolescence.2010.05.014

102. Visser, B. A., Ashton, M. C., & Vernon, P. A. (2008). What makes you think you're so smart? Measured abilities, personality, and sex differences in relation to self-estimates of multiple intelligences. *Journal of Individual Differences, 29*(1), 35–44. doi:10.1027/1614-0001.29.1.35

103. Pallier, G. (2003). Gender differences in the self-assessment of accuracy on cognitive tasks. *Sex Roles, 48,* 265–276.

104. O'Brien, L. T., Major, B. N., & Gilbert, P. N. (2012). Gender differences in entitlement: The role of system-justifying beliefs. *Basic and Applied Social Psychology*, *34*, 136–145. doi:10.1080/01973533.2012.655630

105. Barron, L. A. (2003). Ask and you shall receive? Gender differences in negotiators' beliefs about requests for a higher salary. *Human Relations*, *56*, 635–662. doi:10.1177/00187267030566001

106. Barron, L. A. (2003). Ask and you shall receive? Gender differences in negotiators' beliefs about requests for a higher salary. *Human Relations*, *56*, 635–662. doi:10.1177/00187267030566001

107. Jost, J. T. (1997). An experimental replication of the depressed-entitlement effect among women. *Psychology of Women Quarterly*, *21*, 387–393.

108. Major, B., McFarlin, D. B., & Gagnon, D. (1984). Overworked and underpaid: On the nature of gender differences in personal entitlement. *Journal of Personality and Social Psychology*, *47*, 1399–1412.

109. Experiment 2: Major, B., McFarlin, D. B., & Gagnon, D. (1984). Overworked and underpaid: On the nature of gender differences in personal entitlement. *Journal of Personality and Social Psychology*, *47*, 1399–1412.

110. Hogue, M., & Yoder, J. D. (2003). The role of status in producing depressed entitlement in women's and men's pay allocations. *Psychology of Women Quarterly*, *27*, 330–337.

111. Pelham, B. W. & Hetts, J. J. (2001). Underworked and overpaid: Elevated entitlement in men's self-pay. *Journal of Experimental Social Psychology*, *37*, 93–103. doi:10.1006/jesp.2000.1429

112. Williams, M. J., Paluck, E. L., & Spencer-Rodgers, J. (2010). The masculinity of money: Automatic stereotypes predict gender differences in estimated salaries. *Psychology of Women Quarterly*, *34*, 7–20.

113. Alksnis, C., Desmarais, S., & Curtis, J. (2008). Workforce segregation and the gender wage gap: Is "women's" work valued as highly as "men's"? *Journal of Applied Social Psychology*, *38*, 1416–1441.

114. Moore, D. (1991). Entitlement and justice evaluations: Who should get more, and why. *Social Psychology Quarterly*, *54*, 208–223. doi:10.2307/2786651

115. Hogue, M., Fox-Cardamone, L., & DuBois, C. L. Z. (2011). Justifying the pay system through status: Gender differences in reports of what should be important in pay decisions. *Journal of Applied Social Psychology*, *41*, 823–849.

116. Solnick, S. J., & Schweitzer, M. E. (1999). The influence of physical attractiveness and gender on ultimatum game decisions. *Organizational Behavior and Human Decision Processes*, *79*, 199–215. doi:10.1006/obhd.1999.2843

117. Ridgeway, 1991; 2001, cited in: O'Brien, L. T., & Major, B. (2009). Group status and feelings of personal entitlement: The roles of social comparison and system-justifying beliefs. In J. T. Jost, A. C. Kay, & H. Thorisdottir (Eds.), *Social*

and psychological bases of ideology and system justification (pp. 427–443). Oxford University Press Online.

118. Chowning, K., & Campbell, N. (2009). Development and validation of a measure of academic entitlement: Individual differences in students' externalized responsibility and entitled expectations. *Journal of Educational Psychology, 101,* 982–997. doi:10.1037/a0016351

119. Ciani, K. D., Summers, J. J., & Easter, M. A. (2008). Gender differences in academic entitlement among college students. *The Journal of Genetic Psychology, 169,* 332–344.

120. Holtzman, N. S., Vazire, S., & Mehl, M. R. (2010). Sounds like a narcissist: Behavioral manifestations of narcissism in everyday life. *Journal of Research in Personality, 44,* 478–484. doi:10.1016/j.jrp.2010.06.001

121. Steinmayr, R., & Spinath, B. (2009). What explains boys' stronger confidence in their intelligence? *Sex Roles, 61,*736–749. doi:10.1007/s11199-009-9675-8

122. Nottelmann, E.D. (1987). Competence and self-esteem during transition from childhood to adolescence. *Developmental Psychology, 23,* 441–450.

123. Nottelmann, E.D. (1987). Competence and self-esteem during transition from childhood to adolescence. *Developmental Psychology, 23,* 441–450.

124. National Student Clearinghouse Research Center (2013) Current term enrollment report—Fall 2013 [Webpage]. Retrieved from http://nscresearchcenter.org/currenttermenrollmentestimate-fall2013/

125. These numbers come from the universities' website fact sheets, 2013-2014.

126. National Association of Colleges and Employers (2014, January). NACE salary survey: Starting salaries for new college graduates. Retrieved from https://www.naceweb.org/uploadedFiles/Content/static-assetsdownloads/executive-summary/2014-january-salary-survey-executive-summary.pdf

127. Ewert, S. (2012, February). What it's worth: Field of training and economic status in 2009. U.S. Department of Commerce, Economics and Statistics Administration, U.S. Census Bureau. Retrieved from http://www.census.gov/prod/2012pubs/p70-129.pdf

128. United States Bureau of Labor Statistics (2013,October). Highlight of women's earnings in 2012. Retrieved from http://www.bls.gov/cps/cpswom2012.pdf

For a review of the gender pay gap, see:Lips, H. M. (2013). The gender pay gap: Challenging the rationalizations. Perceived equity, discrimination, and the limits of human capital models. *Sex Roles, 68,* 169–185. doi:10.1007/s11199-012-0165-z

129. Li, Q. (1999). Teachers' beliefs and gender differences in mathematics: A review. *Educational Research, 41*(1), 63–76.

130. Altermatt, E. R., Jovanovic, J. and Perry, M. (1998). Bias or responsivity? Sex and achievement-level effects on teachers' classroom questioning practices. *Journal of Educational Psychology, 90,* 516–27.

131. Tenenbaum, H. R., & Leaper, C. (2003). Parent-child conversations about science: The socialization of gender inequities? *Developmental Psychology, 39*(1), 34–47. doi:10.1037/0012-1649.39.1.34

Andre, T., Whigham, M., Hendrickson, A. and Chambers, S. (1999). Competency beliefs, positive affect, and gender stereotypes of elementary students and their parents about science versus other school subjects. *Journal of Research in Science Teaching, 36*, 719–747.

132. Tenenbaum, H. R. (2009). "You'd be good at that": Gender patterns in parent-child talk about courses. *Social Development, 18*, 447–463. doi:10.1111/j.1467-9507.2008.00487.x

133. Tenenbaum, H. R. (2009). "You'd be good at that": Gender patterns in parent-child talk about courses. *Social Development, 18*, 447–463. doi:10.1111/j.1467-9507.2008.00487.x

134. Bhanot, R. T., & Jovanovic, J. (2009). The links between parent behaviors and boys' and girls' science achievement beliefs. *Applied Developmental Science, 13*, 42–59.

135. Garrahy, D. A. (2001). Three third-grade teachers' gender-related beliefs and behavior. *The Elementary School Journal, 102*, 81–94.

136. Page 20: Kelly, A. (1988). Gender differences in teacher-pupil interactions: A meta-analytic review. *Research in Education, 39*, 1–23.

137. Page 235: Pollack, W. (1998) *Real boys: Rescuing our sons from the myths of boyhood.* New York, NY: Random House.

138. UNESCO: Institute for Statistics (2010). Global education digest 2010: Comparing education statistics across the world. Retrieved from http://www.uis.unesco.org/Library/Documents/GED_2010_EN.pdf

139. O'Brien, L. T., & Major, B. (2009). Group status and feelings of personal entitlement: The roles of social comparison and system-justifying beliefs. *Social and psychological bases of ideology and system justification.* (pp. 427–443). Oxford University Press.

140. Grillo, T., & Wildman, S. M. (1997). Obscuring the importance of race: The implication of making comparisons between racism and sexism (or other isms). In A. K. Wing (Ed.) *Critical race feminism: a reader* (pp 44–50). New York, NY: New York University Press.

141. Twenge, J. M. (2009). Status and gender: The paradox of progress in an age of narcissism. *Sex Roles, 61*, 338–340. doi:10.1007/s11199-009-9617-5

142. Hogue, M., Fox-Cardamone, L., & DuBois, C. L. Z. (2011). Justifying the pay system through status: Gender differences in reports of what should be important in pay decisions. *Journal of Applied Social Psychology, 41*, 823–849.

143. Hogue, M., Fox-Cardamone, L., & DuBois, C. L. Z. (2011). Justifying the pay system through status: Gender differences in reports of what should be important in pay decisions. *Journal of Applied Social Psychology, 41*, 823–849.

5 WOMEN ARE WONDERFUL, BUT MOST ARE DISLIKED

Man is, or should be, woman's protector and defender. The natural and proper timidity and delicacy which belongs to the female sex evidently unfits it for many of the occupations of civil life. The constitution of the family organization, which is founded in the divine ordinance, as well as in the nature of things, indicates the domestic sphere as that which properly belongs to the domain and functions of womanhood.

—BRADWELL V. ILLINOIS, 1873, *U.S. Supreme Court decision upholding the ban on women lawyers.*

Men want to love women, not compete with them. They want to provide for and protect their families—it's in their DNA. But modern women won't let them.

—SUZANNE VENKER, 2012, *"The War on Men"*[1]

Even though these two quotations are 140 years apart, they reflect the historic and contemporary attitudes toward women and their place in Western society. In Chapter 2 we explored the post-9/11 re-traditionalization of gender roles. We examined media reactions to women who spoke out against U.S. government policies in response to the terror attacks and the outspoken women whose loved ones had been killed in the attacks. People don't like women who won't behave, especially in conservative climates. But negative attitudes toward assertive women didn't begin with 9/11. Individuals, both women and men, hold ambivalent attitudes toward women, no matter the political climate. On the one hand, surveys find that women as a group elicit more positive attitudes than do men as a group. On the other hand, when we scratch the surface of these attitudes we find that positive attitudes about women are directed toward a narrow subtype of women—*traditional* women—women who conform to the narrowly prescribed roles of femininity (a category that few women actually satisfy). This chapter explores the attitudes toward most other women—nontraditional women. Because most women, in one way or another, depart from the narrow requirements of so-called tradition, they are vulnerable to the social punishments meted out to women who break gender rules. We look at the research on attitudes toward nontraditional women, exposing and explaining the modern misogyny behind attitudes toward these women.

Ambivalence Toward Women

As mentioned previously, people's attitudes toward women are generally more positive than their attitudes toward men, as a group. Social psychologists Alice Eagly and Antonio Mladinic[2] coined the phrase *women-are-wonderful* to illustrate the fact that the general category "woman" is viewed more positively than the general category "man." The typical woman is viewed as warmer than the typical man.[3] Many individual women embrace and find protection in the warm feelings people tend to have for and attribute to women in general. But being liked and seeming warm come at a cost for any group that elicits such feelings. Groups that are *liked* tend to be *not respected*. In her work on groups that face discrimination, Susan Fiske[4] and her colleagues find that these groups are judged along two dimensions, *warmth* and *competence*. Historically, psychologists have tended to assume that prejudice involves simultaneous dislike and disrespect of an outgroup, but Fiske finds that prejudice results from dislike *or* disrespect, but not necessarily both. Therefore, the content of people's stereotypes may not reflect simple evaluative antipathy but, instead, may reflect separate dimensions of warmth (which includes perceptions of trustworthiness, friendliness, and sociability) and competence (perceptions of capability and skill). For instance, in the United States, Jewish Americans, Asian Americans, and the wealthy are viewed as highly competent but lacking in warmth—they are respected more but liked less than other groups. The elderly, people with disabilities, and homemakers are viewed as warm, but not as competent—they are liked but not respected. Men, relative to women, are liked less but are viewed as more competent.

These patterns of warmth/competence attributed to women reflect the *general* category of women. This chapter addresses *subtypes* of women. Modern misogyny is expressed in people holding different attitudes toward women who are seen as feminine and nonthreatening (i.e., "traditional") versus women who are not. For example, "feminist" tends to be evaluated more negatively than "housewife," even though feminists and homemakers are both part of the larger category of women.[5] Feminists are seen as possessing competence but lacking warmth.[6]

Ambivalent Sexism

How do we understand differing views of women? Susan Fiske and Peter Glick[7] developed a theory of ambivalent sexism to explain both the punishing and pedestal-putting attitudes toward women. Glick and Fiske find that men's (as well as many women's) attitudes toward women can be broken down into two kinds of sexist attitudes that make up ambivalent sexism: *hostile sexism* and *benevolent sexism*. Hostile sexism is what most people think of when they think of sexism. It consists of overtly hostile feelings toward women, with negative feelings toward, and stereotyping of, nontraditional women in particular. Hostile sexism seeks to justify male power, traditional gender roles, and men's exploitation of women as sexual objects through derogatory characterizations of women. Hostile sexists would agree with statements such as, "Most women interpret innocent remarks or acts as being sexist" and "Many women get a kick out of teasing men by seeming sexually available and then refusing male advances." Hostile sexism is correlated with other psychological attitudes such as a social dominance orientation.[8] Those with social dominance attitudes believe in maintaining social hierarchies and in preventing the redistribution of societal resources. When a group that is discriminated against, in this case women, attempts to gain access to societal resources, those with a social dominance orientation will react negatively.

Benevolent sexism is a thornier concept because it involves attitudes toward women that seem positive on the surface but, in fact, are patronizing and disempowering. Benevolent sexists characterize women as pure creatures who need protection from men. It reflects the view that women should be adored by men and women are necessary to make men complete. Benevolent sexism allows men to characterize their privileges as well deserved, even as a responsibility they must bear (akin to the "white man's burden"). Men should be willing to sacrifice their own needs (but not their power) to care for the women in their lives. Benevolent sexists agree with statements such as, "In a disaster, women ought to be rescued before men" and "A good woman should be set on a pedestal by her man." For women, benevolent sexism undermines women's resistance to male dominance. Benevolent sexism is disarming because it is technically favorable and also promises that men's power will be used to women's advantage, as long as they can secure a high-status male protector. Benevolent sexism is a subtle form of sexism. People do not immediately recognize benevolent sexism as sexist, and many women are even flattered by the attitudes of benevolent sexism,[9] just as some women are flattered by so-called chivalry.

Hostile and benevolent sexism are distinct concepts that tap two kinds of sexism; however, people can and often do hold hostile *and* benevolent sexist attitudes simultaneously. In fact, both types work in concert. People can have loving and hating attitudes toward women. People tend to feel hostile sexism toward women who violate traditional gender roles (e.g., feminists, sexually active women, soldiers) and benevolent sexism toward conventional women (e.g., homemakers, secretaries). Benevolent sexism can result in the women-are-wonderful effect in that traditional women are considered to be appealing due to their supposed gentleness, nurturance, and purity (a purity unblemished by participation in the public sphere). Glick and Fiske describe benevolent sexism as the "carrot," the reward of positive feelings toward and the promise of protectiveness, to women who embrace traditional roles; and hostile sexism as the "stick," the hostility directed at women who reject traditional roles.[10] Punishment (through hostile sexism) alone is not the most effective means of shaping behavior because that might result in only resentment and resistance. However, punishment for women who do not cooperate *and* reinforcement for women who do coooperate function together to maintain male dominance and the gender status quo.[11] If we consider the treatment of the Jersey Girls—those 9/11 widows who were vilified when they failed to conform to the 9/11 master narrative of heroes and victims—we can understand how benevolent sexism can quickly turn into hostile sexism if a woman does not conform to gender rules.

Glick and Fiske have analyzed patterns of hostile and benevolent sexism in 16 nations in Latin America, Europe, the Middle East, and Australasia.[12] In general, men's hostile sexism is higher than women's, and women are more likely to be benevolent sexists than hostile sexists. In nations where hostile sexism is high, women are especially likely to embrace benevolent sexism, in some cases even more so than the men. Note the bind women face: they are forced to seek protection from members of the very group that threatens them. The greater the threat, the stronger the incentive to accept benevolent sexism's supposed protective ideology. This dynamic helps to explain the tendency for women in the most patriarchal societies to endorse benevolent sexism. Furthermore, the countries in which women reject both benevolent and hostile sexism are the ones in which men have low hostile sexism scores. As sexist hostility declines, women may feel able to reject benevolent sexism without fear of a hostile backlash. Benevolent sexism helps explain the appeal of so-called chivalry for some women. Some women (specifically traditional women) are protected to some extent by chivalry, but at great cost. In excluding women from the outside world of work and from positions traditionally held by men, benevolent sexists exclude women from roles that offer more status in society. Thus, women are protected but patronized, excluded, and oppressed.

Benevolent sexism, then, is insidious for several reasons. First, it doesn't seem like prejudice to those who perpetrate it because many people do not view it as something negative. Second, women may find the allure of benevolent sexism difficult to resist.[13] Because of its positive valence, women are unlikely to notice it and understand its harmful effects.[14] Third, praising women's nurturing traits is part of a belief system that women are especially suited to domestic roles. However, stereotypes of women as nurturing and communal justify their subordinated status.[15] Fourth, benevolent sexism can drive a wedge between women, preventing them from coming together as activists. Women (e.g., feminists) who reject the overtly negative aspects of hostile sexism, as well as the cloaked negative aspects of benevolent sexism, are at odds with traditional women, who are rewarded by benevolent sexism and reject feminism because they want to hold on to the little power they get as a result of subscribing to traditional attitudes. So while feminists and traditional women should be working in solidarity to fight gender discrimination, they are split by being on opposite sides of benevolent sexism.

The Subtle but Significant Impact of Benevolent Sexism

What kind of impact does benevolent sexism have on women? Imagine how a woman in a job interview might feel when confronted with an interviewer expressing either hostile or benevolent sexism. Muriel Dumont[16] and her colleagues conducted an experiment simulating such an experience. Women college students in France were told that they would receive training for job interviews. They were presented with a job description that contained either hostile sexism, benevolent sexism, or no sexism. So for instance, the job description containing hostile sexism stated that women look for special favors and exaggerate the problems they face to get power and control over men. The job description with benevolent sexism stated that the organization would benefit from the morality and good taste of women. Later, the women were given a cognitive test measuring their ability to distinguish grammatical from ungrammatical sentences. After the cognitive test, the participants were asked to rate how much a specific thought had come to mind during the test. Examples of some thoughts were, "I feel incompetent" and "I must do better." Finally, each participant was asked to recall a situation that made them feel silly or incompetent.

Did the type of sexism the women were exposed to impact their intrusive thoughts or the types of memories they recalled? And which type of sexism made women feel worse in the context of job training? Dumont and her colleagues found that women who were exposed to the benevolent sexist comments experienced greater intrusive thoughts of being incompetent while performing a cognitive task than women exposed to hostile sexism or neutral comments. In addition, the women who were confronted with benevolent sexism generated more memories of their own incompetence than women exposed to hostile or neutral comments. Benevolent sexism actually activated feelings of incompetence in these women. By focusing on positive stereotypical characteristics of women, benevolent sexism implicitly conveys the idea of their incompetence in the workplace, and that idea influenced women's thoughts and memories of their own incompetence. Dumont and her colleagues conclude that benevolent sexism makes women internalize incompetence, which contributes to their accepting or legitimizing their subordinate status.

Another study looked at how observers evaluate women who have been subjected to hostile or benevolent sexism during a job interview. In this experiment,[17] U.S. undergraduates (mostly white or Asian American) read a transcript of an interview during which a male interviewer acted as a benevolent or a hostile sexist or as neutral. So for instance, the benevolent sexist conveyed a protective but patronizing attitude toward the interviewee, and the hostile sexist conveyed resentment toward and competition with women. Participants then evaluated the interviewer as well as the woman applicant's competence, likeability, and hireability. As evidence for the insidiousness of benevolent sexism, benevolent sexist interviewers were viewed more favorably than hostile sexist interviewers. Now, benevolent sexism might seem less harmful than hostile sexism. However, those observers who viewed the benevolent or hostile interviewers favorably tended to perceive the woman applicant to be less competent and less hirable. So while benevolent sexism seems harmless and even positive, in terms of women's legitimate belonging in the workplace, the more subtle, benevolent sexism can be more damaging than even overt, hostile sexism.

Finally, what happens when a woman is confronted with benevolent sexism and either accepts it or reject it? One study[18] looked at those perceptions of warmth and competence outlined by Fiske and her colleagues, as well as the role of benevolent sexism in interpreting women's behavior in the workplace. This experiment asked German college students to read and react to a workplace scenario in which a colleague offers patronizing assistance to another colleague and the colleague either accepts the help or refuses the offer. The researchers were interested in how participants react to patronizing, gender-based offers of help. Not surprising, both women and men who accepted help were perceived as less competent compared to those who refused the help. How were those who refused the help perceived? Only women, not men, who refused help were perceived as less warm than those who accepted help. There were also gendered perceptions of help offerers. A man who offered patronizing help to a woman was perceived as both warmer and more competent than a woman who offered the same assistance to a man. To summarize, women but not men face a warmth penalty for confronting patronizing offers of assistance (the kind of assistance offered by a benevolent sexist). Women, but not men, are seen as ungracious when they reject help. Furthermore, relative to women, men are rewarded by favorable perceptions if they offer patronizing help to a member of the other gender, women are penalized. These findings mirror many women's experiences when they have resisted street harassment or sexual harassment in the workplace, or men running ahead of them to open a door for them. To reject patronizing or even aggressive gendered behavior risks being seen as ungracious, unladylike, or a bitch.

The studies on the impact of benevolent sexism demonstrate how damaging these attitudes are to women. Whereas benevolent sexism seems harmless and even positive, the way chivalry seems, it makes women feel incompetent, it makes others think that women *are* incompetent, and when women resist benevolent sexism, they are disliked.

Double Standards, Discrimination, and the (Dis)Likeability of Women

In July of 2012 tech giant Yahoo rocked the world. They hired a pregnant CEO. The pregnancy of Marissa Mayer, formerly a vice president at Google was described as "a shock to many."[19] "Pregnant Yahoo CEO Ignites Maternity Debate,"[20] "New Yahoo CEO Marissa Mayer Is Pregnant. Does It Matter?,"[21] "Pregnant at Work?,"[22] and "The Pregnant CEO: Should you Hate Marissa Mayer?"[23] were some of the headlines.

The 1873 quotation by a U.S. Supreme Court Justice at the beginning of this chapter invokes the "domestic sphere" as the proper domain of womanhood and therefore as justification for banning women from practicing law. The quotation reflects the historic but also to some degree the current attitude that women's place is ideally in the home. Judging by reactions to women who don't stay in the home, it seems that even today (perhaps only implicitly) many people still believe that women belong in the domestic sphere. Through the lens of modern misogyny, nontraditional women put themselves in bad places; they don't receive the patronizing and condescending benefits of benevolent sexism because they violate gender rules about appropriate femininity and they are therefore targets of hostile sexism.

Let's explore some of the subtypes of nontraditional women. As we see above, people can and often do hold hostile and benevolent sexism simultaneously. However, people tend to express hostile sexism toward women who violate traditional gender roles (e.g., sexually active women, lesbians, professional women) and benevolent sexism toward conventional women (e.g., homemakers, secretaries).[24] For instance, men's hostile sexism scores predict negative attitudes toward career women and their benevolent sexism scores predict positive attitudes toward homemakers.[25]

Professional Women: Competent but Contemptible

Working women, especially women in nontraditional jobs such as management, are one subtype of nontraditional women whose numbers are growing. Much has been made in the media about women's place in the workforce in recent years. Beginning in 2008 with the onset of "The Great Recession," women for the first time in history outnumbered men in U.S. jobs.[26] A 2010/2011 Pew Research Center poll reports that American women place more importance on a career than do men.[27] These recent changes in economic imperatives and in individual priorities conflict with the more primitive beliefs about gender, competence, and warmth. Recall that traditional women tend to be viewed as warm but not very competent. They are low-status, harmless, and nice, and not management material.[28] Professional women elicit the opposite stereotype. They, like most nontraditional women (such as feminists), are seen as relatively competent but not very warm.[29] Extensive research has been done on how professional women and women leaders are perceived. A key part of workplace competence is leadership ability. Obviously being a good leader can lead to promotions, pay increases, and more prestigious positions. If competence and leadership abilities are traits that men and not women are thought to possess, do people recognize when women *do* possess competence and leadership abilities? Do people recognize when men do *not* have these abilities, or do they assume that any man is prepared for leadership?

Study after study finds that competent women are consistently rated as lacking social skills compared to similarly competent men.[30] A study by Madeline Heilman[31] and her colleagues illustrates how the judgments about women who violate these gender expectations play out. American college students evaluated a profile of either a clearly successful or ambiguously successful woman or man in a male-dominated job (assistant vice president in mechanics and aeronautics). All information about the employee was identical except for the employee's gender. Students were asked to rate the candidate on competence, likeability, and interpersonal hostility. When students rated the employee's competence, successful women and men were evaluated equally—they were both given credit for their successes. When information about the candidate's performance was ambiguous, the woman was rated as less competent than the man. So again, men are assumed to be competent and are given credit for competence, even when there is no evidence supporting that assumption.

In addition to ratings of competence, ratings of likeability and hostility are gendered as well. When there was ambiguity about the employee's performance, there was no difference between the likeability ratings of the woman and man targets. But when there was clear evidence of success, the woman was liked less than the man. In fact, the clearly successful woman was liked less than the can-didates in all other conditions: the clearly successful man, the ambiguously suc-cessful man, and the ambiguously successful woman. A similar pattern emerged in terms of judgments of hostility. The woman candidate was rated as less hostile than the man in the ambiguous performance outcome condition but was rated as more hostile than the man in the clearly successful condition. These results suggest the double standard used when evaluating women in male-dominated occupations: When women's success is clear, women are viewed as less likeable than men. Women, although rated less competent than men when information about them was ambiguous, are at least rated as less hostile interpersonally. But the switch when success is clear is dramatic: women who are acknowledged as successful are viewed not merely as indifferent to others but as downright uncivil. And these patterns hold for both women and men evaluators; so women and men are equally likely to penalize women. Heilman further found that dislike was associated with not being recommended for promotions and salary increases. Heilman concludes that while there are many things that lead an individual to be disliked in the job setting, it is only women who are disliked for being successful.

What is it about competent women that puts them at risk for professional rejection? Laurie Rudman has extensively studied the backlash against profes-sional women. In this context, *backlash* refers to social and economic penalties for counterstereotypical behavior. Rudman finds that agentic characteristics (e.g., assertive, competitive, competent, individualist) are associated with people high in status and with men. People believe men should possess agency but women should not—women should remain warm and less competent. By exhibiting traditionally masculine competencies, agentic women undermine the presumed differences between the genders and discredit the system in which men have more access to power and resources for ostensibly legitimate reasons.[32] Dominant traits are viewed as extreme in agentic women but merely normal in agentic men. Women face, what is referred to as a *dominance penalty*. For instance, in one study[33] Rudman and her colleagues created fictitious recommendation letters for professors eligible for promotion at Yale University. The highly competent can-didates were portrayed as either agentic (e.g., the agentic candidate was described as brutally honest toward critics) or communal (e.g., overly polite toward critics) and either women or men, resulting in four versions of the recommendation let-ter. Evaluators were asked to assess the candidate's chances at promotion. Rudman found evidence for a dominance penalty for the agentic woman candidate. The agentic woman was judged to be less likeable and less hirable than the identi-cally portrayed agentic man. Having outstanding achievements did not protect a woman from the dominance penalty when she displayed high-status behaviors typically reserved for men, even when such behaviors are necessary for effective leadership (i.e., frank assessment to maintain high standards). In fact, Rudman and her colleagues found that participants engaged in sabotage against agentic women compared to agentic men.[34] So while participants recognized the accomplishments of agentic women, they don't like them, don't want to hire them, and are willing to undermine them, relative to men with identical characteristics. This is the problem of nontraditional women.

Two sets of attitudes help fuel the backlash against agentic women.[35] First, those who endorse the gender status quo—those who hold traditional gender attitudes and believe that the current gender system is just and appropriate—are especially likely to penalize agentic women relative to agentic men. These *gender system justifiers* dislike agentic women and are less likely to endorse their hiring compared to agentic men. Second, reaction to perceived *threats to the system* fuel the backlash toward agentic women.[36] Recall the discussion in Chapter 2 of *terror management theory*. Terror management theory predicts that when people are faced with actual or symbolic mortality, they cling tightly to their worldviews, they denigrate those who are perceived to threaten their worldview, and they adhere to attitudes and beliefs that make them feel safe. For instance, according to a study conducted by Laurie Rudman[37] and her colleagues, when people have been exposed to a threat, a woman job candidate is seen as more dominant, less likeable, and less hirable, compared to those not exposed to a threat. Men are equally hirable regardless of a presence of a threat. Backlash serves a system-justifying purpose. Rudman's research finds that defending the gender hierarchy—keeping men in high-status, leadership positions and keeping women out of those positions—is the primary motivation for backlash against competent women. Women are in a Catch 22. Because of their low gender status, they must enact agency to be viewed as fit for leadership, but when they do, they experience backlash. In her research Rudman did find that when women leveled their status by behaving with extreme diplomacy or low agency, they avoided the backlash and the dominance penalty. When women lead by "not leading" they are spared backlash. But when women use these tempering strategies, their competence and status are jeopardized.[38]

During the 2008 U.S. presidential campaign, there were many strong opinions about Hillary Rodham Clinton as a *woman* running for president. Few voters doubted her competence, but some were put off by it. Her competence worked against her in that she was viewed as less warm than, for instance, Sarah Palin. In contrast, during her run for Vice President, Sarah Palin generated different attitudes from the voters. Unlike Clinton, Palin was not seen as very competent and was seen as more feminine.[39] Palin was dismissed by some because of her apparent lack of competence. If we consider the role of ambivalent sexism we can make predictions about support for each of these politicians based on voter sexism scores. Benevolent sexists were likely to vote for Palin and hostile sexists were not likely to vote for Clinton.[40] Because Palin was viewed as warmer, more feminine, and less competent than Clinton, she fit a more traditional female role than did Clinton. Therefore, benevolent sexists were likely to reward her with support. Because Clinton was viewed as relatively nontraditional compared to Palin, hostile sexists—those individuals who seek to punish gender transgressions in women—were likely to not vote for Clinton. Voters are put off by power-seeking, competent women—a scenario reflecting more of Clinton than Palin. At the same time, as we saw in the studies just reviewed, people easily detect incompetence in women—a scenario reflecting more of Palin than Clinton—and tend to ignore incompetence in men and instead grant men points for competence even when it is undeserved. It is worth noting that the these attitudes about Sarah Palin described here were prominent during the 2008 election. Since that time, Palin has become a more complicated character—engendering praise and hostility from a variety of constituents.

What does it mean that voters were *put off* by Clinton? Some voters have a visceral reaction to assertive and competent women. Consistent with the other studies reviewed here, women who seek power pay a heavy political price. Power-seeking women are perceived to have a communality/warmth deficit. Compared to power-seeking men, power-seeking women are seen as less caring and sensitive. Power-seeking women actually elicit feelings of moral outrage, including contempt, anger, and disgust.[41] Voters tend to think it inappropriate for a woman to seek power, whereas it is natural and normative for a man to seek power.[42] Like professional women in general, women politicians have to demonstrate competence, but in order to not pay a dominance penalty they must also convey warmth—but not too much warmth, as doing so will undermine their perceived competence.

Employers use strategies to keep these competent yet contemptible women out of their workplace. One phenomenon that happens in hiring is a shifting of the job criteria to emphasize attributes that assertive women supposedly lack. That is, if professional women are believed to lack warmth, communal characteristics suddenly become important for the job.[43] Shifting job criteria is a convenient way to subtly edge out women from jobs. One study[44] revealed that for the traditionally male job of police chief, evaluators defined merit in a manner that favored men over women applicants. When considering an educated, media-savvy family man, evaluators inflated the importance of those qualities for success in the job. But when a male applicant lacked those qualities, and instead was "streetwise," being streetwise was inflated in importance. No such favoritism was extended to the woman applicant. In other words, when the evaluators wanted to hire the man and not the woman, they used whatever characteristics the man had as important to edge out the woman. An alarming finding in this study was that the more objective evaluators believed they were, the more gender bias they engaged in. This pattern is dangerous because it allows evaluators to discriminate and feel falsely confident in their objectivity.

A 2012 Gallup poll of American women found that mothers who are employed outside the home are happier than stay-at-home mothers.[45] Gallup surveyed more than 60,000 women and found that employed women (with and without children) worried less, felt less sadness, stress, anger, and depression than did stay-at-home mothers. If professional women have a perceived warmth deficit—they are viewed as colder than professional men and colder than the "typical" woman—what is the effect of a professional woman becoming a mother? Does becoming a mother "warm up" the professional woman, making her more appealing? It does, but at a price. Amy Cuddy[46] and her colleagues asked respondents to rate fictitious consultants on traits reflecting warmth and competence. The consultants were either women or men, and in their portfolios there was either mention of a child or not—so there were four versions of the consultant. How did the competence ratings relate to interest in hiring the mothers? Participants expressed more interest in hiring, promoting, and educating the childless woman and the man who was or was not a father. Indeed, consultants who were mothers were viewed as warmer than women who were not mothers—but that gain in perceived warmth resulted in a loss of perceived competence. The same was not the case for men with children. Working men who were fathers gained perceived warmth and maintained their perceived competence. When working women become mothers, they unwittingly trade perceived competence for perceived warmth. This trade unjustly costs them professional credibility and hinders their chances of being hired, promoted, and generally supported in the workplace. Men, on the other hand, are not fated to lose perceived competence when they gain a child, and becoming fathers does not diminish their professional opportunities. This study complements other studies[47] and anecdotal evidence that indicates women workers who have children are perceived as a bad risk, whereas men workers who have children are viewed as well-balanced and gain social points for being responsive dads. Like many of the studies on perceptions of professional women and men, the gender of the evaluators did not matter—both women and men respondents have these biases.[48]

The experimental research on criteria necessary for success for women in the workplace is solidly convincing. However, it has an important limitation because the stimulus materials—the fictitious women and men job candidates created for these studies—are either white or presumed to be white through the use of white-sounding applicant names. Even when race or ethnicity is not made explicit, whites are presumed to be the target race because whites tend to be viewed as the default, "normal," "regular" person in the United States.[49] There are few studies that consider the price that nonwhite women pay for agency and competence. The lack of studies examining the intersection of gender and race/ethnicity is a major gap in the research on gender roles and rules because specific stereotypes about women of color would no doubt affect their perceived warmth and competence. For instance, African American women, compared to white women, are perceived to be loud, tough, dominating, and less educated.[50] How then are African American women professionals likely to be perceived? Asian Americans (both women and men) are perceived to be more competent, but less warm and less dominating than whites.[51] How do gender and race stereotypes interact in perceptions of professional Asian women? When experiments are conducted that take into account the interaction of gender and race/ethnicity we do find different patterns. For instance, U.S. Latinas tend to be viewed as more warm than Anglo (white) women and Latino men.[52] A study on students' perceptions of professors found that Latina and Anglo women were penalized when they violated gender role prescriptions by teaching with strict, authoritarian teaching styles, but Anglo men who taught with the same teaching style were not similarly penalized.[53] A similar study found that Latinas with authoritarian teaching styles were viewed as less warm and less competent than Anglo women with the same teaching style.[54]

Women Who Are Athletes

There is a cultural assumption that I think persists even to this day, that because of the definition of masculinity and sport, part of the birthright of being male in this culture is owning sport. You own sport. As women move into this once exclusive domain of male power and privilege and identity, there's been a tremendous backlash, and a desire to push back, and either to push women out of sport altogether or certainly to contain their power within it and keep them on the margins.

—MARY JO KANE in *Playing Unfair: The Media Image of the Female Athlete*[55]

Another subtype of nontraditional women is women who play sports, especially professional sports. Like professional women, women athletes are thought to be interlopers, trespassing a domain in which they do not belong and to which they are not entitled. Media coverage of women's sports reflects this assumption. Women's sports coverage is less than 2% of all the coverage on ESPN and the three major U.S. television networks.[56] When women athletes are shown, they tend to be used by sportscasters and commentators as the butt of sexual jokes presumably to entertain young male heterosexual viewers. Rather than covering actual sports, news coverage frequently contains stories on scantily-clad women wrestlers, nude bungee jumpers, and cheerleaders.[57] Women who are featured in sports news and highlights are often wives, girlfriends, or mothers of male athletes.[58] This coverage conveys that real sports are men's sports and that women serve as support to men's sports or as comic relief.

There are other ways women professional athletes are portrayed that convey their lack of belonging. In his analysis of television sports coverage, Michael Messner[59] observes that newscasts lead with men's sports using video, graphics, interviews, and higher production value relative to coverage of women's sports. The specific women's sports that are covered tend to be more traditionally feminine sports such as figure skating and tennis, rather than basketball or boxing. Sports such as figure skating and gymnastics require strength, flexibility, and discipline, but women in these sports tend to be very young with small bodies, conveying a less powerful female athlete. Men's gymnastics has adult men whose athleticism focuses on their strength and power. Women's gymnastics tends to not involve women at all; it involves girls with tiny bodies. What would it mean for women's gymnasts to be fully grown adult women with muscles and power?

Messner also notes that women competitors are more likely to be described by their first names, whereas men are more likely to be described by their last names or first and last names. Names and the terms of address convey power and legitimacy. Similar to workplace differences in power that occurs when bosses are called Mr. or Ms. so-and-so and secretaries are called by their first name, this distinction in sports coverage suggests an informality, unwarranted familiarity, and a lack of respect for women athletes.[60]

One of the most vexing problems for women's sports is lesbian-baiting. In Chapter 1 we considered the sexualization and hyperfeminization of the woman athlete. Because power, strength, and athletic aptitude are *prescriptive* stereotypes for men (what men *should* be like) but *proscriptive* stereotypes for women (what women should *not* be like) women professional athletes are nontraditional women who excel in a masculine domain and therefore are subject to questions about their sexuality. Lesbian-baiting—accusations of homosexuality—is common in professional sports. Women who are too good in their sports or who do not readily appear to be attached to a man are accused of being lesbians (of course some women athletes *are* lesbians). Lesbian-baiting is a useful strategy to contain women's power and progress in sport. Consider women's sports through an ambivalent sexism lens. Those women who present themselves as objects of feminine beauty by posing in popular magazines, conveying heterosexuality, and presenting themselves as nonthreatening to the male-dominated sports establishment, are rewarded with and supposedly protected by benevolent sexism. Unfortunately, their power and strength is undermined, so they are not taken seriously as athletes. For those women who do not adhere to feminine standards of beauty and heterosexuality, who show-case their strength or play in sports that threaten the sports establishment, we have hostile sexism to punish them with lesbian-baiting.

Although the presence of women in sports challenges the historical and traditional association between masculinity and sport, media representations of women athletes sadly emphasize gender difference through a focus on the femininity of the athlete rather than athletic strength and skill. This process of feminization constructs differences between women and men athletes and reinforces the gender order.[61] For instance, the magazine *Sports Illustrated* reinforces men's ownership of sports by presenting women athletes with a focus on their domestic status—featuring them as wives and mothers. Women are more likely to be presented *off* the court and field, out of uniform, and in domestic settings, whereas men are more likely to be featured *on* the field and court—actually doing their sport.[62] Of course, the annual Swimsuit issue of *Sports Illustrated* is the one time a year that women dominate the magazine but the women in the Swimsuit issue are models, not athletes.

The gender constructions behind the pressure to appear feminine are informed by constructions of race and sexuality. Recall from Chapter 1 our discussion of Victoria Carty's[63] argument that because African American women were historically denied access to full-time homemaking and sexual protection, they did not tie womanhood to a specific, limited set of activities and attributes defined as separate and opposite from masculinity. African American women historically have been situated outside dominant culture's definition of acceptable (white) femininity and tend to be seen as more athletic than white women. Their strength is less threatening to traditional definitions of femininity and beauty because they are disallowed from being there in the first place. Therefore, media coverage of black women is more about their athletic accomplishments compared to coverage of white women. Carty says that African American women athletes may be represented in a wider range of roles and traverse the boundaries of traditional standards of femininity because they have never been fully included in the stringent ideals of femininity and heterosexuality to begin with.[64] But African American women pay a price for being represented as crossing gendered boundaries, as evidenced in the discussions later in this chapter on rape.

Women in the Military

Like the domain of sports, the military is historically and currently an institution inextricably tied to masculinity. Military service, constructed as strength and aggression, is fundamentally incompatible with femininity and therefore women who do enter the military are often viewed as interlopers. The impact of stereotypic beliefs in military settings is problematic for women because of the discrepancy between the stereotyped attributes associated with women and the attributes required for effective military performance. Like professional sports, the predominantly male institution of the military is also a hypermasculine culture, in which anything identified as feminine is devalued as "other" and counter to the masculine ideal, with negative consequences for women.

Jennifer Boldry[65] shows the stark contrast between the *perceptions* of female and male cadets and their actual *performance*. Her colleagues surveyed members of the Texas A&M Corps of Cadets about their evaluations of women and men in military training. Cadets rated themselves, the typical woman/man cadet, and each individual cadet in the outfit. The typical man cadet was perceived to be more motivated, dedicated to physical fitness, and diligent, with more leader-like qualities, and more self-confidence. In contrast, women were rated as selfless, tactful, respectful of authority, lacking in arrogance, and having integrity. There were no rater gender differences of the typical woman and man cadet, meaning actual women and men cadets agreed on these descriptions.[66] What is especially noteworthy is that while all this stereotyping was happening about women and men cadets, actual performance measures did not correspond to the gender differences of the evaluations of women and men. In fact, no gender differences emerged in any performance measure, thus indicating that actual performance differences do not account for the differences in assumptions about women and men cadets—stereotypes account for the differences. So even though there were no performance differences among the women and men, there's a belief that women are somehow different from the men. Women *must* be seen as different from men, otherwise there is no justification for excluding women from certain jobs.

This chapter began with a discussion of hostile and benevolent sexism. In the next section, we consider rape survivors as yet another category of nontraditional women who are denigrated, marginalized, and are blamed for being victimized. On a continuum of hostility toward women, rape is at a violent extreme. Sexual assault can be a systematic way to humiliate, and terrorize. Before we leave the topic of women in the military, a discussion of rape in the military is necessary, as rape is a tactic used by some men in the military against women service members. In 2011 there were more than 3,000 reported sexual assaults involving U.S. service members.[67] A 2012 report from the U.S. Department of Defense finds that incidents of reported rape and sexual assault of women in military academies has increased every year since 2008.[68] And a U.S. Department of Defense study estimates that there were 26,000 sexual assaults in the armed services in 2012.[69]

A CNN investigation[70] of reported rapes in the military found disturbing patterns in how cases were handled. The report profiles several women who were forced out of the military after they reported a sexual assault. The women report that their superior officers dismissed the charges and punished the victim. For example, in one case, the victim and attacker were ordered to clean out an attic on base together in order "to work out their differences." (This should remind us of our discussion in Chapter 3 of sexual harassment being dismissed as simply "miscommunication" between the sexes.) In other cases, the superior officer *was* the perpetrator. According to CNN, rather than investigating the allegations, the investigators diagnosed the victims with personality disorders and discharged them from the military. Personality disorders are long-term psychiatric disorders with symptoms beginning in adolescence and early adulthood. Experts say that a victim of sexual assault might experience posttraumatic stress disorder after an assault but not, suddenly, a personality disorder. The women victims were apparently healthy and sane enough to be screened by and join the military but after they reported a rape they were discharged due to a hastily diagnosed psychiatric illness. And if the rape and the discharge from the military weren't traumatizing enough for these women, CNN found that the military considers a personality disorder a preexisting condition and not a service-related disability, and thus sexual assault survivors with such a diagnosis may not receive military health benefits like other veterans.[71] It is difficult to imagine a more callous response, a response that can only be understood as attributing blame for the rape to victims.

Rape Survivors: Hostile and Benevolent Victim-Blaming

It might seem odd that women who have been raped are constructed into another subtype of nontraditional women. Of course, any woman or girl of any age, of any dress, in any circumstance can be raped—not just nontraditional women. What puts rape survivors alongside other types of nontraditional women is not *who* they are but rather how individuals and the legal system *react* to them. It is because of how rape survivors are blamed and stigmatized after the crime that they become viewed as nontraditional women, as not having stayed in their place, and, tragically, as being viewed as responsible for what has happened to them.

Fox News contributor Liz Trotta reflects some people's view about women in the military and the perceived role they play in their own victimization. In her response to news reports of increased sexual assaults against military women, Trotta[72] states,

> But we have women once more, the feminist, going, wanting to be warriors and victims at the same time…And the sexual abuse report says that

there has been, since 2006, a 64% increase in violent sexual assaults. Now, what did they expect? These people are in close contact, the whole airing of this issue has never been done by Congress, it's strictly been a question of pressure from the feminist. And the feminists have also directed them, really, to spend a lot of money. They have sexual counselors all over the place, victims' advocates, sexual response coordinators.... So, you have this whole bureaucracy upon bureaucracy being built up with all kinds of levels of people to support women in the military who are now being raped too much.

There are a number of troubling aspects of Trotta's remarks. First, Trotta states that women desire to be both warriors and victims at the same time, and when they put themselves in a nontraditional, inappropriate location, she implies women should be expected to be raped. For trouble-making women, stepping out of the domestic realm, they simply deserve to be raped. Second, the role that feminists appear to play is curious. Trotta claims that feminists are to blame for women wanting to be in the military and then being raped; and feminists are blamed for creating a bloated bureaucracy of support services for the rape victims they themselves have created; and feminists are responsible for the rapes; and feminists are bad because they insist on rape being taken seriously as a crime. Third, Trotta's last sentence suggests that women complain about being raped when they are raped *too much*—as if there is an optimum level of rape and sometimes that number is exceeded. Finally, like many anti-feminist victim-blamers, Trotta believes that when women and men are put in the same place, rape is inevitable, as if men cannot help themselves. How ironic it is that feminists are accused of man-hating, when it is anti-feminists like Liz Trotta who hold such demeaning and dehumanizing attitudes toward men, believing they have no control over themselves and cannot be responsible for their behavior.

Liz Trotta's sentiments and the inadequate response by military personnel to rape reflects the classic response to rape survivors: victim blaming. Victim blaming is perpetuated by *rape myths*—attitudes about rape that are false but widely held and serve to excuse and justify men's sexual aggression against women. Rape myths include the belief that women asked to be raped by their behavior, dress, or location; that women lie about being raped;[73] that women enjoy being raped; and that only "bad" women are raped. In short, if a woman has been raped, she probably did something to deserve it.

Victim-blaming ideology is reflected in the rhetoric of media coverage of rape cases. For instance, when professional basketball player Kobe Bryant was under investigation for rape, news agencies tended to use the term "accuser" rather than "alleged victim." "Accuser" shifts the attention from the alleged perpetrator to the woman,[74] suggesting that the woman may have played a role in her victimization, or that there may have been no victim at all, in which case the alleged perpetrator, the alleged rapist, is actually the victim of a misguided, reckless, or vindictive woman. Similarly describing rape in the passive voice such as, "On the evening of June 2, a woman was raped near. . ." rather than the active voice such as, "On the evening of June 2, a man raped a woman near. . ." puts the focus on the victim rather than the criminal perpetrator. Passive sentence constructions imply that in a rape the characteristics of the victim are more important than the characteristics of the perpetrator, or that there was no perpetrator at all—a rape just happened almost by magic.

"Bad" women—those who do not adhere to gender role conventions such as sexual purity, modesty, and chastity—are more likely to be blamed for being raped than "virtuous" women. And again, because most women do not adhere to strict gender-role conventions, most rape survivors can easily be constructed as bad for one reason or another. For instance, police officers are less likely to believe a victim who reports a rape if she is not a virgin or if she had a prior relationship with the suspect.[75] In rape cases, jurors often base their judgments not on legal factors (e.g., that there was no consent) but instead on *extralegal* factors such as the behavior of the victim *prior* to the rape. An appalling finding is that jurors' beliefs in rape myths have been found to be the single best predictor of their decisions in rape case verdicts. Studies have found that those who subscribe to rape myths are less sympathetic to victims.[76]

In addition to victim-blaming interpretations of survivor characteristics, attitudes about gender roles predict attributions about guilt in rape cases involving woman victims. For example, individuals with traditional gender role attitudes are more judgmental toward rape victims and more lenient toward rapists than are people with nontraditional attitudes. The more participants endorse traditional attitudes about women's place in society the more likely they are to blame rape on the victim.[77] Gender role stereotyping has also been linked to self-reported propensity toward sexual coercion (i.e., rape proclivity). Men who believe in male domination are more likely than other men to have engaged in verbal sexual coercion and even rape.[78] For instance, those with traditional gender role attitudes tend to believe a woman rape survivor to be more culpable than do those with nontraditional attitudes. This pattern was particularly true if the survivor is an African American woman compared to a white woman.[79] Recall from the earlier discussion of women athletes: African American women tend not to be afforded the paternalistic protections of benevolent sexism offered to white women. Angela Davis and other feminists of color have written powerfully about the construction of women of color as not *rapeable* historically and in the present. "In conjunction with the sexual exploitation of black women, the stereotypical image of the black woman branded her as a creature motivated by base, animal-like sexual instincts. It was therefore no sin to rape her."[80] The stereotype of the promiscuous African American woman we can see historically going back to slavery, during which white men could justify the rape of black women. If black women were presumed highly sexual and animal-like, which contrasted with the presumed chaste and modest femininity of white women, raping black women was no crime at all. The stereotype of the promiscuous African American woman we can see presently in how they are depicted in music videos—as lustful "bitches" and "hos."[81]

Benevolent sexism predicts victim blame when the survivor's behavior is seen as inconsistent with traditional gender roles.[82] For instance, benevolent sexists attribute less blame and recommend shorter sentences for a perpetrator of date rape than do people who do not hold benevolent sexist beliefs. There was no such difference for a stranger rape case.[83] In other words, for those with traditional gender attitudes, women who are raped by someone they know were probably up to something unladylike and deserve what they get. Those who believe women should be pure and traditional punish women who violate those assumptions. That benevolent sexists are more accepting of sexual violence against certain types of women than those who are not benevolent sexists is important because benevolent sexism is seen on the surface as positive, harmless, and even chivalrous toward women. But benevolent sexism's protection is not available to all women.

Popular culture does its part to perpetuate the punishment of sexually active women. In a content analysis of slasher/horror films, for example, Andrew Welsh[84] analyzed the fate of women in these films and found that female characters who were involved in sexual activity were depicted more negatively and were punished more severely than women who were not sexually active. Sexually active women were more likely to be killed and murder scenes were actually longer in duration for sexually active women than the murder scenes for other women characters. This type of film genre teaches the viewer lessons about the fate of women who have sex. Other film genres and pop culture in general are rife with the punishment of women who dare to be sexual agents (or even just single and independent).[85]

Trans Women and Lesbians

Misogyny and sexism intertwine with heterosexism, homophobia, transphobia, and other forms of prejudice and discrimination. Richard Mohr, in his discussion of antigay stereotypes, argues that homophobic stereotypes are a means of reinforcing traditional gender roles and maintaining men's high status in society. Mohr contends, if "one is free to choose one's social roles independently of gender, many guiding social divisions both domestic and commercial might be threatened. The socially gender-linked distinctions would blur between breadwinner and homemaker, protector and protected, boss and secretary..." Accusations such as "fag" and "dyke" are used to "keep women in their place and to prevent men from breaking ranks and ceding away theirs."[86] This dynamic can target people whether or not they are themselves gay or lesbian.

Transgender individuals are those who identify with a gender that is not the sex they were assigned at birth or those who do not conform to one particular gender or another.[87] Trans people face high rates of violence, from school bullying and family violence to street violence and sexual abuse.[88] Trans individuals experience widespread discrimination in health care, education, housing, and employment.[89]

According to trans activist and author Julia Serano, discrimination against trans women isn't solely about the societal disruption when individuals who are assigned as males at birth give up their power and status as males to become females. Rather, Serano argues that contempt for trans women stems from a key aspect of sexism: *anti-femininity*.

Trans women and trans men threaten the gender status quo. Activist Laverne Cox (acclaimed for her portrayal of a trans woman in the Netflix series *Orange Is the New Black*) attributes the high rates of violence against trans people in part to the belief of some that transgender "identities are inherently deceptive, our identities are inherently sort of suspect."[90] In addition, trans people disrupt the cultural idea that gender is a binary, two-category system that is natural, unchanging, and fixed at birth. The patriarchal system that relegates women to second-class status is disrupted if we no longer believe that there are two and only two genders that are fundamentally different and based in nature. Furthermore, the fact that trans women were assigned the male sex category at birth but have rejected that sex category may be particularly confusing and frustrating to gender normative individuals because trans women have ceded their power and status in the way Mohr describes. Serano says:

> Examining the society-wide disdain for trans women also brings to light an important yet often overlooked aspect of traditional sexism: that it targets people not only for their femaleness, but also for their expressions of femininity...The idea that masculinity is strong, tough, and natural while femininity is weak, vulnerable, and artificial continues to proliferate even among people who believe that women and men are equals...[91] And now, as an out transsexual woman, I find that those who wish to ridicule or dismiss me do not simply take me to task for the fact that I fail to conform to gender norms—instead, more often than not, they mock my femininity.[92]

Part of the complexity of misogyny is that women can be punished for stepping outside the bounds of femininity, *and* for residing within those boundaries.

Whether they present as feminine, masculine, androgynous, or somewhere else in the gender galaxy,[93] lesbians violate gender norms by virtue of the fact that they affiliate romantically and sexually with women and not men, and are therefore outside the traditional heterosexual family arrangement. Like other nontraditional women, lesbians are viewed as less warm than the women who reside in the heteronormative domestic sphere.[94] Like other categories of nontraditional women, lesbians do not receive the patronizing protection of benevolent sexism, and like feminists, lesbians are targets of hostile sexism—punishment for not adhering to the stereotypes of the traditional woman as gentle, nurturing, unthreatening, and compliant with heterosexual norms.

Despite the numerous advances in lesbian and gay rights over the last three decades, lesbians continue to face violence and discrimination.[95] As a result, lesbian-baiting continues to be a potent weapon in the attempt to keep all women—lesbian or not—in line. As we found in Chapter 3, lesbian-baiting has served as a form of sexual extortion in the military, particularly prior to the lifting of the ban on homosexuals in the military.[96] The military's antigay policy gave harassers and rapists an additional tool of sexual extortion, as allegations of lesbianism could ruin a woman's career. It mattered little whether the allegations were true. Women soldiers who refused sexual advances from men could be accused of being lesbians and subjected to investigation for homosexual conduct. Thus, the ban against homosexuals in the military could be used as a weapon of retaliation against women who reported sexual harassment or rape, or against women who rebuffed sexual advances. Now that lesbians and gay men can serve openly in the military, lesbian-baiting ought to be a less effective weapon against women service members, although it still continues, just as it does in nonmilitary society, so long as there are negative consequences of being identified as a lesbian. Those negative consequences persist because, even in the absence an overtly discriminatory policy (such as "Don't Ask, Don't Tell"), lesbians are still perceived as stepping outside the sphere of traditional womanhood.

Both lesbians and feminists are understood as women who disrupt and threaten gender. Both lesbians and feminists are viewed as unladylike, assertive, and outspoken, and women like this threaten the gender status quo.[97] We discussed in Chapter 3 the faulty assumption that feminists are all lesbians and lesbians are all feminists. Because *lesbian* is often linked with *feminist*, feminists sometimes feel compelled to prove they are not lesbians. Linking lesbianism and feminism serves an ideological purpose. Lesbian-baiting is an effective form of silencing women who may not be romantically interested in men (or in a particular man), may not cooperate with gender roles, or who might call attention to inequality.[98] Accusations of lesbianism work alongside descriptions of feminists as angry, unladylike, and unfeminine to make feminists, and by extension, the goals of feminism, unattractive and repellent. Lesbian-baiting is a scare tactic that provides a disincentive for women to take collective action to challenge gender inequality.

Conclusion

This chapter examined several ways that sexism persists even as women (as a group) are perceived positively relative to men. Those positive feelings are narrow in scope and are reserved for an ever-shrinking category—traditional woman—a category most women do not fit into. Traditional women are viewed as warm but not very competent. These positive feelings turn into punishment for women who are perceived as departing from tradition. Nontraditional women such as professionals and feminists (and, as it turns out, most women) are viewed as competent but not very warm. Benevolent sexism is directed toward traditional women, offering them the promise of paternalistic protection by men, whereas hostile sexism is directed toward nontraditional women—penalizing them for not knowing their place and for potentially competing with men.[99] In her 1988 book, *Homophobia: A Weapon of Sexism*, Suzanne Pharr aptly critiqued this process by pointing out that sexism stays in place with the promise to women that they will not suffer violence as long as they attach themselves to a man for protection.[100]

Dividing women into good (traditional) and bad (nontraditional) allows for reinforcement of the good and punishment for the bad. The homemaker subtype and its close associates (such as secretaries or other women in traditional jobs) epitomize *paternalistic stereotypes* that portray them as warm, nonthreatening, not competent, and needing male protection. Paternalistic stereotypes contribute to justifying and maintaining a social system of gender inequality. These gender stereotypes are not merely descriptive but prescriptive, expressing expectations about how women ought to be. The favorable traits attributed to traditional women suit them to their low-status roles in society.[101] Many women are comforted by benevolent sexism because they view it as chivalrous behavior designed to protect women and to make them feel special and different from men. Many men are taught that chivalrous behavior is the polite and proper way to treat women. However, the research on benevolent sexism finds that its consequences are less than benevolent. Because it assumes that women are weak, fragile, and incompetent, women who are subjected to benevolent sexism view themselves as less competent; such women are viewed by others as less competent; moreover, women who reject benevolent sexism are viewed as ungracious and cold.

On the other hand, career women, feminists, and other nontraditional subgroups are targets of *envious stereotypes* that portray them as competent but not warm. Endowing nontraditional women with respected traits like competence, part of stereotypes for typical men, may nonetheless serve to justify discrimination against them because they are viewed as potentially dangerous or as unfair competitors with men. Attributions of nontraditional women's supposed lack of warmth further serve to rationalize acts of discrimination.[102] Other kinds of nontraditional women—such as athletes, sexually active women, and women in the military—face discrimination because they are viewed as violating traditional gender roles and needing to be put in their place. An extreme form of punishment for nontraditional women is sexual violence. When men rape women, individuals justify and rationalize their abuse by maintaining rape myths and victim-blaming ideology, assuming the victim did something to bring it on. Any departure from the "proper" domain of womanhood, including independence, sexual agency, and military service, can be invoked to blame the victim.

Many women, of course, do succeed in nontraditional realms. In the case of competent professionals, women who temper their agentic qualities with a declaration that they are "team players" and are more interested in "helping others" than "getting ahead" can convey their competence and lessen the risk of backlash.[103] But this is an additional burden for women leaders that men do not have, and it is another cost of modern misogyny.

An important psychological function of the division of women into subtypes is that it allows both benevolent and hostile sexists to believe that they are not prejudiced against women—only against women who challenge gender norms. Subtyping women supports the maintenance of the gender hierarchy by allowing individuals to hold sexist views without seeing themselves as prejudiced and by helping them manage their ambivalence toward women.[104] This convoluted system keeps sexism in place, blames women for any harm that befalls them, and informs everything from job interviews and sports pages to slasher films and courtroom verdicts.

Notes

1. Venker, S. (2012, November 26). The war on men. *FoxNews.com*. Retrieved from http://www.foxnews.com/opinion/2012/11/24/war-on-men/
2. Eagly, A. H., & Mladinic, A. (1994). Are people prejudiced against women? Some answers from research on attitudes, gender stereotypes and judgments of competence. In W. Stroebe & M. Hewstone (Eds.), *European review of social psychology* (pp. 1–35). New York, NY: Wiley.

3. Eckes, T. (2002). Paternalistic and envious gender stereotypes: Testing predictions from the stereotype content model. *Sex Roles*, *47*, 99–114.

4. Fiske, S. T., Cuddy, A.J.C., Glick, P., & Xu, J. (2002). A model of (often mixed) stereotype content: Competence and warmth respectively follow from perceived status and competition. *Journal of Personality and Social Psychology*, *82*, 878–902. doi:10.1037//0022-3514.82.6.878

5. Haddock, G., & Zanna, M. P. (1994). Preferring "housewives" to "feminists": Categorization and the favorability of attitudes toward women. *Psychology of Women Quarterly*, *18*, 25–52.

6. Cuddy, A., Fiske, S. T., & Glick, P. (2007). The BIAS map: Behaviors from intergroup affect and stereotypes. *Journal of Personality and Social Psychology*, *92*, 631–648. doi:10.1037/0022-3514.92.4.631

7. Glick, P., & Fiske, S.T. (2001). An ambivalent alliance: Hostile and benevolent sexism as complementary justifications for gender inequality. *American Psychologist*, *56*, 109–118. doi:10.1037//0003-066X.56.2.109

8. Serano says:Christopher, A. N., & Mull, M. S. (2006). Conservative ideology and ambivalent sexism. *Psychology of Women Quarterly*, *30*, 223–230.

9. Barreto, M., & Ellemers, N. (2005). The burden of benevolent sexism: How it contributes to the maintenance of gender inequalities. *European Journal of Social Psychology*, *35*, 633–642. doi:10.1002/ejsp.270

10. Robnett, R. D., Anderson, K. J., & Hunter, L. E. (2012). Predicting feminist identity: Associations between gender-traditional attitudes, feminist stereotyping, and ethnicity. *Sex Roles*, *67*, 143–157. doi:10.1007/s11199-012-0170-2

11. Glick, P., & Fiske, S.T. (2001). An ambivalent alliance: Hostile and benevolent sexism as complementary justifications for gender inequality. *American Psychologist*, *56*, 109–118. doi:10.1037//0003-066X.56.2.109

12. Glick, P., Lameiras, M., Fiske, S.T., Eckes, T., Masser, B., Volpato, C.,...Wells, R. (2004). Bad but bold: Ambivalent attitudes toward men predict gender inequality in 16 nations. *Journal of Personality and Social Psychology*, *86*, 713–728. doi:10.1037/0022-3514.86.5.713

13. Page 114–115: Glick, P., & Fiske, S.T. (2001). An ambivalent alliance: Hostile and benevolent sexism as complementary justifications for gender inequality. *American Psychologist*, *56*, 109–118. doi:10.1037//0003-066X.56.2.109

14. Bosson, J. K., Pinel, E. C., & Vandello, J. A. (2010). The emotional impact of ambivalent sexism: Forecasts versus real experiences. *Sex Roles*, *62*, 520–531. doi:10.1007/s11199-009-9664-y

15. Jost, J. T., & Kay, A. C. (2005). Exposure to benevolent sexism and complementary gender stereotypes: Consequences for specific and diffuse forms of system justification. *Journal of Personality and Social Psychology*, *88*, 498–509. doi:10.1037/0022-3514.88.3.498

16. Dumont, M., Sarlet, M., Dardenne, B. (2010). Be too kind to a woman, she'll feel incompetent: Benevolent sexism shifts self-construal and autobiographical memories toward incompetence. *Sex Roles, 62*, 545–553. doi:10.1007/s11199-008-9582-4

17. Good, J. J., & Rudman, L. A. (2010). When female applicants meet sexist interviewers: The costs of being a target of benevolent sexism. *Sex Roles, 62*, 481–493. doi:10.1007/s11199-009-9685-6

18. Becker, J. C., Glick, P., Ilic, M., Bohner, G. (2011). Damned if she does, damned if she doesn't: Consequences of accepting versus confronting patronizing help for the female target and male actor. *European Journal of Social Psychology, 41*, 761–773. doi:10.1002/ejsp.823

19. Duerson, M. H. (2012, July 17). Pregnant Google exec name Yahoo CEO. *NY Daily News.* Retrieved from http://articles.nydailynews.com/2012-07-17/news/32717940_1_ceo-ross-levinsohn-zachary-bogue-yahoo-board

20. Petrecca, L. (2012, July 19). Pregnant Yahoo CEO ignites maternity debate. *USA Today.* Retrieved from www.usatoday.com/money/workplace/story/2012-07-17/yahoo-ceo-pregnant-marissa-mayer/56323292/1

21. Goudreau, J. (2012, July 17). New Yahoo CEO Marissa Mayer is pregnant. Does it matter? *Forbes.* Retrieved from http://www.forbes.com/sites/jennagoudreau/2012/07/17/new-yahoo-ceo-marissa-mayer-is-pregnant-does-it-matter/

22. Clark, D. (2012, July 23). Pregnant at work? Follow Marissa Mayer's playbook. *Forbes.* Retrieved from http://www.nbcnews.com/id/48259962/ns/business-forbes_com/t/pregnant-work-follow-marissa-mayers-playbook/

23. Keyishian, A. (2012, July 19). The pregnant CEO: Should you hate Marissa Mayer? *Forbes.* Retrieved from http://www.forbes.com/sites/learnvest/2012/07/19/the-pregnant-ceo-should-you-hate-marissa-mayer/

24. Glick, P. & Fiske, S. T. (2001). An ambivalent alliance: Hostile and benevolent sexism as complementary justifications for gender inequality. *American Psychologist, 56*, 109–118. doi:10.1037//0003-066X.56.2.109

25. Glick, P., Diebold, J., Bailey-Werner, B., & Zhu, L. (1997). The two faces of Adam: Ambivalent sexism and polarized attitudes toward women. *Personality and Social Psychology Bulletin, 23*, 1323–1334. doi:10.1177/01461672972312009

26. Rampell, C. (2010, February 6). Women now a majority in American workplaces. *The New York Times.* Retrieved from http://www.nytimes.com/2010/02/06/business/economy/06women.html

27. Patten, E., & Parker, K. (2012, April 19). A gender reversal on career aspirations. *Pew Research Center.* Retrieved from http://www.pewsocialtrends.org/2012/04/19/a-gender-reversal-on-career-aspirations/

28. Fiske, S. T. (2012). Managing ambivalent prejudices: Smart-but-cold and warm-but-dumb stereotypes. *The ANNALs of the American Academy of Political and Social Science, 639*, 33–48. doi:10.1177/0002716211418444

29. Fiske, S. T. (2012). Managing ambivalent prejudices: Smart-but-cold and warm-but-dumb stereotypes. *The ANNALs of the American Academy of Political and Social Science, 639*, 33–48. doi:10.1177/002716211418444

30. Rudman, L. A., & Glick, P. (1999). Feminized management and backlash toward agentic women: The hidden costs to women of a kinder, gentler image of middle managers. *Journal of Personality and Social Psychology, 77*, 1004–1010.

31. Heilman, M. E., Wallen, A. S., Fuchs, D., & Tamkins, M. M. (2004). Penalties for success: Reactions to women who succeed at male gender-typed tasks. *Journal of Applied Psychology, 89*, 416–427. doi:10.1037/0021-9010.89.3.416

32. Rudman, L. A., Moss-Racusin, C. A., Phelan, J. E., & Nauts, S. (2012). Status incongruity and backlash effects: Defending the gender hierarchy motivates prejudice against female leaders. *Journal of Experimental Social Psychology, 48*, 165–179.

33. Study 2: Rudman, L. A., Moss-Racusin, C. A., Phelan, J. E., & Nauts, S. (2012). Status incongruity and backlash effects: Defending the gender hierarchy motivates prejudice against female leaders. *Journal of Experimental Social Psychology, 48*, 165–179.

34. Study 5: Rudman, L. A., Moss-Racusin, C. A., Phelan, J. E., & Nauts, S. (2012). Status incongruity and backlash effects: Defending the gender hierarchy motivates prejudice against female leaders. *Journal of Experimental Social Psychology, 48*, 165–179.

35. Study 3: Rudman, L. A., Moss-Racusin, C. A., Phelan, J. E., & Nauts, S. (2012). Status incongruity and backlash effects: Defending the gender hierarchy motivates prejudice against female leaders. *Journal of Experimental Social Psychology, 48*, 165–179.

36. Study 4: Phelan, J. E., Moss-Racusin, C. A., & Rudman, L. A. (2008). Competent yet out in the cold: Shifting criteria for hiring reflect backlash toward agentic women. *Psychology of Women Quarterly, 32*, 406–413.

37. Rudman, L. A., Moss-Racusin, C. A., Phelan, J. E., & Nauts, S. (2012). Status incongruity and backlash effects: Defending the gender hierarchy motivates prejudice against female leaders. *Journal of Experimental Social Psychology, 48*, 165–179.

38. Rudman, L. A., Moss-Racusin, C. A., Phelan, J. E., & Nauts, S. (2012). Status incongruity and backlash effects: Defending the gender hierarchy motivates prejudice against female leaders. *Journal of Experimental Social Psychology, 48*, 165–179.

39. Gervais, S. J., & Hillard, A. L. (2011). A role congruity perspective on prejudice toward Hillary Clinton and Sarah Palin. *Analyses of Social Issues and Public Policy, 11*, 221–240. doi:10.1111/j.1530-2415.2011.01263.x

40. Gervais, S. J., & Hillard, A. L. (2011). A role congruity perspective on prejudice toward Hillary Clinton and Sarah Palin. *Analyses of Social Issues and Public Policy, 11*, 221–240. doi:10.1111/j.1530-2415.2011.01263.x

41. Okimoto, T. G., & Brescoll, V. L. (2010). The price of power: Power seeking and backlash against female politicians. *Personality and Social Psychology Bulletin, 36,* 923–936. doi:10.1177/0146167210371949

42. Okimoto, T. G., & Brescoll, V. L. (2010). The price of power: Power seeking and backlash against female politicians. *Personality and Social Psychology Bulletin, 36,* 923–936. doi:10.1177/0146167210371949

43. Phelan, J. E., Moss-Racusin, C. A., & Rudman, L. A. (2008). Competent yet out in the cold: Shifting criteria for hiring reflect backlash toward agentic women. *Psychology of Women Quarterly, 32,* 406–413.

44. Uhlmann, E. L., & Cohen, G. L. (2005). Constructed criteria: Redefining merit to justify discrimination. *Psychological Science, 16,* 474–480.

45. Rampell, C. (2012, May 18). At-home vs. employed mothers: Who's happier. *The New York Times.* Retrieved from http://economix.blogs.nytimes.com/2012/05/18/at-home-vs-employed-mothers-whos-happier/

46. Cuddy, A. J. C., Fiske, S. T., & Glick, P. (2004). When professionals become mothers, warmth doesn't cut the ice. *Journal of Social Issues, 60,* 701–718. doi:10.1111/j.0022-4537.2004.00381.x

47. For a review, see: Cuddy, A. J. C., Fiske, S. T., & Glick, P. (2004). When professionals become mothers, warmth doesn't cut the ice. *Journal of Social Issues, 60,* 701–718. doi:10.1111/j.0022-4537.2004.00381.x

48. Cuddy, A. J. C., Fiske, S. T., & Glick, P. (2004). When professionals become mothers, warmth doesn't cut the ice. *Journal of Social Issues, 60,* 701–718. doi:10.1111/j.0022-4537.2004.00381.x

49. For a longer discussion, see Chapter 5 in: Anderson, K. J. (2010). *Benign bigotry: The psychology of subtle prejudice.* Cambridge, UK: Cambridge University Press.

50. Donovan, R. A. (2011). Tough or tender: (Dis)similarities in white college student's perceptions of black and white women. *Psychology of Women Quarterly, 35,* 458–468. doi:10.1177/0361684311406874

51. Berdahl, J. L., & Min, J.-A. (2012). Prescriptive stereotypes and workplace consequences for East Asians in North America. *Cultural Diversity and Ethnic Minority Psychology, 18,* 141–152. doi:10.1037/a0027692

52. Anderson, K. J. (2010). Students' stereotypes of professors: An exploration of the double violations of ethnicity and gender. *Social Psychology of Education, 13,* 459–472. doi:10.1007/s11218-010-9121-3

53. Anderson, K. J. (2010). Students' stereotypes of professors: An exploration of the double violations of ethnicity and gender. *Social Psychology of Education, 13,* 459–472. doi:10.1007/s11218-010-9121-3

54. Anderson, K. J., & Smith, G. (2005). Students' preconceptions of professors: Benefits and barriers according to ethnicity and gender. *Hispanic Journal of Behavioral Sciences, 27,* 184–201. doi:10.1177/0739986304273707

55. Jhally, S. (Producer) & Alpert, L. (Director). (2002). *Playing unfair: The media image of the female athlete [Motion Picture]*. USA: Media Education Foundation.

56. Messner, M. A., & Cooky, C. (2010, June). Gender in televised sports: News and highlights shows, 1989–2009. Retrieved from https://dornsifecms.usc.edu/assets/sites/80/docs/tvsports.pdf

57. Messner, M. A., Duncan, M. C., & Cooky, C. (2003). Silence, sports bras, and wrestling porn: Women in televised sports news and highlights shows. *Journal of Sport & Social Issues, 27*(1), 38–51. doi:10.1177/0193732502239583

58. Messner, M. A., & Cooky, C. (2010, June). Gender in televised sports: News and highlights shows, 1989–2009. Retrieved from https://dornsifecms.usc.edu/assets/sites/80/docs/tvsports.pdf

59. Jhally, S. (Producer) & Alpert, L. (Director). (2002). *Playing unfair: The media image of the female athlete [Motion Picture]*. USA: Media Education Foundation.

60. Jhally, S. (Producer) & Alpert, L. (Director). (2002). *Playing unfair: The media image of the female athlete [Motion Picture]*. USA: Media Education Foundation.

61. Carty, V. (2005). Textual portrayals of female athletes: Liberation or nuanced forms of patriarchy? *Frontiers, 26*, 132–155.

62. Jhally, S. (Producer) & Alpert, L. (Director). (2002). *Playing unfair: The media image of the female athlete [Motion Picture]*. USA: Media Education Foundation.

63. Carty, V. (2005). Textual portrayals of female athletes: Liberation or nuanced forms of patriarchy? *Frontiers, 26*, 132–155.

64. Carty, V. (2005). Textual portrayals of female athletes: Liberation or nuanced forms of patriarchy? *Frontiers, 26*, 132–155.

65. Boldry, J., Wood, W., & Kashy, D. A. (2001). Gender stereotypes and the evaluation of men and women in military training. *Journal of Social Issues, 57*, 689–705.

66. Matthews, M. D., & Ender, M. G. (2009). Role of group affiliation and gender on attitudes toward women in the military. *Military Psychology, 21*, 241–251. doi:10.1080/08995600902768750

67. U.S. Department of Defense. (2012). DOD releases annual sexual assault response and prevention report. Retrieved from http://www.defense.gov/releases/release.aspx?releaseid=15185

68. Roulo, C. (2012, December 21). DOD: Sexual assault reporting up at service academies. Retrieved from http://www.defense.gov/news/newsarticle.aspx?id=118860

69. Department of Defense Sexual Assault Prevention and Response. (2013). Department of Defense annual report on sexual assault in the military, Vol. 1 (RefID: 5-9DB8000). Retrieved from http://www.sapr.mil/index.php/annual-reports

70. Martin, D. S. (2012, April 14). Rape victims say military labels them 'crazy.' *CNN Health*. Retrieved from http://www.cnn.com/2012/04/14/health/military-sexual-assaults-personality-disorder/index.html

71. Martin, D. S. (2012, April 14). Rape victims say military labels them 'crazy.' *CNN Health.* Retrieved from http://www.cnn.com/2012/04/14/health/military-sexual-assaults-personality-disorder/index.html

72. Newbold, A. [AU: Correct?] (2012, February 12). Fox's Liz Trotta on sexual assault in military: "What did they expect? These people are in close contact." [Web log post]. Retrieved from http://mediamatters.org/blog/2012/02/12/foxs-liz-trotta-on-sexual-assault-in-military-w/184046

73. Edwards, K. M., Turchik, J. A., & Dardis, C. M., Reynolds, N., Gidycz, C. A. (2011). Rape myths: History, individual and institutional-level presence, and implications for change. *Sex Roles, 65,* 761–773. doi:10.1007/s11199-011-9943-2

74. Katz, J. (2006). *The macho paradox: Why some men hurt women and how all men can help.* Naperville, IL: Sourcebooks.

75. For a review, see: Edwards, K. M., Turchik, J. A., & Dardis, C. M., Reynolds, N., Gidycz, C. A. (2011). Rape myths: History, individual and institutional-level presence, and implications for change. *Sex Roles, 65,* 761–773. doi:10.1007/s11199-011-9943-2

76. For a review, see: Edwards, K. M., Turchik, J. A., & Dardis, C. M., Reynolds, N., Gidycz, C. A. (2011). Rape myths: History, individual and institutional-level presence, and implications for change. *Sex Roles, 65,* 761–773. doi:10.1007/s11199-011-9943-2

77. Grubb, A., & Turner, E. (2012). Attribution of blame in rape cases: A review of the impact of rape myth acceptance, gender role conformity and substance use on victim blaming. *Aggression and Violent Behavior, 17,* 443–452. doi:10.1016/j.avb.2012.06.002

78. Grubb, A., & Turner, E. (2012). Attribution of blame in rape cases: A review of the impact of rape myth acceptance, gender role conformity and substance use on victim blaming. *Aggression and Violent Behavior, 17,* 443–452. doi:10.1016/j.avb.2012.06.002

79. Esqueda, C. W., & Harrison, L. A. (2005). The influence of gender role stereotypes, the woman's race, and level of provocation and resistance on domestic violence culpability attributions. *Sex Roles, 53,* 821–834. doi:10.1007/11199s-005-8295-1

80. Davis, A. (2002, Spring). Joan Little: The dialectics of rape (1975). Ms. Magazine. Retrieved from http://www.msmagazine.com/spring2002/davis.asp

81. Harris-Perry, M. V. (2011). *Sister citizen: Shame, stereotypes, and black women in America.* New Haven, CT: Yale University Press.

82. Duran, M., Moya, M., Megías, J. L., & Viki, G. T. (2010). Social perception of rape victims in dating and married relationships: The role of the perpetrator's benevolent sexism. *Sex Roles, 62,* 505–519. doi:10.1007/s11199-009-9676-7

83. Viki, G. T., Abrams, D., & Masser, B. (2004). Evaluating stranger and acquaintance rape: The role of benevolent sexism in perpetrator blame and recommended sentence length. *Law and Human Behavior, 28,* 295–303.

84. Welsh, A. (2010). On the perils of living dangerously in the slasher horror film: Gender differences in the association between sexual activity and survival. *Sex Roles, 62,* 762–773. doi:10.1007/s11199-010-9762-x

85. Faludi, S. (1991). *Backlash: The undeclared war against American women.* New York, NY: Crown.

86. Page 587 in: Mohr, R. D. (2014/1988). Anti-gay stereotypes. In P. S. Rothenberg, & K. S. Mayhew (Eds.) *Race, class, and gender in the United States* (pp. 585–591). New York, NY: Worth Publishers.

87. *Transgender* is a broad term to include those who transition from one gender to another (transsexuals), *and* those who may not, including genderqueer people, cross-dressers, the androgynous, and those whose gender nonconformity is a part of their identity. This definition comes from: Grant, J. M., Mottet, L. A., & Tanis, J. (2011, February 3). *Injustice at every turn: A report of the National Transgender Discrimination Survey.* Retrieved from http://www.thetaskforce.org/reports_and_research/ntds

88. Bradford, J., Reisner, S. L., Honnold, J. A., & Zavier, J. (2013). Experiences of transgender-related discrimination and implications for health: Results from the Virginia Transgender Health Initiative Study. *American Journal of Public Health, 103,* 1820–1829.

89. Grant, J. M., Mottet, L. A., & Tanis, J. (2011, February 3). Injustice at every turn: A report of *the National Transgender Discrimination Survey.* Retrieved from http://www.thetaskforce.org/reports_and_research/ntds

90. Burk, M., Feltz, R., Maté, A., Shaikh, N., Guzder, D., Alcoff, S.,…Littlefield, A. (Producers). (2014, February 19). "Black trans bodies are under attack:" Freed activist CeCe McDonald, actress Laverne Cox speak out. Retrieved from http://www.democracynow.org/2014/2/19/black_trans_bodies_are_under_attack

91. Page 5 in: Serano, J. (2007). *Whipping girl: A transsexual woman on sexism and the scapegoating of femininity.* Emeryville, CA: Seal Press.

92. Page 3 in: Serano, J. (2007). *Whipping girl: A transsexual woman on sexism and the scapegoating of femininity.* Emeryville, CA: Seal Press.

93. The gender galaxy is a three-dimensional nonlinear space in which every gender has a location that may or may not be fixed. Vade, D. (2005). Expanding gender and expanding the law: Toward a social and legal conceptualization of gender that is more inclusive of transgender people. *Michigan Journal of Gender and Law, 11,* 253.

94. Brambilla, M., Carnaghi, A., & Ravenna, M. (2011). Status and cooperation shape lesbian stereotypes: Testing predictions from the stereotype content model. *Social Psychology, 42,* 101–110. doi:10.1027/1864-9335/a000054.

95. Guequierre, P. (2012, December 10). FBI: Reported hate crimes based on sexual orientation on the rise. Retrieved from https://www.hrc.org/blog/entry/fbi-reported-hate-crimes-based-on-sexual-orientation-on-the-rise

96. Corbett, K. M. (1997, November). Lesbian-baiting: A threat to all military women. *Lesbian News, 23*, 16–18.

97. Alexander, S., & Megan, R. (1997). Social constructs of feminism: A study of undergraduates at a women's college. *College Student Journal, 31*, 555–567.

98. Pharr, S. (1988). *Homophobia: A weapon of sexism*. Inverness, CA: Chardon Press.

99. Eckes, T. (2002). Paternalistic and envious gender stereotypes: Testing predictions from the stereotype content model. *Sex Roles, 47*, 99–114.

100. Pharr, S. (1988). *Homophobia: a weapon of sexism*. Inverness, CA: Chardon Press.

101. For a review, see: Eckes, T. (2002). Paternalistic and envious gender stereotypes: Testing predictions from the stereotype content model. *Sex Roles, 47*, 99–114.

102. Eckes, T. (2002). Paternalistic and envious gender stereotypes: Testing predictions from the stereotype content model. *Sex Roles, 47*, 99–114.

103. Rudman, L. A., & Glick, P. (2001). Prescriptive gender stereotypes and backlash toward agentic women. *Journal of Social Issues, 57*, 732–762.

104. Fowers, A. F., & Fowers, B. J. (2010). Social dominance and sexual self-schema as moderators of sexist reactions to female subtypes. *Sex Roles, 62*, 468–480. doi:10.1007/s11199-009-9607-7

6 IS FEMINISM GOOD FOR WOMEN?

Feminism has fought no wars. It has killed no opponents. It has set up
no concentration camps, starved no enemies, practiced no cruelties.
Its battles have been for education, for the vote, for better working
conditions for women and children; for property rights for women,
for divorce, for custody rights, for the right to safety on the streets.
Feminists have fought for child care, for social welfare, for greater vis-
ibility for people with disabilities.

—DALE SPENDER[1]

Although much of the U.S. mainstream has embraced feminist initiatives such as advances in women's paid employment, the recognition
of sexual harassment in the workplace, and Title IX for girls' education, feminists find themselves portrayed as objects of scorn and pity.
In a variety of mass media contexts feminists have been described vari-
ously as "angry women"[2] with "persecution fantasies,"[3] who "shame
the males"[4] and are "chronically dissatisfied."[5] With descriptions like
these, one might reasonably assume that feminists suffer from mental disorders, psychological adjustment problems, and relationship
maladies. However, feminists themselves view feminism as a "life raft"
protecting them against discrimination.[6] Contrary to popular representations, feminist psychologists have long demonstrated that a feminist identity is psychologically good for women.

It is unlikely that women consciously and deliberately adopt a
feminist identity in order to achieve psychological benefit. Instead,
research suggests that women adopt a feminist identity to help them
understand, manage, and resist male dominance and to achieve some
solidarity with other women. While the central focus of feminism is
social change, psychological health turns out to be a side benefit of
feminist identification. There exists a body of literature that examines the role of feminism in general, and feminist identification in
particular, with various aspects of psychological health. This chapter
reviews the empirical research that examines feminism as a *protective identity*—as a healthy and empowering identity—for American
women. A few studies look at the role of feminism in men's lives,
and those are discussed here as well. Does feminism protect against

ordinary psychological distress that befalls traditional women? First, we examine psychological theory and research on the role that feminism plays in women's psychological well-being. Issues such as self-efficacy, mental health, body image, eating disorders, and heterosexual relationships are of particular interest here. Do women differ in terms of psychological well-being in these areas depending on whether or not they hold traditional gender role attitudes? Do women differ in these areas depending on whether or not they label themselves as feminists? In addition to these questions, we address the empirical research on the impact of women's and gender studies courses on women. A growing body of research on the benefits of these courses finds positive changes in critical thinking skills, open mindedness, participatory learning, and increased self-efficacy.

Feminist Identity: Two Constructs

Before we begin, some definitions are in order. There are a variety of definitions of a feminist, but common to most definitions is the idea that a feminist recognizes that discrimination against women exists, experiences a sense of shared fate with women as a group, and wants to work with others to improve women's status.[7] In the psychological literature on feminism, there are generally two ways of categorizing feminist status in individuals—first, determining pro-feminist *attitudes* via survey questions and, second, determining feminist *identity* by simply asking the individual if she is a feminist. In determining pro-feminist attitudes, researchers use surveys such as Betsy Morgan's[8] Liberal Feminist Attitude and Ideology Scale, or Nancy Henley and her colleagues'[9] Feminist Perspectives Scale. These scales ask respondents about their degree of agreement with statements such as, "A woman should have the same job opportunities as a man," "Women have been treated unfairly on the basis of their gender throughout most of human history," and "Pornography exploits female sexuality and degrades all women."

The most common method of assessing pro-feminist attitudes is by measuring feminist identity development with Nancy Downing and Kristin Roush's[10] stage model. Downing and Roush propose that feminist identity development progresses through a series of five stages: passive acceptance, revelation, embeddedness-emanation, synthesis, and active commitment. *Passive acceptance* describes women who are unaware of or deny the existence of sexism. Movement into the second stage, *revelation*, is precipitated by a crisis that forces the woman to recognize inequality. This crisis might be a personal experience of discrimination. The *embeddedness-emanation* stage represents a time for discovery of sisterhood. Women in this stage look for support from other women and begin to appreciate creative work by women (e.g., art, music, drama). Stage four, *synthesis*, is achieved when women value the positive aspects of being women and integrate these qualities with their own personal attributes for a positive and realistic self-concept. Finally, *active commitment* involves translating the newly consolidated feminist identity with action for social change. Various paper-and-pencil measures have been used to measure individuals' stages of feminist identity development. Interestingly, the scales that assess pro-feminist attitudes and feminist identity development do not assess explicit feminist self-identification (e.g., "I am a feminist") and rarely even use the word *feminist*.

The second way of measuring feminist status is by assessing feminist *identification*. This typically involves simply asking the respondent, "Do you consider yourself a feminist?" One limitation of this approach is that some contemporary young people do not necessarily know what a feminist is (likely due to misrepresentation or marginalization by the media). For instance, one study[11] found that when asked to define feminism, some respondents confused it with "feminine" or described feminism as "When women think they are superior to men." Thus, when assessing feminist identification it is important to make sure respondents have a basic definition of feminism.

Pro-feminist *attitudes*, which assess one's support of feminism's goals, and *feminist identity*, which measures one's self-labeling as a feminist, are correlated, but they remain distinct constructs.[12] Alyssa Zucker and Laina Bay-Cheng[13] distinguish *self-identified feminists, nonlabelers*, and *nonfeminists*. Nonlabelers are those who hold pro-feminist attitudes but reject the feminist label. In their work, many more women identify as nonlabelers than as feminists. They find important similarities and differences among the three groups of women. For instance, they have found no differences in the prioritization of achievement and power between the three groups of women. Importantly, however, nonlabelers tend to have more in common with nonfeminists than with feminists. For example, nonlabelers are indistinguishable from nonfeminists in terms of valuing adherence to social conventions and norms, their lower concern for social justice and equality, and their support for hierarchy and the myth of meritocracy compared to feminists. Nonlabelers are more aligned with the neoliberal principles of individualism described in Chapter 1.

Whereas most women do endorse feminist *attitudes*, relatively few women call themselves feminists. As we consider the relationship between feminism and mental health, these two measures of feminism should be kept in mind, because outcomes differ depending on whether a woman identifies as a feminist or merely holds pro-feminist attitudes.

Mental Health and Well-Being

Psychological Well-Being and Feminism

Psychological well-being refers to people's cognitive and affective evaluations of their lives. Well-being is indicated by a wide variety of psychological constructs, such as "happiness" and "life satisfaction," and it is examined by measures of self-esteem, purpose in life, autonomy, and mastery of one's environment. Oksana Yakushko[14] classified a sample of mostly white U.S. women as those with traditional values (nonfeminists), those with moderate values, and those with feminist values, based on their responses on a measure of feminist identity development. She examined several aspects of psychological well-being such as *autonomy in life* (the degree to which someone is self-determining, independent, able to resist social pressure); *personal growth* (the feeling of continued development, openness to new experiences); *environmental mastery* (a sense of competence in managing one's environment); *self-acceptance* (possessing a positive attitude about the self, accepting good and bad qualities); *purpose in life* (having goals and a sense of directedness); and *positive relations with others* (having warm, trusting relationships with others, concern about the welfare of others). In general, scores on these measures of psychological well-being were higher among women with feminist values than for women with traditional values. Specifically, traditional women had lower scores on autonomy in life and personal growth than did moderate women and women with feminist values. Women with traditional values also had lower scores on sense of purpose in life than feminists. The three groups of women did not differ on measures of environmental mastery, positive relationships with others, self-acceptance, and general satisfaction with life.

The differences between those with traditional, moderate, and feminist values suggest that women who hold traditional values may experience lower levels of well-being in life than women who ascribe partially or fully to the tenets of feminism. Specific aspects of these women's identities that may especially contribute to their lower sense of well-being are their lower scores in the areas of autonomy, personal growth, and purpose in life. Perhaps traditional women do not view these aspects of well-being as significant to their lives. Instead, they may see their role in life as being supportive of others, promoting the growth and well-being of others around them, rather than seeing themselves as autonomous individuals.[15] At the same time, other research finds a link between feminist attitudes and a *generativity identity*—having a conscious concern for the next generation and concern for the welfare of others—and higher self- and life satisfaction.[16] Women with traditional gender role attitudes might be more likely to focus on the lives of their immediate family, which could be associated with lower levels of some aspects of well-being. In contrast, women who are concerned with others at the generational level, and have a feminist consciousness, report higher levels of satisfaction.

Another study[17] explored the relationship between feminist identity development, and psychological well-being and gender-role self-concept, in an ethnically and socioeconomically diverse sample of women. *Gender-role self-concept* refers to people's ratings of themselves in terms of agentic/instrumental characteristics (stereotypically associated with men) and communal/expressive characteristics (stereotypically associated with women). Higher levels of feminist identity development were associated with psychological well-being. In addition, agentic/instrumental and androgynous (i.e., both female- and male-stereotyped) gender role self-concepts were associated with psychological well-being.

The two studies described above measured pro-feminist attitudes via measures of feminist identity development. Other studies also have found that having a feminist orientation or being a member of a feminist organization is positively related to a more androgynous or stereotypically masculine gender role self-concept, though well-being is not specifically examined.[18] Further studies[19] find that feminist *attitudes* tend to be indirectly related to self-efficacy—the expectation that one has the ability to carry out chosen actions—whereas the link between feminist *identity* and self-efficacy is direct. That is, feminist attitudes alone, without explicit feminist identification, are only weakly related to self-efficacy.[18]

The Angry Feminist?

In addition to the feminist-as-manhater stereotype we address in Chapter 3, another pervasive stereotype about feminists is that they are bitter, angry, and hostile. Feminist consciousness provides a cognitive framework for women to understand the world, especially their experiences of prejudice and discrimination. Feminists have the tools to frame sexist discrimination they may experience as unjust and as a result of their status as women. Feminists are more likely to attribute sexism to society and gender oppression and are less likely to blame themselves for the sexist treatment they experience. But do these views predict anger? Ann Fischer and Glenn Good[19] assessed United States, mostly white women's feminist identity development and compared the stages of development to anger measures. The respondents completed the State-Trait Anger Expression Inventory, and the Symptoms Checklist, which measures a range of problems such as anxiety, phobias, and paranoia. Are any of the stages of feminist identity development linked to psychological distress and anger? Only the *revelation* stage showed a substantial link to psychological distress and anger. Revelation is the second stage of feminist identity development and does not represent a feminist identity or consciousness; it is the stage at which women first begin to recognize gender inequality (perhaps because they have experienced discrimination). Revelation-like experiences may be overwhelming and could contribute to a generalized state of anger, particularly given that the awareness of gender inequality is a new recognition for women at this stage. So contrary to the angry feminist stereotype, it is only early awareness of sexism, not identifying as a feminist, that is associated with anger. The more sophisticated stages of feminist identity—those stages that are compatible with a feminist identity—are not associated with anger. It is surprising that there are not more studies on the relationship (or lack of) between feminist identity and anger given the prevalence of the stereotype of the angry feminist in Western culture. Like the feminist-manhater myth debunked in Chapter 3, those who perpetuate the angry-feminist stereotype have little need to verify their belief with empirical support because the belief is consistent with their worldview. Also, like the feminist-manhater myth—perpetuated in part because people confuse hating male dominance and patriarchal hegemony with actually hating men—people tend to mistake the righteous anger directed toward injustice with individual-level personal anger and resentment.

Body Image

The damaging effects of impossible beauty standards and the internalization of objectified representations of women in culture have been concerns of feminists for decades. Feminist psychologists have argued that a feminist identity protects women from internalizing the damaging effects of female body objectification so common in Western cultures. Women tend to have more negative views of their bodies than do men; individuals (both women and men) with fewer instrumental/agentic traits (those stereotypically associated with men) have more negative evaluations of their appearance than those with many instrumental/agentic traits.[20] At the beginning of this chapter we discussed the difference between feminist *attitudes*, measured by surveys, and feminist *self-identity*. Self-identified feminists may be more likely than women who simply hold feminist beliefs (nonlabelers—those who do not embrace the socially stigmatized label) to reap benefits associated with rejecting the restrictive norms of beauty and thinness. Sarah Murnen and Linda Smolak[21] conducted a meta-analysis compiling the results from 26 studies (most from North America) examining whether a feminist identity protects women from body image problems. They predicted that women who identify as feminists would have more positive body attitudes and less disordered eating than those who simply agreed with feminist principles. Consistent with much of the work we have reviewed thus far, this association was strongest when feminist identity, as opposed to feminist attitudes, was the measure of feminism. Those women who call themselves feminists are more likely to have positive attitudes about their bodies compared to women who simply hold feminist attitudes and nonfeminists. Specifically, feminist identity was associated with a lower preoccupation with thinness and with lower scores on eating disorder inventories. Also, feminists were less likely to internalize media messages about thinness than were nonfeminists. That is, feminist women are more resistant to media images that glorify thinness. Women who report body shame are believed to have internalized the cultural messages that they should be thin, that they should be able to control their weight, and that they are not valued as women otherwise. A feminist identity seems to provide some protection against this internalization.

It is likely that feminism helps women critically evaluate, and perhaps avoid, harmful cultural messages. Overall, Murnen and Smolak report that, compared to other meta-analytic findings, the association between feminist identity and (lack of) body shame is one of the strongest "protective" effects they have found. It should be noted that none of the studies Murnen and Smolak analyzed looked at adolescents or younger girls—and these younger years are often when problematic eating habits begin. Also, there were no identified differences in the relationship between feminist identity and body image by ethnicity, although few studies actually included diverse samples of women. Research on body dissatisfaction that has compared women by race has found that African American women have more satisfaction than do white women, and Asian American women tend to have body dissatisfaction similar to white women[22] although this research did not examine the role of feminist identity. A different study found that racial centrality may be a buffer against body dissatisfaction for African American women. This means that African American women, for whom their race is a central aspect of their identity, may be protected against the body dissatisfaction issues more typical of white women.[23]

Murnen and Smolak's meta-analysis does not analyze research on lesbians or bisexual women, but a different study finds that women who are in the commitment stage of feminist identity development are less likely to engage in disordered eating related to anorexia and bulimia than are women with traditional gender roles. This pattern held for both lesbian and heterosexual women (bisexual women were not included in the study) and both "older" (about 38 years old) and younger (about 20 years old) women.[24]

Overall, Murnen and Smolak's meta-analysis indicates that feminism is a protective factor against body image issues in three ways: (1) A feminist identity should lead to an elevation of critical thought, (2) encourage collective action, and (3) such thought and action may empower women to act more in their own self-interest than to blindly follow the dictates of society that women should obsess over their bodies.[25]

Relationships

In addition to the angry-feminist stereotype, another set of stereotypes about feminists is that they do not have successful relationships with men, may even be scorned women, and are lesbians.[26] In his book *Manliness*, Harvey Mansfield describes feminists as "none too pleased with men and not shy about letting them know it."[27] Anti-feminist author Kate O'Beirne said, "I have long thought that if high-school boys had invited homely girls to the prom we might have been spared the feminist movement."[28] These stereotypes can serve as a barrier to feminist identification, preventing young women (and men) from identifying as feminists and working on behalf of women's rights.

Is Feminism Bad for Relationships?

Women and men alike tend to think that feminism is incompatible with heterosexual romance. For instance, people tend to believe that unattractive women are likely to be feminists, just as people assume lesbians to be feminists (and vice versa). And women who rate themselves as attractive tend to have more anti-feminist attitudes than women who do not rate themselves as attractive.[29] Of course these findings may speak more to the *perceptions* that feminists are unattractive than the reality that feminists are unattractive. More likely, feminists resist traditional heterosexual beauty norms and are less likely to define themselves in terms of physical attractiveness. Also, women who are not feminists may be more committed to romantic ideals and may report themselves to be more attractive to be consistent with these ideals.

In terms of heterosexual relationships, those who believe that feminism is threatening to romance also show less enthusiasm for feminism and for policies that support women.[30] Indeed the belief that feminism is problematic for heterosexual relationships negatively predicts feminist identity, feminist attitudes, and support for women's rights.[31] In other words, those who think that being a feminist will bring problems to heterosexual relationships will avoid feminism. If intimate relationship concerns undermine feminism's appeal, these concerns will also undermine collective action on women's behalf. Is feminism actually incompatible with heterosexual relationships? A study on feminists' and nonfeminists' romantic relationships does not find support for such a belief. Laurie Rudman and Julie Phelan[32] examined whether (mostly white) heterosexual feminists (or men paired with feminists) have troubled romantic relationships, as is popularly perceived. Contrary to stereotypes, feminists were *more* likely to be in romantic relationships than nonfeminist women. Feminist women did not report decreased relationship quality and stability, although they tended to report more conflict regarding equality in the relationship compared with nonfeminist women.

Feminist men are important for heterosexual women's relationship health. Heterosexual women report greater relationship quality, equality, stability, and sexual satisfaction if their partner is a feminist.[33] To the extent that feminist women select feminist men as partners, feminism for women may have an indirectly positive influence on their relationships. What about men who are in relationships with women? Feminist men report greater agreement about the importance of equality in their relationships than do nonfeminist men. Men also report greater relationship stability and sexual satisfaction if their partner is a feminist. Therefore, feminism may also be healthy for men's relationships. Thus, the overall pattern suggests that for men, feminism (for self and partners) may be beneficial for their relationships, rather than problematic.

Expectations and Inequality

Feminist attitudes and gender-role attitudes predict women's (and men's) expectations about equality in intimate heterosexual relationships. For instance, women with traditional gender-role attitudes tend to have lower expectations for egalitarian romantic relationships than those with nontraditional attitudes.[34] In fact, compared to women who endorse feminist attitudes, women with traditional gender-role attitudes have lowered expectations for egalitarian long-term relationships. This holds in general and across specific aspects of long-term relationships, including the balance of power in the relationship, the division of household labor, sharing of child care, participation in social and community activities outside the home, the importance placed on education for each spouse, employment options and responsibilities, and having good qualities in a spouse. Not endorsing feminist attitudes is also associated with less sexual assertiveness overall, and in the areas of initiation and safe sexual practices in particular.[35] A related study found that women and men with nontraditional gender role attitudes expect to share in child care (although, curiously, not in household chores) with their partners, whereas women and men with traditional attitudes expect the traditional unequal division of labor.[36] Alarmingly, nonfeminist women are more likely than feminist women to endorse problematic aspects of masculinity in potential partners. Specifically, nonfeminist women consider emotional control, exerting power over women, and dominance as desirable characteristics in a potential mate, compared to feminist women.[37]

Feminists, and those with nontraditional gender attitudes, put a high premium on equity in relationships compared to nonfeminists and those with traditional gender attitudes. Women and men with traditional gender role self-concepts (i.e., men as agentic, women as expressive) accept greater inequality in their relationships compared to women and men with nontraditional gender role self-concepts.[38] Women and men with nontraditional gender role self-concepts report that a change in the equity of their relationship would be disturbing. That is, nontraditional women are sensitive to being put in the traditional position of underbenefiting in the relationship in terms of domestic duties; and nontraditional men are sensitive to being in a privileged, overbenefiting, position. However, this is not the case for traditional women and men. Traditional men report being concerned about losing their privileged position. Traditional women do not expect that they would be highly affected by a lack of equity in their relationships; perhaps reflecting the belief that women and men contribute different things to their relationships and that a comparison of the relative value of these contributions is unhelpful or irrelevant.[39] In summary, women and men with nontraditional attitudes put a premium on equity, whereas traditional women and men are more accepting of inequity and are less disturbed by it, with the exception of men losing their privileged status in a household. Traditional women and men are more expecting and accepting of the status quo that keep men privileged relative to women.

Sexual Relations and Sexual Health

Gender-related attitudes particularly affect one specific aspect of heterosexual relationships, namely sexual behavior. Women who endorse feminist attitudes feel a greater sense of sexual subjectivity—awareness of sexual desires and agency necessary to advocate for one's sexual safety and pleasure. Women who endorse feminist attitudes are more inclined to have sex as a result of their own sexual interests and wishes rather than in response to extrinsic forces (e.g., pressure from their male partners).[40] Feminist attitudes are linked to both sexual subjectivity and sexual motivation. Given the relations of sexual subjectivity and sexual motivation to condom-use, self-efficacy, and sexual satisfaction, these findings suggest that young women who endorse feminist beliefs may be sexually safer, as well as more satisfied with their sexual experiences.[41] These findings complement other research finding that women with traditional gender-role attitudes tend to demonstrate less sexual assertiveness and are less likely to practice safe sex.[42] Women who endorse traditional gender roles are even less knowledgeable about sexual health, reproductive health, and pregnancy prevention than women with nontraditional attitudes.[43] Women with traditional gender roles are more self-conscious and less comfortable with their bodies during sex than women with nontraditional gender role attitudes.[44]

Laina Bay-Cheng and Alyssa Zucker[45] compared self-identified *feminists* with *nonfeminists* and *nonlabelers* (women who endorse feminist ideology but do not identify as feminist) on a variety of measures related to sexual beliefs and behavior.

Feminists expressed greater erotophilia (one's positive affective and evaluative responses to sexual cues) than nonfeminists, and nonlabelers did not differ from either group. Feminists expressed significantly less support for the sexual double standard (e.g., believing that promiscuity is OK for men, but not for women) than nonfeminists and nonlabelers. There were no significant differences among feminists, nonlabelers, and nonfeminists on measures of sexual assertiveness or sexual satisfaction. One curious difference between nonlabelers and the other two groups is that nonlabelers felt more confident in their abilities to assert their wishes regarding condom use than did nonfeminists and feminists. Why do feminists feel less confident than nonlabelers in their ability to assert the need for condom use? One possibility, according to the study's authors, is that feminists may be more aware of and therefore feel more susceptible to gendered power differences between women and their male partners. This reasoning suggests that feminists believe larger social conditions, such as sexism and inequality, impinge on individual women's ability to advocate for themselves in the sexual arena regardless of their interest in doing so. Nonlabelers, on the other hand, empowered by the discourse of self-determination and individual entitlement, may not perceive gendered scripts or sexism as threats to their own sexual agency. As a result, nonlabelers may have the subjective perception of greater self-efficacy with regard to condom use assertiveness. It's important to note that this difference between feminists and nonlabelers is limited to subjective *perception*; nonlabelers did not report higher rates of *actual* condom use than their feminist or nonfeminist counterparts.

The internalization of traditional feminine gender socialization plays a role in women's sexual behavior. *Sexual compliance* is having sex when one does not want to. Sexually compliant women report a greater investment in ideal womanhood compared to other women.[46] The investment in feminine gender norms may lead women to submit to unwanted sex, avoiding deviation from their prescribed gender role as passive keepers of peace and relational harmony. Because sexually compliant women report less relationship satisfaction than other women, it appears that women who adhere to gender socialization messages fostering sexual compliance are at risk for feeling resentful, used, or having negative emotions about the relationship. One might anticipate—at least in the context of traditional heterosexual relationships—that women's sexual compliance might enhance romantic well-being. However, the data fail to show a connection between women's sexual compliance and romantic well-being. Sexually compliant women report less relationship satisfaction, although they do not differ in their commitment to their relationship from noncompliant women.[47] Women who engage in compliant sex do it because they think it will make their partners happy. However, the evidence failed to show that compliance helps women feel more romantically happy themselves.

Internalizing the norms of traditional femininity might conform to society's expectations about how to be a good girl or woman but it can have a negative effect on negotiating sexuality issues. For instance, one study found that among 12th grade Latina and Anglo girls from the United States, those who internalize norms of traditional femininity tend to be unable to act on their own desires in sexual relationships. Specifically, girls who have an objectified relationship with their body (e.g., the view that a girl has to be thin to be beautiful; being concerned with how one's body looks rather than feels) and an inauthentic self in relationships (e.g., telling people what they want to hear; holding back opinions) are less likely to refuse unwanted sex, less likely to insist on using condoms, and less likely to enjoy sex.[48]

Looking at friendships among women, Suzanna Rose and Laurie Roades[49] compared the types of friendships between women who identified as heterosexual feminists, heterosexual nonfeminists, and lesbian feminists (no information on ethnicity, and bisexual women were not part of the sample). First, there were no differences between feminists (lesbian or heterosexual) and nonfeminists in number of close women or men friends—another debunking of the myth that feminists (and lesbians) dislike men. Second, no differences emerged between the three groups in satisfaction with the friendships, or importance of the relationships to the individual. The most significant differences were between heterosexual feminists and heterosexual nonfeminists. First, feminists avoided friendships with nonfeminist women. Second, compared to nonfeminists, feminists had more women friends at least ten years older or younger than themselves. This finding about intergenerational friendships among feminist women is significant because one disappointment regarding the lack of a coherent feminist movement in the early 21st century, is the absence of an intergenerational transfer of feminist consciousness from older to younger emerging feminists.[50] And finally, feminists' friendships were reported to be more equal and democratic than nonfeminists' friendships.[51]

The literature on the connection between feminism and relationships demonstrates that being a feminist or holding feminist attitudes does not negatively influence women in heterosexual relationships. In fact, the preponderance of the research suggests that feminism is good for relationships, especially for women and perhaps even for men.

The Impact of Women's and Gender Studies

The 1970s ushered in a high point of feminism in the U.S. as feminist scholars launched women's studies programs and courses in college curricula. Women's studies coursework offered entirely new subject matter, as well as a rereading of conventional curricula. The main contribution of women's studies curricula was

(1) the shift in scholarly attention from women as marginal subjects to central subjects and (2) the shift from a focus on white heterosexual male authors as the dominant source of knowledge to women, people of color, and LGBT people as central in intellectual work. This final section looks at the impact that women's and gender studies courses have on women students.

If feminist attitudes and feminist identity have a generally positive impact on women, is feminist coursework likely to influence women in positive ways? Do these courses influence women to become feminists? And do women's and gender studies courses influence women in other ways that we have examined, such as self-esteem/self-efficacy, empowerment, and likelihood of engaging in activism? Much of the empirical research on the experience of women's and gender studies (WGS) courses entails pre-/posttest research designs in which students are assessed on various dimensions at the beginning and then the end of a course. Pre- and posttest scores are compared between students taking WGS courses and "control" students taking non-WGS courses. Unfortunately, like the work we have reviewed thus far, much of this work includes mostly white samples and thus few ethnic comparisons are made.

WGS students tend to become more politically liberal in their gender-related attitudes than those students who take non-WGS coursework.[52] Also, women in WGS courses are more likely to identify as feminists by the end of the course than those in non-WGS courses.[53] Students who have taken a women's studies course are more likely to view gender differences as a result of socialization rather than biology.[54]

When WGS courses were first developed, one of the hopes was that these courses would empower women students. Some studies have examined empowerment directly or indirectly. Karen Harris[55] and her colleagues examined locus of control before and after a women's studies course. *Locus of control* refers to an individual's sense of personal control over the events in her life. Individuals with an internal locus of control believe they have agency and they have an impact on determining their own fate. In their study of mostly white U.S. college students, Harris and her colleagues found that by the end of their course WGS students displayed a more internal locus of control than did non-WGS students. The change in locus of control occurred in both women and men. Another study[56] examined whether or not students' general personal self-efficacy scores change over the course of a semester. Personal self-efficacy scores of African American and white women increased over the course of the semester, but men's personal self-efficacy declined somewhat over the semester. Perhaps some of the men in the sample had not been exposed to awareness of male privilege. Maybe this new information dampened their feelings of self-efficacy with the realization that their successes may not be based solely on their effort and talents but also on unearned privilege.

The influence of WGS coursework on self-esteem is somewhat unclear. For example, one study[57] found that WGS students had higher posttest scores on performance self-esteem than did students taking other courses. This was the case for both women and men WGS students. Other work[58] has found no changes in self-esteem after taking WGS. Finally, an early study[59] found a pattern associated with self-esteem and undergraduate grade/class level. Lower-level WGS students experienced a decline in self-esteem, whereas upper-level students experienced an increase in self-esteem after having taken a women's studies course. These data suggest that WGS classes might serve different purposes for younger and older students: younger students may be gaining awareness about sexism and inequality rather than building self-esteem, whereas older students might be gaining empowerment.

Women's Studies: A Training Ground for Man-Hating?

A common caricature coming from the political right is that women's studies programs are antimale training grounds. Recall from Chapter 3 when President of the Center for Military Readiness Elaine Donnelly reacted to the U.S. Pentagon's attempt to establish the Office of the Victim Advocate to handle hundreds of sexual assault claims made by women soldiers against men soldiers. Elaine Donnelly described the effort as establishing an "Office of Male-Bashing."[60] She predicted the office would "create a new job market for 'women's studies' graduates schooled in man-hating ideology." The impact on gender-related attitudes after exposure to WGS courses has been a central question for feminists as well.

Dan Pence[61] addressed this alleged relationship between man-hating and women's studies when he compared attitudes toward men among women (mostly white) taking a women's studies course with those taking an African American studies or general sociology course. Using the typical pre-/posttest procedure, Pence found that over the course of the semester the women's studies students' attitudes toward both nontraditional masculine behaviors (e.g., men taking care of children) and attitudes toward men in general actually became *more* positive. This attitude change occurred in women taking the women's studies course but not women taking the African American studies or sociology course. Furthermore, those women who enrolled in women's studies for personal interest had more positive attitudes toward men during the pre- *and* posttest than those who took the course because of a requirement. In other words, the women who were attracted to the women's studies course came into the course with more positive attitudes toward men in the first place and finished the course with even higher levels of positive attitudes than did the women taking the non–women's studies courses. Pence explains that even though men were, at most, peripheral to the course content, by semester's end these students saw men as gendered beings whose roles and behaviors were also socially constructed, thus providing a context for why men act the way they do. By the end of the course, students establish a gendered framework for understanding women's and men's attitudes and behaviors. Findings from Pence's study is consistent with another study finding that feminists actually have more positive attitudes toward men than do nonfeminists[62]—a topic we examined in Chapter 3. Unfortunately, the assumption that WGS is hostile toward men trivializes what is actually occurring in these courses, and marginalizes the faculty who teach them and the students who take them.

With political activism being supplanted by individualism and consumerism, as we discussed in Chapter 1, an important antidote to the self-centered individual empowerment of post-feminism is the creation of new activists spawned by WGS courses. Jayne Stake[63] found that among African American and white (but not Asian American) women and men students, those who took WGS courses were more likely to engage in activism than students who did not take WGS courses. Activism is important for meaningful social and political change because it involves personal, direct, grassroots efforts on the part of students. WGS students have increased feelings of empowerment and believe they can have an impact on the world. Women's commitment to meaningful activism is linked to expectations for egalitarian partnerships in general, as well as for authority, homemaking, child care, education, and employment support.[64] In the same study, Stake[65] found that the emotional responses of the WGS students included little increase in distress or anger but a substantial increase in feelings of empowerment. Interestingly, although activist *intentions* were predicted by both awareness of sexism and pro-feminist attitudes, only awareness of sexism predicted activist *behaviors*. Stake notes that flexible, egalitarian attitudes may be useful in getting individuals to consider the possibility and viability of participating in a women's movement, yet egalitarian attitudes by themselves may not be enough to propel them to action.

The empirical research on the impact of women's and gender studies courses demonstrates a variety of positive effects on women (and, in some cases, men as well), such as increased locus of control, self-efficacy, feelings of empowerment and activism—and even positive attitudes toward men. Although one study found that students' lessons from the courses were sustained over a nine-month period,[66] an important area for further study is the long-term effects of taking such classes.

Conclusion

Many political commentators, and some women themselves, dismiss feminism as part of the past and unnecessary for women today. Those who insist on identifying as feminists or insist on the relevance of a feminist movement are viewed as angry, dissatisfied, and hostile toward men.[67] In this chapter, we examined the role that feminism plays in women's psychological well-being, in heterosexual relationships, and in body image, as well as the research on the influence of women's and gender studies courses on women. Contrary to popular stereotypes, in almost all areas of review, feminist attitudes and feminist identity, in particular, have positive effects on women's psychology and relationships.

Women's holding of feminist attitudes is beneficial. However, taking the extra step, with the additional consciousness of *identifying* as a feminist is better. We find this for self-efficacy,[68] heterosexual relationships,[69] sexual behavior (with the exception of assertiveness in condom use),[70] and in body image. An important point about the work reviewed in this chapter is that the associations found are correlational. It is not clear whether psychological well-being in the form of self-efficacy, internal locus of control, and feelings of empowerment create the opportunity to become a feminist or whether feminism causes positive changes in well-being.

Finally, most of the research studies examined here include samples consisting of white women. Like much psychological research, even in the 21st century, too few studies include significant numbers of people of color and people from various social class backgrounds. American women of color have had an ambivalent relationship with the women's movement,[71] making the impact of feminist attitudes and identity in women of color a most necessary area of research. Similarly, much of the recent psychology studies on feminism and feminists include heterosexual women but not lesbians, bisexual or transgender women. Lesbians have also had an ambivalent relationship with the women's movement, and the impact that feminist consciousness has on sexual minority women needs to be studied. In particular, the work on feminism and relationships almost exclusively examines heterosexual relationships. The role that feminist consciousness plays in lesbian relationships is understudied. The role of being a feminist who is also a sexual minority should impact well-being, although it is not clear how.

This chapter reveals many positive (and essentially no negative) relationships between feminism and psychological well-being. This fact makes all the more curious the stigmatization of feminists and feminism. What function is served by maintaining the fiction that feminism is bad for women? What institutions and individuals benefit from the maintenance of this myth?

Notes

1. Spender, D. (1993, July/August). An alternative to Madonna: How to deal with the "I'm not a feminist, but..." *Ms. 4*(1), 44–45.

2. Page xviii: O'Beirne, K. (2006). *Women who make the world worse: And how their radical feminist assault is ruining our families, military, schools, and sports*. New York, NY: Sentinel.

3. Page xvi: O'Beirne, K. (2006). *Women who make the world worse: And how their radical feminist assault is ruining our schools, families, military, and sports*. New York, NY: Sentinel.

4. Page 11: Mansfield, H. C. (2006). *Manliness*. New Haven, CT: Yale University Press.

5. p. xv: O'Beirne, K. (2006). *Women who make the world worse: And how their radical feminist assault is ruining our schools, families, military, and sports*. New York, NY: Sentinel.

6. Klonis, S., Endo, J., Crosby, F., & Worell, J. (1997). Feminism as life raft. *Psychology of Women Quarterly*, *21*, 333–345.

7. Murnen, S. K., & Smolak, L. (2009). Are feminist women protected from body image problems? A meta-analytic review of relevant research. *Sex Roles*, *60*, 186–197. doi:10.1007/s11199-008-9523-2

8. Morgan, B. L. (1996). Putting the feminism into feminism scales: Introduction of a Liberal Feminist Attitude and Ideology Scale (LFAIS). *Sex Roles*, *34*, 359–390.

9. Henley, N. M., Meng, K., O'Brien, D., McCarthy, W. J., & Sockloskie, R. J. (1998). Developing a scale to measure the diversity of feminist attitudes. *Psychology of Women Quarterly*, *22*, 317–348.

10. Downing, N. E., & Roush, K. L. (1985). From passive acceptance to active commitment: A model of feminist identity development for women. *The Counseling Psychologist*, *13*, 695–709.

11. Anderson, K. J., Kanner, M., & Elsayegh, N. (2009). Are feminists man haters? Feminists' and nonfeminists' attitudes toward men. *Psychology of Women Quarterly*, *33*, 216–224. doi:10.1111/j.1471-6402.2009.01491.x

12. Eisele, H., & Stake, J. (2008). The differential relationship of feminist attitudes and feminist identity to self-efficacy. *Psychology of Women Quarterly*, *32*, 233–244. doi:10.1111/j.1471-6402.2008.00432.x

13. Zucker, A. N., & Bay-Cheng, L. Y. (2010). Minding the gap between feminist identity and attitudes: The behavioral and ideological divide between feminists and non-labelers. *Journal of Personality*, *78*, 1896–1924. doi:10.1111/j.1467-6494.2010.00673.x

14. Yakushko, O. (2007). Do feminist women feel better about their lives? Examining patterns of feminist identity development and women's subjective well-being. *Sex Roles*, *57*, 223–234. doi:10.1007/s11199-007-9249-6

15. Yakushko, O. (2007). Do feminist women feel better about their lives? Examining patterns of feminist identity development and women's subjective well-being. *Sex Roles*, *57*, 223–234. doi:10.1007/s11199-007-9249-6

16. Rittenour, C. E., & Colaner, C. W. (2012). Finding female fulfillment: Intersecting role-based and morality-based identities of motherhood, feminism and generativity as predictors of women's self satisfaction and life satisfaction. *Sex Roles, 67*, 351–362. doi:10.1007/s11199-012-0186-7

17. Saunders, K. J., & Kashubeck-West, S. (2006). The relations among feminist identity development, gender-role orientation, and psychological well-being in women. *Psychology of Women Quarterly, 30*, 199–211. doi:10.1111/j.1471-6402.2006.00282.x

18. Baucom, D. H., & Sanders, B. S. (1978). Masculinity and femininity as factors in feminism. *Journal of Personality Assessment, 42*, 378–384.
    Jordan-Viola, E., Fassberg, S., & Viola, M. T (1976). Feminism, androgyny, and anxiety. *Journal of Consulting and Clinical Psychology, 44*, 870–871.

19. Fischer, A. R., & Good, G. E. (2004). Women's feminist consciousness, anger, and psychological distress. *Journal of Counseling Psychology, 51*, 437–446. doi:10.1037/0022-0167.51.4.437

20. Gillen, M. M., & Lefkowitz, E. S. (2006). Gender role development and body image among male and female first year college students. *Sex Roles, 55*, 25–37. doi:10.1007/s11199-006-9057-4

21. Murnen, S. K., & Smolak, L. (2009). Are feminist women protected from body image problems? A meta-analytic review of relevant research. *Sex Roles, 60*, 186–197. doi:10.1007/s11199-008-9523-2

22. Grabe, S., & Hyde, J. S. (2006). Ethnicity and body dissatisfaction among women in the United States: A meta-analysis. *Psychological Bulletin, 132*, 622–640. doi:10.1037/0033-2909.132.4.622

23. Oney, C. N., Cole, E. R., Sellers, R. M. (2011). Racial identity and gender as moderators of the relationship between body image and self-esteem for African Americans. *Sex Roles, 65*, 619–631. doi:10.1007/s11199-011-9962-z

24. Guille, C., & Chrisler, J. C. (1999). Does feminism serve a protective function against eating disorders? *Journal of Lesbian Studies, 3*, 141–148. doi:10.1300/J155v03n04_18

25. Murnen, S. K., & Smolak, L. (2009). Are feminist women protected from body image problems? A meta-analytic review of relevant research. *Sex Roles, 60*, 186–197. doi:10.1007/s11199-008-9523-2

26. Anderson, K. J. (2010). *Benign bigotry: The psychology of subtle prejudice.* Cambridge, UK: Cambridge University Press.

27. Pages 4–5 in: Mansfield, H. C. (2006). *Manliness.* New Haven, CT: Yale University Press.

28. Lopez, K. J. (2005, December 29). Women who make the world worse: Kate O'Beirne calls feminists on their bad ideas. *National Review Online.* Retrieved October 31, 2010, from www.nationalreview.com/interrogatory/obeirne200512290819.asp

29. Rudman, L. A., & Fairchild, K. (2007). The *F* word: Is feminism incompatible with beauty and romance? *Psychology of Women Quarterly, 31*, 125–136. doi:10.1111/j.1471-6402.2007.00346.x

30. Rudman, L. A., & Fairchild, K. (2007). The *F* word: Is feminism incompatible with beauty and romance? *Psychology of Women Quarterly, 31*, 125–136. doi:10.1111/j.1471-6402.2007.00346.x

31. Rudman, L. A., & Fairchild, K. (2007). The *F* word: Is feminism incompatible with beauty and romance? *Psychology of Women Quarterly, 31*, 125–136. doi:10.1111/j.1471-6402.2007.00346.x

32. Rudman, L. A., & Phelan, J. E. (2007). The interpersonal power of feminism: Is feminism good for romantic relationships? *Sex Roles, 57*, 787–799. doi:10.1007/s11199-007-9319-9

33. Rudman, L. A., & Phelan, J. E. (2007). The interpersonal power of feminism: Is feminism good for romantic relationships? *Sex Roles, 57*, 787–799. doi:10.1007/s11199-007-9319-9

34. Yoder, J. D., Perry, R. L., & Saal, E. I. (2007). What good is a feminist identity?: Women's feminist identification and role expectations for intimate and sexual relationships. *Sex Roles, 57*, 365–372. doi:10.1007/s11199-007-9269-2

35. Yoder, J. D., Perry, R. L., & Saal, E. I. (2007). What good is a feminist identity? Women's feminist identification and role expectations for intimate and sexual relationships. *Sex Roles, 57*, 365–372. doi:10.1007/s11199-007-9269-2

36. Askari, S. F., Liss, M., Erchull, M. J., Staebell, S. E., & Axelson, S. J. (2010). Men want equality, but women don't expect it: Young adults' expectations for participation in household and child care chores. *Psychology of Women Quarterly, 34*, 243–252. doi:10.1111/j.1471-6402.2010.01565.x

37. Backus, F. R., & Mahalik, J. R. (2011). The masculinity of Mr. Right: Feminist identity and heterosexual women's ideal romantic partners. *Psychology of Women Quarterly, 35*, 318–326. doi:10.1177/0361684310392357

38. Donaghue, N., & Fallon, B. J. (2003). Gender-role self-stereotyping and the relationship between equity and satisfaction in close relationships. *Sex Roles, 48*, 217–230.

39. Donaghue, N., & Fallon, B. J. (2003). Gender-role self-stereotyping and the relationship between equity and satisfaction in close relationships. *Sex Roles, 48*, 217–230.

40. Schick, V. R., Zucker, A. N., & Bay-Cheng, L. Y. (2008). Safer, better sex through feminism: The role of feminist ideology in women's sexual well-being. *Psychology of Women Quarterly, 32*, 225–232. doi:10.1111/j.1471-6402.2008.00431.x

41. Schick, V. R., Zucker, A. N., & Bay-Cheng, L. Y. (2008). Safer, better sex through feminism: The role of feminist ideology in women's sexual well-being. *Psychology of Women Quarterly, 32*, 225–232. doi:10.1111/j.1471-6402.2008.00431.x

42. Yoder, J. D., Perry, R. L., & Saal, E. I. (2007). What good is a feminist identity? Women's feminist identification and role expectations for intimate and sexual relationships. *Sex Roles, 57*, 365–372.

43. Curtin, N., Ward, L. M., Merriwether, A., & Caruthers, A. (2011). Femininity ideology and sexual health in young women: A focus on sexual knowledge, embodiment, and agency. *International Journal of Sexual Health*, *23*(1), 48–62. doi:10.10 80/19317611.2010.524694

44. Curtin, N., Ward, L. M., Merriwether, A., & Caruthers, A. (2011). Femininity ideology and sexual health in young women: A focus on sexual knowledge, embodiment, and agency. *International Journal of Sexual Health*, *23*(1), 48–62. doi:10.10 80/19317611.2010.524694

45. Bay-Cheng, L. Y., & Zucker, A. N. (2007). Feminism between the sheets: Sexual attitudes among feminists, nonfeminists, and egalitarians. *Psychology of Women Quarterly*, *31*, 157–163. doi:10.1111/j.1471-6402.2007.00349.x

46. Katz, J., & Tirone, V. (2009). Women's sexual compliance with male dating partners: Associations with investment in ideal womanhood and romantic well-being. *Sex Roles*, *60*, 347–356. doi:10.1007/s11199-008-9566-4

47. Katz, J., & Tirone, V. (2009). Women's sexual compliance with male dating partners: Associations with investment in ideal womanhood and romantic well-being. *Sex Roles*, *60*, 347–356. doi:10.1007/s11199-008-9566-4

48. Impett, E. A., Schooler, D., & Tolman, D. L. (2006). To be seen and not heard: Femininity ideology and adolescent girls' sexual health. *Archives of Sexual Behavior*, *35*, 131–144. doi:10.1007/s10508-005-9016-0

49. Rose, S. & Roades, L. (1987). Feminism and women's friendships. *Psychology of Women Quarterly*, *11*, 243–254.

50. Anderson, K. J. (2011). Anti-feminism. In M. Z. Stange, C. K. Oyster, & J. E. Sloan (Eds.) *The multimedia encyclopedia of women in today's world*. Sage Publications. Retrieved from http://www.sage-ereference.com/womentoday/Article_n39.html

51. Rose, S. & Roades, L. (1987). Feminism and women's friendships. *Psychology of Women Quarterly*, *11*, 243–254.

52. For a review, see: Macalister, H. E. (1999). Women's studies classes and their influence on student development. *Adolescence*, *34*, 283–292.

53. Bargad, A., & Hyde, J. S. (1991). Women's studies: A study of feminist identity development in women. *Psychology of Women Quarterly*, *15*, 181–201. doi:10.1111/j.1471-6402.1991.tb00791.x

54. Yoder, J. D., Fischer, A. R., Kahn, A. S., & Groden, J. (2007). Changes in students' explanations for gender differences after taking a psychology of women class: More constructionist and less essentialist. *Psychology of Women Quarterly*, *31*, 415–425. doi:10.1111/j.1471-6402.2007.00390.x

55. Harris, K. L., Melaas, K., & Rodacker, E. (1999). The impact of women's studies courses on college students of the 1990s. *Sex Roles*, *40*, 969–977. doi:10.1023/A:1018885407873

56. Eisele, H., & Stake, J. (2008). The differential relationship of feminist attitudes and feminist identity to self-efficacy. *Psychology of Women Quarterly*, *32*, 233–244. doi:10.1111/j.1471-6402.2008.00432.x

57. Stake, J. E., & Gerner, M. A. (1987). The women's studies experience: Personal and professional gains for women and men. *Psychology of Women's Quarterly*, *11*, 277–287.

58. Harris, K. L., Melaas, K., & Rodacker, E. (1999). The impact of women's studies courses on college students of the 1990s. *Sex Roles*, *40*, 969–977. doi:10.1023/A:1018885407873

59. Zuckerman, D. M. (1983). Women's studies, self-esteem, and college women's plans for the future. *Sex Roles*, *9*, 633–642. doi:10.1007/BF00290070

60. Page 7: Donnelly, E. (2005, December 5). Pentagon doesn't need an office of male-bashing. *Human Events*, *61*, 7.

61. Pence, D. (1992). A woman's studies course: Its impact on women's attitudes toward men and masculinity. *NSWA Journal*, *4*, 321–335.

62. Anderson, K. J., Kanner, M., & Elsayegh, N. (2009). Are feminists man haters? Feminists' and nonfeminists' attitudes toward men. *Psychology of Women Quarterly*, *33*, 216–224. doi:10.1111/j.1471-6402.2009.01491.x

63. Stake, J. E. (2007). Predictors of change in feminist activism through women's and gender studies. *Sex Roles*, *57*, 43–54. doi:10.1007/s11199-007-9227-z

64. Yoder, J. D., Perry, R. L., & Saal, E. I. (2007). What good is a feminist identity? Women's feminist identification and role expectations for intimate and sexual relationships. *Sex Roles*, *57*, 365–372. doi:10.1007/s11199-007-9269-2

65. Stake, J. E. (2007). Predictors of change in feminist activism through women's and gender studies. *Sex Roles*, *57*, 43–54. doi:10.1007/s11199-007-9227-z

66. Stake, J. E., & Rose, S. (1994). The long-term impact of women's studies on students' personal lives and political activism. *Psychology of Women Quarterly*, *18*, 403–412. doi:10.1111/j.1471-6402.1994.tb00463.x

67. Anderson, K. J. (2011). Anti-feminism. In M. Z. Stange, C. K. Oyster, & J. E. Sloan (Eds.) *The multimedia encyclopedia of women in today's world*. Sage Publications. Retrieved from http://www.sage-ereference.com/womentoday/Article_n39.html

68. Eisele, H., & Stake, J. (2008). The differential relationship of feminist attitudes and feminist identity to self-efficacy. *Psychology of Women Quarterly*, *32*, 233–244. doi:10.1111/j.1471-6402.2008.00432.x

69. Rudman, L. A., & Phelan, J. E. (2007). The interpersonal power of feminism: Is feminism good for romantic relationships? *Sex Roles*, *57*, 787–799. doi:10.1007/s11199-007-9319-9

70. Bay-Cheng, L. Y., & Zucker, A. N. (2007). Feminism between the sheets: Sexual attitudes among feminists, nonfeminists, and egalitarians. *Psychology of Women Quarterly*, *31*, 157–163. doi:10.1111/j.1471-6402.2007.00349.x

71. Anderson, K. J. (2010). *Benign bigotry: The psychology of subtle prejudice*. Cambridge, UK: Cambridge University Press.

CONCLUSION

The truth is—despite stereotypes that paint feminists as forever
negative—doing feminist work requires boundless optimism. It means
believing that people have the ability to be better, that culture can
change, and maybe even that people who hate can learn to love.

—JESSICA VALENTI, 2013[1]

This book began with a quotation about the premature burial of feminism. Activists have responded for more than a century to the notion
that feminism is obsolete, irrelevant, and dead. If feminism were
truly dead no one would be fighting it, insisting on its irrelevance,
and demonizing it. Insistence on the irrelevance of feminism and the
supposed threat it presents to society means feminism is successful,
necessary, and very much alive. Feminism *does* threaten the gender
order and the status quo; feminism is inspirational and transformative
for women (and men). It is the power of feminism today that makes
anti-feminists nervous and desperate to undermine it.

The claim that feminism is no longer necessary denies the reality
of many women's and girls' lives, particularly poor, ethnic, and sexual
minority women and girls. In addition, post-feminist discourse encourages young women to believe that they were born into a free society, so
if they experience discrimination, it is an individual, isolated problem
that may even be their own fault. Increased consumerism among some
Western women further divides them from the women in developing nations who make their consumer goods. Portraying feminism as
irrelevant silences and marginalizes feminists, making feminism seem
unpalatable and any kind of feminist movement invisible and immate-
rial. Consequently, the transfer of feminist power to younger activists
coming into consciousness is discouraged both actively and passively.
This belief in the irrelevance of activism and a focus on the individual
preempts and effectively prevents the solidarity among women that is
a feature of any feminist movement.

Every day there are women and men taking paradigm-shifting
women's and gender studies courses, and many such programs now
are combined with ethnic studies and queer studies for a vibrant inter-
sectional analysis of sexism, racism, heterosexism, and classism. There

are hundreds of blogs, magazines, books, websites, and organizations that are expressly and exuberantly feminist. Young feminists have skillfully utilized social media to organize online protests, real-life marches, the election of progressive political candidates, subversive culture jamming, and clever subvertising. The bad news is that feminism's work is not nearly done. The good news is that there are brilliant individuals and coalitions engaging in this vital work.

Privatization, Consumerism, Individualism, and Resistance

Anti-feminism and sexism are fueled by recent moves away from collective action and toward individualism, consumerism, and privatization brought on in part by the neoliberal politics that took hold during the Reagan presidency and continue into the present. War, terrorism, and natural disasters all provide opportunities for antigovernment privateers to push through rebuilding efforts by private, for-profit corporations—projects that were previously carried out by the government. As Naomi Klein outlines in her book *The Shock Doctrine*, regions that are traumatized by disaster are softened up by the collective terror they experience, making them vulnerable to greedy corporations. In turn, these corporations demolish public schools for private/charter schools and privatize security using mercenary firms, such as Blackwater, rather than government agencies to keep peace and protect the public.

The United States prison industrial complex incarcerates a larger percentage of the country's population than any other nation in the world. With private prisons, these corporations depend on new inmates to feed the private prison beast. Corporate exploitation of prison labor corporatizes even public prisons, which also increase the profits of companies that provide food, security, and technology.

By 2012, union membership in the United States was at its lowest point in 97 years after legislatures in several states passed punishing anti-union legislation.[2] Unions are a crucial form of collective resistance against the neoliberal politics of extreme individualism. In the second decade of the 21st century, union membership and influence seem to be at a low point. In September of 2013, however, the AFL-CIO, the largest federation of unions in the United States, with nearly half its members women, made an announcement that could empower millions of low-wage workers and radically change the power behind unions. The AFL-CIO announced a plan to work with tens of millions of *nonunion* workers, including immigrants and low-wage workers who have traditionally not been part of its federation.[3] This historic move has the potential to unite millions of workers who have been prevented from collective bargaining in their work by recent anti-union legislation.

As actual political freedom was not the agenda of the post-9/11 presidential administrations, freedom has come to imply the freedom to consume. Consumption is the arena in which the liberal idea of "choice" has become operative in new and powerful ways. In the aftermath of 9/11, consumer culture has become ever more central to neoliberalism, endlessly promoting the idea of so-called choice as central to a liberated person and enabling the hegemony of both American-style capitalist democracy and the supposed self-actualizing and identity-producing possibilities of American-style consumption.[4] The rhetoric of neoliberalism co-opts themes from the feminist movement of the 1960s and 1970s. Terms such as "empowerment" and "choice" are applied to individual consumer behavior rather than collective action or even individual women feeling empowerment in their choices in personal relationships and private lives. Modern misogyny says women can exert their power through their pocketbooks by purchasing consumer goods and products for self-improvement to make themselves beautiful and sexy (and in the process enriching a range of corporations dependent on our artificially created need to change our bodies).

But women exert their power in other ways that actually *are* empowering. In November 2002 with the United States on the brink of invading Iraq, 100 women staged an antiwar vigil outside the White House that lasted four months. The group, CODEPINK, was founded as a women-driven antiwar organization for peace and justice. A decade later, its members still routinely protest at congressional hearings and political speeches, critiquing U.S. drone strikes, Pentagon funding, threats of war with Syria and Iran, and violations of human rights.

The focus on consumerism pitches middle-class American women against poor and working class women who do not share their incomes and consumer capacities—and whose domestic labor often assists the choice-making capacity of middle-class women. Empowerment through consumerism also pitches Western women against the girls and women in the developing world who work for poverty wages making the products that Western women are encouraged to purchase, use, throw away, and purchase again, as demonstrations of their "freedom" and "empowerment." So there is little opportunity for solidarity between middle- and upper-class women and poor and working-class women in their own nations and across the globe. Dismantling the antihierarchical struggles of social movements is also a priority within the discourses of neoliberalism. An attack on disadvantaged social groups is masked by the ostensibly nonracist and nonsexist language of self-esteem, empowerment, and personal responsibility.[5]

But still there is resistance. On August 29, 2013, thousands of fast food workers across 60 U.S. cities walked off the job in a one-day strike to protest their paltry $7.25 an hour wages.[6] Thirty years ago, the typical fast food worker was a middle-class teenager earning extra money during summer break or between college semesters. By 2013, the typical fast food worker is 28 years old and two-thirds are women, many women of color. Underpaid fast food labor is a woman's issue.[7] Workers resist, collectively, and with results. In response to fast-food worker strikes, the California legislature in September 2013, with the governor's support, voted to raise the state's minimum wage to $10 an hour by 2016.[8] And with such a huge labor market, this move in California could spur changes in other states.

In September 2013 hundreds of feminists marched on Capitol Hill in the United States to fight for immigration reform and address the issues of women's rights and reproductive health. Jessica González-Rojas, executive director of the National Latina Institute for Reproductive Health, and Kimberly Inez McGuire, associate director for government relations and public affairs, were arrested for their participation in a peaceful act of civil disobedience.[9] This action works alongside the young, mostly Latino immigrant "DREAMers," who support a U.S. Senate bill named the DREAM Act[10] that would provide a pathway to citizenship to those living in the United States since childhood but without citizenship. These young activists have compelled the U.S. Congress to consider immigration reform even as they risk their own deportation as U.S. activists without documents.

Sociologists refer to a *values stretch*—when individuals dilute their original expectations and goals to adapt to changing circumstances.[11] In psychology, we have the theory of *cognitive dissonance* to help explain how individuals psychologically accommodate contradictory, absurd or unjust circumstances. When people find themselves in situations that put them so fundamentally at odds with their values, desires, or worldview, if they do not or cannot resist those conditions and fight back, their minds find ways to accommodate the untenable circumstances. It is too unpleasant to live in a state of cognitive dissonance—the state of tension when our attitudes, values, or beliefs conflict with our circumstances.[12] It is easier for some people to believe in the myth of meritocracy and that their own efforts will pay off in the face of more and more difficult economic conditions than it is to realize the extent to which the American Dream is a myth. The U.S. populace has internalized the belief that individual success can be achieved by hard work alone. Regardless of political circumstances or economic exigencies, when individualism trumps collectivism and active resistance, we cannot expect a collective consciousness to resist these current oppressive and unfair trends in any sustained way.

Nevertheless, while some capitulate, many resist. In recent years, we have seen inspiring resistance to the neoliberal policies described in Chapter 1 of this book: the protests of the World Trade Organization at the turn of the century;

the Occupy protests in New York and across the United States in 2011 and 2012; protests in Wisconsin against Governor Scott Walker's anti-union legislation in 2011; and protests against climate change in 2013. Many of the protests have occurred outside the United States, including movements against austerity measures in Greece, Spain, and France, and the Arab Spring pro-democracy demonstrations beginning in late 2010 in Tunisia, Egypt, Libya, Bahrain, and Syria, and the 2013 protests in Turkey. Blithe claims that we have arrived and that all is well in the world ring hollow in the face of such concerted efforts to create change.

The "End-of Men," the "Crisis" for Boys, and the Promise of Feminism

Modern misogyny rests on the assumption of an already secured feminist victory—the belief that feminism has accomplished its goals and is thus no longer relevant. This post-feminist fiction is also tied to backlash and center-stealing. Trina Grillo and Stephanie Wildman coined the term *center-stage problem* to describe what happens when attention is turned away from the dominant group and toward a marginalized group. Members of the dominant group and supporters of the status quo rush to take back the center. Focusing on those who have not been given attention and seemingly do not deserve it threatens the dominant worldview, encouraging even some in the marginalized group to come to the defense of the dominant group who seem to have lost the center for a brief moment.

The boy-crisis authors focus on boys and men primarily in the education arena. The perceived takeover by women and girls has no foundation in reality. These authors are not interested in equality: they are interested in keeping boys and men at the center. But not any men, white men in particular. Boy-crisis authors such as Christina Hoff Sommers and Kathleen Parker talk about a monolithic boy and man being shafted by feminism. If the boy-crisis authors were truly interested in equality, and truly concerned about men who struggle in our society, they would be concerned about men and youth of color in the United States who are arrested and incarcerated at dramatically higher rates than whites, who are presumed to be criminals when they are young, and who feed the prison industrial complex.[13]

In Chapter 3 we debunked the tired but durable feminists-are-man-haters stereotype. In Chapter 4 we debunked the fictional boy crisis and the belief that now *men* are the marginalized, oppressed gender. Still, many people think that feminism leads to women having negative and problematic relationships with men. Research contradicts this belief. First, one study found that heterosexual feminist women were more likely to be in romantic relationships than were heterosexual nonfeminists.[14] Feminism can be good for heterosexual relationships and for heterosexual men. Heterosexual women who are involved in romantic relationships with feminist men report greater relationship quality, equality, stability, and sexual satisfaction than women whose partners are not feminists. Furthermore, feminist men report greater agreement about the importance of equality in the relationships than did nonfeminist men. Significantly, men also report greater relationship stability and sexual satisfaction if their partner is a feminist.[15] It is too bad that those who believe that feminism is threatening to romance also show less enthusiasm for feminism and for policies that support women.[16] These negative and inaccurate attitudes about feminists create barriers to activism.

Patronize Traditional Women, Demonize Nontraditional Women, but They Fight Back

Women who do not cooperate with gender rules—and most women do not in one way or another—are trivialized, marginalized, and demonized. Social control is exerted over girls and young women, for example, with the monitoring of their virginity through purity balls. At the same time, in the wider culture girls and women are hypersexualized through the mainstreaming of pornography and through the dual processes of what Susan Douglas refers to as embedded feminism and enlightened sexism. Now that gender equality has been supposedly achieved, girls and women can go back to having fun by putting their energy and power into being *hot*. At the same time, sexually active women are punished in a variety of ways—from being murdered in horror films to being blamed as rape survivors. Women who seek abortions or even birth control are punished, as we saw in the treatment of student Sandra Fluke during her 2012 testimony in the U.S. congress about contraceptive access. Fluke was excoriated as a "slut" by right-wing talk show host Rush Limbaugh. But her treatment also prompted nationwide outrage (along with magazine cover stories and a prime-time speaking slot at the Democratic National Convention). Also meeting nationwide scorn were the bizarre comments about rape made from various politicians such as U.S. Congressmember Todd Akin who distinguished between "legitimate" and not-legitimate rape during the 2012 election season; or U.S. Senator Ron Paul parsing an imaginary difference between "honest rape" and, apparently, dishonest rape[17] in 2012; or Congressmember Trent Franks claiming (falsely) that pregnancy resulting from rape is "very low" in 2013.[18] Significantly, Akin's remarks led not only to a lost bid for the U.S. Senate but also to Republican hand-wringing.

The comments were even suggested as a factor in Mitt Romney's failed presidential campaign.[19]

In March 2011, an anti-abortion group launched a billboard campaign on the South Side of Chicago targeting African American women. The billboard featured President Obama's picture alongside the words, "Every 21 minutes, our next possible leader is aborted." Less than a week after 30 billboards went up, most were covered with red paint by those who protested its message.[20] Another set of anti-abortion billboards accuses African American women who exercise their reproductive rights of committing "genocide." In response, the Trust Black Women partnership was born,[21] focusing on reproductive justice issues for African American women and refusing the antiwoman terms of this cynical campaign. This vibrant coalition works for affordable health care, education, child care, and access to contraception and abortion.

We find many examples of powerful resistance to the regressive antiwoman legislation in the second decade of the 21st century. In June 2013, in the face of Texas Governor Rick Perry signing sweeping legislation that would severely limit the ability of the women of Texas to obtain birth control and abortion services, Texas state senator Wendy Davis launched an historic 11-hour filibuster in the state house.[22] News of Davis's filibuster brought thousands of Texas feminists to the state house for weeks of protests. While Rick Perry's bill survived in the short-term, this political work sets in place a framework for ongoing resistance as these antiwomen politicians run for reelection.

Social control is exerted over women by demonizing and denigrating nontraditional women and by nominally putting traditional women on a pedestal. In the aftermath of the 9/11, women widowed by the attacks who did not follow the male-hero/female-victim narrative in the media were denigrated and rendered invisible. Women professionals, soldiers, and athletes do not receive the patronizing "protection" of benevolent sexism but instead are targets of hostile sexism. A special ire is directed at feminists and supported by the myth that feminists are male-bashers. Keeping this allegation in the public discourse perpetuates this myth but also forecloses any opportunity to talk about real-life issues such as men's actual bashing of women. One contingent of women constructed as nontraditional (and sometimes conflated) are rape survivors and sexually active women. In January 2011 a police constable in Toronto advised a group of students to "avoid dressing like sluts" in order to prevent sexual assault. The comments, perfectly in line with the phenomenon of victim-blaming we address in Chapter 5, sparked protests known as SlutWalks all over Canada and the United States.[23] In addition to reappropriating the word "slut," the aim of the SlutWalk movement is to resist the tendency that blames women for rape based on how they are dressed or whether they are seen as promiscuous and, therefore, deserving of rape. In her article "SlutWalks and the Future of Feminism," Jessica Valenti finds great promise in this movement:

> Not because an entire generation of women will organize under the word "slut" or because these marches will completely eradicate the damaging tendency of law enforcement and the media to blame sexual assault victims...But the success of SlutWalks does herald a new day in feminist organizing. One when women's anger begins online but takes to the street, when a local step makes global waves and when one feminist action can spark debate, controversy and activism that will have lasting effects on the movement.[24]

SlutWalk is now a global phenomenon that fights the global issue of victim-blaming and violence against women.

Transgender people face a shocking range of violence, including beatings, rape, and murder, and discrimination in the workplace, housing, and in access to health care.[25] The courage, persistence, and resistance of out trans women activists such as Janet Mock, CeCe McDonald, Laverne Cox, and Julia Serano, has forced a reframing of the trans conversation from an obsession with body parts[26] and pathology to the recognition of trans individuals' humanity. Transgender activist organizations—ranging from youth groups such as BreakOUT! in New Orleans to legal centers such as the Sylvia Rivera Law Project—exist across the United States and globally, and they actively build coalitions with other movements. While some trans activists have critiqued aspects of mainstream feminism, many have also spearheaded "transfeminism" as an academic and activist movement.

2013 saw several victories for the trans community, including trans-inclusive language in the Violence Against Women Act passed by the U.S. Congress; the U.S. Social Security Administration's easing of rules for changing one's gender on driver's licenses and passports; and the new edition of the Diagnostic and Statistical Manual of Mental Disorders renaming "Gender Identity Disorder" to a less pathologizing "Gender Dysphoria." This change in the DSM emphasizes that it is not a person's innate gender identity that may call for psychiatric treatment but rather the distress that some may feel about an identity, body, and social role that do not line up with one's assigned gender.[27] One piece of evidence for how far society has come in understanding gender as a complex and constructed category is Facebook's 2014 change in gender options for its users.[28] The seemingly mundane modification to a social networking site's option for gender identity goes a long way in raising people's consciousness about the complicated and fluid category of "gender."

Feminism Is Good

As we saw in the final chapter of this book, feminist attitudes are associated with numerous positive psychological attributes for individual women. Women with feminist attitudes have higher levels of psychological well-being, such as autonomy, personal growth, and sense of purpose in life, than women with traditional attitudes. Women with feminist attitudes are more likely than women with traditional gender attitudes to have a generativity identity—having a conscious concern for the next generation and the welfare of others. Women with feminist attitudes are more likely to engage in sex as a result of their own sexual wishes than in response to outside forces such as pressure from their partners, are more likely to practice safer sex, and are more knowledgeable about sexual and reproductive health.

Women who identify as feminists, rather than simply holding pro-feminist attitudes, have higher levels of psychological well-being and higher levels of self-efficacy. Women who call themselves feminists are more likely to have positive attitudes about their bodies compared to nonfeminists and women who simply hold feminist attitudes. A feminist identity is associated with a lower preoccupation with thinness and fewer eating disorders.

In addition to the concrete examples of feminist resistance described earlier, feminist activism in the academy, with women's and gender studies offerings, provides women an intellectual frame for understanding privilege and inequality. Women's and gender studies courses offer a range of benefits to women (and men) who take them. Taking these courses has been shown to increase individuals' sense of agency, self-determination, and personal control over the events in their lives, for both women and men.[29] And contrary to some beliefs that these courses are a breeding ground for man-hating, the courses can have a positive impact on women's attitudes toward men. [30]

With some political activism being supplanted by individualism and consumerism in so many ways, an important antidote to the self-centered individual "empowerment" of post-feminism is the creation of new activists spawned by women's and gender studies courses. Women and men who take these courses are more likely to engage in activism than students who do not. Activism is important for meaningful social and political change because it involves personal, direct, grassroots efforts on the part of students. Women's and gender studies students have increased feelings of empowerment and believe they can have an impact on the world. Rather than increasing distress and anger, these courses increase feelings of empowerment.

Feminist consciousness provides a cognitive framework for women to understand the world, especially their experiences of prejudice and discrimination.

Feminists have the tools to frame sexist discrimination they may experience as unjust and as stemming from their status as women. Feminists are more likely to attribute sexism to society and gender oppression and are less likely to blame themselves for the sexist treatment they experience. I hope that material in this book, the studies described, the arguments made, the brilliant work of others cited, and the examples of recent activism and resistance make clear the present need of a robust feminist movement and a future of opportunities for feminist activists.

Notes

1. Valenti, F. (2013, June 3). Fuck the high road: The upside of sinking to their level. Retrieved from http://www.thenation.com/blog/174624/fuck-high-road-upside-sinking-their-level#axzz2WRBk12zt

2. Greenhouse, S. (2013, January 23). Share of the work force in a union falls to a 97-year low, 11.3%. The New York Times. Retrieved from http://www.nytimes.com/2013/01/24/business/union-membership-drops-despite-job-growth.html?r=0

3. Trottman, M. (2013, September 9). AFL-CIO members back link to outside groups. The Wall Street Journal. Retrieved from http://online.wsj.com/article/SB10001424127887323864604579065491962718868.html

4. Grewal, I. (2003). Transnational America: Race, gender and citizenship after 9/11. *Social Identities, 9*, 535–561.

5. McRobbie, A. (2009). *The aftermath of feminism: Gender, culture and social change.* London, UK: Sage.

6. Petroff, A., & O'Toole, J. (2013, August 29). Wave of fast food strikes hits 60 cities. Retrieved from http://money.cnn.com/2013/08/29/news/fast-food-strikes/index.html

7. Bhutada, Y. (2013, August 25). Fast-food workers will strike on August 29—here's what you need to know. Retrieved from http://www.policymic.com/articles/60771/fast-food-workers-will-strike-on-august-29-here-s-what-you-need-to-know

8. Fields, L. (2013, September 15). California to raise minimum wage to $10 by 2016. Retrieved from http://abcnews.go.com/Business/california-raise-minimum-wage-10-2016/story?id=20258394

9. White, E. (2013, September 12). National Latina Institute for Reproductive Health leaders arrested in act of civil disobedience for immigration reform. Retrieved from http://latinainstitute.org/media/releases/National-Latina-Institute-for-Reproductive-Health-leaders-arrested-in-act-of-civil-di

10. DREAM stands for Development, Relief, and Education for Alien Minors.

11. Coontz, S. (2013, February 16). Why gender equality stalled. *The New York Times.* Retrieved from http://www.nytimes.com/2013/02/17/opinion/sunday/why-gender-equality-stalled.html?pagewanted=all

12. For a review of cognitive dissonance theory, see: Tavris, C., & Aronson, E. (2007). *Mistakes were made (but not by me)*. New York, NY: Harcourt.

13. Alexander, M. (2010). *The new Jim Crow: Mass incarceration in the age of colorblindness*. New York, NY: The New Press.

14. Rudman, L. A., & Phelan, J. E. (2007). The interpersonal power of feminism: Is feminism good for romantic relationships? *Sex Roles, 57*, 787–799. doi:10.1007/s11199-007-9319-9

15. Rudman, L. A., & Phelan, J. E. (2007). The interpersonal power of feminism: Is feminism good for romantic relationships? *Sex Roles, 57*, 787–799. doi:10.1007/s11199-007-9319-9

16. Rudman, L. A., & Fairchild, K. (2007). The F word: Is feminism incompatible with beauty and romance? *Psychology of Women, 31*, 125–136. doi:10.1111/j.1471-6402.2007.00346.x

17. Gray, K. J. (2012, February 6). Ron Paul okay with emergency contraception in cases of 'honest rape.' Retrieved from http://www.dailykos.com/story/2012/02/06/1062186/-Ron-Paul-okay-with-emergency-contraception-in-cases-of-honest-rape?detail=hide

18. Clawson, L. (2013, June 12). Non-Todd Akin GOP congressman: "The incidence of rape resulting in pregnancy are very low." Retrieved from http://www.dailykos.com/story/2013/06/12/1215656/-Non-Todd-Akin-GOP-congressman-The-incidence-of-rape-resulting-in-pregnancy-are-very-low

19. Kraske, S., & Helling, D. (2013, August 18). One year later, Todd Akin's "legitimate rape" remark holds lessons for Republicans. Retrieved from http://www.kansascity.com/2013/08/18/4419689/akins-legitimate-rape-remark-one.html

20. Bassett, L. (2011, April 22). Anti-abortion movement targets black women in latest efforts. Retrieved from http://www.huffingtonpost.com/2011/04/22/black-women-anti-abortion-movement_n_852591.html

21. See: http://www.trustblackwomen.org/about-trust-black-women/our-story

22. Lavender, P. (2013, August 15). Wendy Davis in *Vogue*: "I do hate losing." Retrieved from http://www.huffingtonpost.com/2013/08/15/wendy-davis-vogue_n_3761576.html

23. Stampler, L. (2011, April 20). SlutWalks sweep the nation. Retrieved from http://www.huffingtonpost.com/2011/04/20/slutwalk-united-states-city_n_851725.html

24. Valenti, J. (2011, June 3). SlutWalks and the future of feminism. Retrieved from http://www.washingtonpost.com/opinions/slutwalks-and-the-future-of-feminism/2011/06/01/AGjB9LIH_story.html?wpisrc=emailtoafriend

25. Bradford, J., Reisner, S. L., Honnold, J. A., & Zavier, J. (2013). Experiences of transgender-related discrimination and implications for health: Results from the Virginia Transgender Health Initiative Study. *American Journal of Public Health, 103*, 1820–1829.

Grant, J. M., Mottet, L. A., & Tanis, J. (2011, February 3). Injustice at every turn: A report of the National Transgender Discrimination Survey. Retrieved from http://www.thetaskforce.org/reports_and_research/ntds

Burk, M., Feltz, R., Maté, A., Shaikh, N., Guzder, D., Alcoff, S.,... Littlefield, A. (Producers). (2014, February 19). "Black trans bodies are under attack:" Freed activist CeCe McDonald, actress Laverne Cox speak out. Retrieved from http://www.democracynow.org/2014/2/19/black_trans_bodies_are_under_attack

26. Hess, A. (2014, February 7). Piers Morgan's interview with Janet Mock was not a failure of sensitivity. It was a failure of reporting. Retrieved from http://www.slate.com/blogs/xx_factor/2014/02/07/_piers_morgan_s_janet_mock_interview_why_journalists_get_coverage_of_the.html

27. Keisling, M. (2013, December 30). 10 transgender wins of 2013 you should know about. Retrieved from http://www.huffingtonpost.com/mara-keisling/10-transgender-wins-of-20_1_b_4505453.html

28. Mendoza, M. (2014, February 13). Facebook offers new gender options for users. Retrieved from http://bigstory.ap.org/article/apnewsbreak-new-gender-options-facebook-users

29. Harris, K. L., Melaas, K., & Rodacker, E. (1999). The impact of women's studies courses on college students of the 1990s. *Sex Roles, 40,* 969–977. doi:10.1023/A:1018885407873

30. Pence, D. (1992). A woman's studies course: Its impact on women's attitudes toward men and masculinity. *NSWA Journal, 4,* 321–335.

INDEX

Made in the USA
Coppell, TX
17 January 2022

71806807R00116